THE ROYAL FLYING CORPS:

A History

Also by Geoffrey Norris:

THE WRIGHT BROTHERS—A BIOGRAPHY

JET ADVENTURE

Geoffrey Norris

THE ROYAL FLYING CORPS:

A History

with a Foreword by
Marshal of the Royal Air Force
Sir John Slessor, G.C.B., K.C.B., C.B., D.S.O., M.C.

FREDERICK MULLER LIMITED
LONDON

First published in Great Britain in 1965
by Frederick Muller Limited

Printed in Great Britain by Ebenezer Baylis and Son, Ltd.
The Trinity Press, Worcester, and London

Contents

Illustrations

Acknowledgements

ANYONE who researches into First World War Aviation very soon becomes aware that there is a bewildering amount of often conflicting material available. One unmistakeable landmark in this sea of information is *The War in the Air*, the official history started by Sir Walter Raleigh and completed by H. A. Jones. My first acknowledgement must be to this magnificent, thorough and extremely readable work. I am glad that subsequent researches have enabled me to uncover the small, dramatic and heroic part which Jones himself played in the air war—the one omission that can be found in the official history.

For access to and guidance among pertinent literature I am indebted to Miss R. Coombs, Librarian of the Imperial War Museum, and to her staff. Her enthusiasm never flagged and was often instrumental in keeping mine going.

To Cassell and Company Limited go my thanks for permission to quote from *The Central Blue* by Marshal of the Royal Air Force, Sir John Slessor.

But, of course, this work could never have been written without the generous help of the men who served in the Royal Flying Corps. It would be wrong to single out any one person for individual mention. Their willingness to talk or to write to me or to loan documents, their cheerfulness and spirit have made the compilation of this book a pleasant task.

Finally, a word of thanks to my wife and children who have cheerfully endured the domestic upheavals caused by this work.

GEOFFREY NORRIS
Belfast, 1965

Acknowledgements

[illegible]

[illegible]

[illegible]

[illegible]

[illegible]

Foreword

by

Marshal of the Royal Air Force, Sir John Slessor, G.C.B., K.C.B., C.B., D.S.O., M.C.

IN AN AGE when a single military aeroplane can cost anything up to two million pounds, flies at more than twice the speed of sound and packs a punch that could eliminate a fair-sized city, it is difficult even for those of us who were in the old R.F.C. in the early days to recapture the memory—the look and the feel and the smell (burnt castor oil) of the primitive stick-and-string contraptions of fifty years ago. A fighting aeroplane today is really a mass of electronics with wings—a guided missile with a man in it. I don't mean that the manned aircraft has had its day, on the contrary I believe the R.A.F. will need young men of high quality for as far ahead as we need look. But aviation today is as different from fifty years ago as a tank is from an Egyptian war-chariot.

This book will bring back nostalgic memories to many old gentlemen who are still proud to wear the rather gaudy tie of the Royal Flying Corps. It is obviously many years since I last flew as a pilot, but I find it hard to believe that flying is as much fun today as it was in the dim ages. It is far more skilful, of course; all these marvellous modern navigational aids don't make it easy. What they are doing is to take the meaning out of the word impossible, and I am always filled with rather uneasy admiration of the men who fly these great modern jets in weather in which—as the old saying had it—even the gulls are walking.

The chaps are much the same. A bit more serious perhaps, less irresponsible—you'd have to be pretty irresponsible to take the same liberties with a V-bomber that we used to take with our old Henri Farmans, Camels and D.H. fours, each of which cost a good deal less than one leg of the undercarriage of a Vulcan II. They obviously enjoy flying, but I wonder if they get the same thrill out of it as we did? Not the same sort of thrill, I suspect. Fifty years ago it was an adventure which drew added zest from being something completely novel—something that very very few other people had ever done before. I am sure my son, commanding a V-bomber squadron, gets no more kick out of slipping across to Canada for a couple of days than I did from my first cross-country in an old 50 Blériot from Gosport to Farnborough, when I recall having some doubts about my ability to climb over the Hog's Back. The modern pilot has to be more serious than his father was in the maternity jacket and puttees of the R.F.C. He has to be, and is, a superbly-trained, highly-disciplined professional. There is no place in a modern air force for the light-hearted amateur—that is why, regrettably but inevitably, the Auxiliary squadrons had to go. In the old days there was an agreeably amateur status about most regular officers (not all, but most). In a way that was a source of strength; it certainly made them take life (and death) less seriously. But it had its disadvantages. We cannot, for instance, blame the politicians or the Treasury entirely for the ludicrous inadequacy of the equipment of the R.F.C. in 1914 compared with the French, of which Mr. Norris reminds us. Naval officers were more professional, but they, too, neglected some vitally important aspects of their profession; if they had thought more about what we should now call "operational requirements", Beatty would have been less surprised than he was by our battle-cruisers blowing up at Jutland.

The stirring tale that Mr. Norris tells should not obscure the fact that the Royal Flying Corps in its first and only war was an ancillary Service. The influence of aircraft in the war at sea was virtually negligible. In the great, grim siege that was the Western Front the R.F.C. was an ancillary of great and increasing importance—but an ancillary. Its primary job remained reconnaissance and observation for the guns and that it did, on the whole, extremely well, undeterred by heavy loss. We saw in the old Independent Force the rudiments of what came to be known as strategic bombing and, for those with eyes to see, the writing was on the wall. It is too often forgotten that 1939/45 was the first air war, in the sense of air power as a decisive factor in itself. That the men who had to plan the operations and composition of the Royal Air Force in that war did not make more mistakes than they did was surely due in part to their experience a generation earlier in the old Royal Flying Corps.

JOHN SLESSOR

CHAPTER ONE

Britain, the Poor Relation

WHEN the Wright brothers made the world's first successful powered, heavier-than-air flight in December, 1903, the event passed almost without notice. The little news which did appear in the press was greeted with disbelief. There was every excuse for this, for numerous others had attempted this feat over a span of many years, and all had failed. The Wrights' achievement was just not credible. By 1909, however, the art of flying had progressed beyond all recognition, a fact which the Frenchman, Louis Blériot, dramatically demonstrated in July of that year by successfully flying from France to England. He had also shown that, with the advent of the air age, Britain was no longer an island.

The German Government had realized the value of aviation to the Army some time earlier and, in the year that Blériot had crossed the Channel, had earmarked the sum of £40,000 for military aviation. During the same year the British Government suddenly realized that it had already spent the vast sum of £2,500 on some rather inconclusive aerial experiments. In its wisdom, it decided that matters had got out of hand. It immediately curtailed any further payment. The following year there came a much-discussed report which revealed that there were twenty-six military airships in existence in Europe. Of these, Germany possessed fourteen, Great Britain one. The Government remained unimpressed.

Two years later came the Turco-Italian war. Italy's army had a small aviation detachment at its disposal, and the first blooding of the aeroplane in war was on October 22nd, 1911, when Captain Moizo, piloting a Nieuport machine, flew out to observe ground movements of Turkish troops. In his anxiety to bring back as much information as possible, he descended to 600 feet. The angry Turks were firing at him with rifles. Several bullets ripped through his wings and one smashed a wing rib, but Moizo returned safely with his information. Three days later, Moizo, accompanied by Captain Piazza, who was flying a Blériot, made another reconnaissance and brought back the news that concentrations of Turkish and Italian troops were advancing. On receipt of this information, the Italians were able to prepare their defences so effectively that 3,000 Turkish soldiers died the following day at the Battle of Sciara-Sciat. During the battle Captain Piazza and Lieutenant Gavotti flew over the fighting in their aeroplanes, directing the guns from the battleship *Carlo Alberto* and those from the mountain artillery. Again the aircraft were shot at from the ground but, although the blast from some of the larger guns gave the pilots a bumpy ride, they returned safely.

On November 1st, the aircraft gave help to the army in a more active manner. Lieutenant Gavotti, in an Etrich monoplane, flew over Turkish troops, carrying four small bombs in a leather bag and, with careless regard for his own safety, detonators in the pocket of his flying suit. When he came across an enemy camp, he put one of the bombs on his knee, took out a detonator and prepared the missile for dropping. The bomb was by no means large but this unexpected attack from the air caused gratifying panic among the Turkish troops, and Gavotti circled to prepare, and drop, his other three bombs. Four days later, two more bombs were dropped, this time on some Arabs. "They fell," said an official communiqué, "with effect."

Thus, in 1911, the aeroplane was already a proven instrument of war. Had the official British attitude changed by this time?

"Aviation is a useless and expensive fad advocated by a few individuals whose ideas are unworthy of attention," pronounced the Chief of the Imperial General Staff, Sir W. G. Nicholson.

A general uneasiness about Britain's lack of airpower in the face of a steady and alarming growth of aerial forces in France and Germany was given wide expression, both in the press and in Parliament, during the years 1910 and 1911. Continued agitation, however, produced little effect on either the War Office or the Admiralty. Their head-in-the-sand attitude could be explained, perhaps, by the fact that, at that time, peace in Europe seemed secure. But, in July, even this flimsy excuse was swept away. There was anarchy in Morocco and the Sultan found himself incapable of controlling his unruly subjects. France, whose interest in Morocco was officially recognized, marched troops into the capital city to restore order. This was a purely domestic move, but Germany chose to assume that this operation was a preliminary step to the partition of Morocco between France and Spain, and despatched the corvette *Panther* to Agadir. This ship was later replaced by the cruiser *Berlin*.

It was an unmistakable threat of war from Germany. It was a threat which eventually came to nothing, but distrust of Germany prevailed throughout Europe from that time. This distrust, allied with the much-reported growth of Germany's aerial forces, should have made Britain's politicians wake up, but it did not. To the natural reluctance of any government to spend money was added the outdated views of the Army. "We have got quite enough complications in modern war already, you know. It's all very well saying that we should saddle ourselves with a lot of these aeroplanes, but in nine cases out of ten they would not be a scrap of good. We should only be adding to our worries, and perhaps we might get ourselves into a bad tangle by relying on them."

This view was put forward by someone who has remained anonymous over the years but who was described at the time as "a very influential officer".

Despite this appalling laxity in pursuing the new art of aviation, Great Britain was able to send four squadrons of aircraft across to France within a few weeks of Europe erupting into war a few years later. This has been hailed as a tremendous achievement. Certainly it was; but it must not be allowed to whitewash the fact that, in the first years of fighting, many brave officers died because they were insufficiently trained, or because their aircraft were unreliable and inferior to those of Germany. Without a doubt, casualties would have been very much lower if only the War Office and the Government had opened their eyes to the obvious uses of the aeroplane a little earlier than they did.

It was not as if the subject of aviation was new to the War Office. The first human flight had been made in 1783 by Pilâtre de Rozier in a hot-air balloon built by the Montgolfier brothers. From that time the art of ballooning progressed rapidly. The hot-air balloon gave way to the hydrogen-filled balloon and, in January, 1785, the art had progressed sufficiently for an Englishman, J. P. Blanchard, and an American, Dr. John Jeffries, to cross the English Channel by balloon.

Almost a century passed before any interest was shown in the balloon as a military vehicle in Great Britain. Credit for a grudging interest by the War Office in this method of transportation and reconnaissance must be given to Lieutenant G. E. Grover and Captain F. Beaumont, both of the Royal Engineers. Between 1862 and 1873 these two badgered the War Office continually, stressing the obvious value of the balloon for reconnaissance, and in 1863, made some experimental reconnaissance flights from both Woolwich and Aldershot with a balloon and equipment borrowed from Henry Coxwell, a famous civilian balloonist. Their balloon was filled with coal gas from a War Department gasworks. The War Office was unimpressed by their efforts. There was not, at that time, a material available which could efficiently contain the hydrogen, and the generating equipment which would have to be carried around was cumbersome. In 1865, following recommendations from its chief chemist, the War Office decided that there was no reason to continue experimenting with balloons "in times of profound peace".

Grover and Beaumont continued to advocate the use of balloons for some years after this, but it was not until 1878 that the practical development of ballooning in the British Army began. Captain H. P. Lee and Captain J. L. B. Templer were appointed to Woolwich Arsenal and a grant of £150 was made for the construction of a balloon and experiments in its use. This led, the following year, to the constitution of the Balloon Equipment Store. Its equipment was one balloon, of 10,000 cubic feet capacity, named *Pioneer*.

Experiments continued and the number of balloons in the Army increased. Many officers were keen on experimenting; that they often discovered this sedate form of flying was not without its dangers did nothing to deter them. In December, 1881, Captain Templer made an ascent in the balloon *Saladin* to make meteorological observations. Templer was accompanied by Mr. Walter Powell, M.P. for Malmesbury, and Lieutenant Agg-Gardner. The flight was to end in tragedy.

The fateful trip started at Bath and the first interesting meteorological observation made was that the cloud base was very low. This fact was driven home, somewhat forcibly, when the ground disappeared from view soon after the ascent had started. The wind freshened and, with the daylight departing at an alarming rate, Templer decided that the flight should be terminated. He freed some of the coal gas with which the balloon was filled and, on breaking the clouds, found that he was approaching the sea near Bridport. Ballast was discharged to stop the descent into what looked like an extremely cold sea and Templer just managed to clear a village which was directly in his path. On the far side of the village, he valved hard and the balloon descended rapidly, to crash on land just 150 yards short of the cliff edge.

Deciding that the grappling iron, which was carried to prevent the balloon from being dragged by the wind on landing, would not hold, Templer yelled to his passengers to jump clear. He set the example himself and the others attempted to follow him. Agg-Gardner succeeded, but at the expense of a broken leg. Powell, however, became tangled in the rigging and could not free himself. Templer, who was already badly bruised, hung on to the valve until his fingers were cut to the bone but the balloon, freed of the weight of two of its passengers, rose at speed and disappeared over the sea. Powell remained trapped in the basket and was never seen again.

British Army balloons had their first "use in anger", as it were, in 1885, when balloon detachments accompanied British forces in the Bechuanaland Expedition and in the Red Sea littoral operations in Eastern Sudan. The balloons were intended only for observation purposes and were used with some success in Bechuanaland. In the Sudan, however, lack of transport severely hampered operations and few positive results could be obtained, although there was an unlooked for bonus. Convoys passing through without balloons were invariably attacked by hostile tribesmen but, on the one occasion when the balloon was used, there was no opposition. So great was the effect on Arab morale, that tribesmen were seen to be dispersing rapidly in the path of the balloon.

The long-standing tradition of the Army often made it even more difficult to assimilate the balloon into its everyday life. Marching order consisted of tunic, riding breeches, jackboots, spurs, helmet, belt, sword and sabretache. On one field day exercise a senior staff-officer was scandalized at seeing an officer-aeronaut about to ascend in clothing which was sensible rather than ceremonially correct. The senior officer rode up and stopped the launching. Did not the ballooning officer know, he asked, that a visit was expected from the Princess Beatrice that day; and what was the officer doing without his spurs, helmet, belt, sword and sabretache? Only with difficulty could he be persuaded that this paraphernalia had to be discarded if the balloon's load was to be made light enough for an ascent.

Balloons did not have a very dramatic history in the British Army for the first few years. In 1886 the Army was granted a mere £2,000 for ballooning and in 1888 this was reduced to £1,600. In the following year, however, a balloon section and depot was constituted under the command of Lieutenant H. B. Jones, R.E., at Aldershot. For the first time, the British Army had an air unit among its establishments. Nevertheless, lighter-than-air craft were regarded with continued scepticism by the War Office, and by 1899, there was still only one section and the depot in the British Army.

Then came the Boer War, which gave ballooning a boost. More balloon sections were built up and balloons were used with great success, both in the purely observation role and for directing the fire of artillery. The Boers had no balloons of their own and had an intense dislike of those used by Britain. They did their best to destroy them but were never successful, although they did succeed in perforating them occasionally, and once wounded an observer with their rifle fire.

After the Boer War the peace establishment of the ballooning branch was fixed at five sections, with one officer in charge of each. More experiments were made and the art brought a stage nearer perfection. Experiments were also made with man-lifting kites, which could be used in high wind conditions when balloons could not. Despite this activity, the War Office was by no means air-minded. Any progress made could be directly attributed to the zeal and foresight of individual officers. One of these was Lieutenant-Colonel J. E. Capper, C.B., R.E., later Major-General Sir John Capper, who was made Officer Commanding Balloon Sections in 1903, the year when the Wright Brothers made their first successful flight.

Capper was convinced of the value of balloons and intrigued by the prospect of heavier-than-air craft. He visited the Wrights while they were experimenting at Dayton, Ohio, was extremely impressed by their knowledge of the art of flying and confident that, with adequate resources, great progress could be made. The Wrights had achieved no recognition in their own country, and Capper sounded them informally on the terms they would expect if asked to come and work in England for the War Office. The brothers stated that for the sum of £20,000 they would work in England for four years and impart all their knowledge to the War Office and to no one else—unless their own country requested their help.

On his return to England, Capper reported to the War Office and strongly recommended that the Wrights' offer should be accepted. It was turned down. A little later, the Wrights approached the War Office directly, and this resulted in some lengthy correspondence and tentative discussions on the subject of an airworthy machine being supplied to Britain, together with instruction in flying it. Eventually, the War Office informed the Wrights that it had been decided not to buy an aeroplane. And so Britain lost the chance of becoming the first European power—in fact, the first power anywhere—whose army had a workable aeroplane. If Britain had begun building an air force from this moment, she would have been able to put experienced units into France from the start and the First World War could well have been shortened.

Capper did not let this failure to use the Wright brothers deter him in advocating the use of aeroplanes. In a lecture on ballooning, delivered at the Royal United Service Institution in 1906, he ended with the prophetic words:

"There is another and far more important phase of aerial locomotion which, in the near future, will probably have to be reckoned with. In a few years we may expect to see men moving swiftly through the air on simple surfaces just as a gliding bird moves. Such machines will move very rapidly, probably never less than twenty, and up to a hundred miles an hour. Nothing but the heaviest storms will stop them. They will be small and difficult to hit, and very difficult to damage and their range of operations will be very large."

By this time, the ballooning activities in the Army stemmed from what was known as the Balloon Factory at South Farnborough, Hants. In 1908, this was graced with the prefix "His Majesty's", and, in the same year, Capper made two recommendations to the War Office. The first was to buy any practical flying machines which came on the market, and the second was that the Farnborough factory should make strenuous efforts towards powered heavier-than-air flight. At this time, there were two men seriously experimenting with aeroplanes in Great Britain, Mr. S. F. Cody and Lieutenant J. W. Dunne.

Cody, an American, was a huge, flamboyant, mustachioed character. He did not have a great deal of technical knowledge but had much imagination and enthusiasm for flying. He was, moreover, a persuasive talker and had already done work for the British Army on man-lifting kites. Capper took him under his wing at the Balloon Factory and Cody started work on an aeroplane proudly called *British Army Aeroplane, No. 1*. Because of the nature of its designer, this aircraft was built amid considerable publicity. Dunne, on the other hand, was encouraged by Capper to work in some secrecy at Blair Atholl, in Scotland.

Despite his growing interest in aeroplanes, Capper did not cease experiments with lighter-than-air craft. In September, 1907, the first British Army airship, named *Nulli Secundus*, sausage-shaped, 130 feet long and less than 30 feet in diameter, took to the air for the first time and passed successfully through its trials. It was powered by an Antoinette engine of some 50 h.p. and with that the airship attained a speed of sixteen miles an hour. On October 5th, this airship made a flight from Farnborough to London, where it circled around St. Paul's Cathedral, manoeuvred over the grounds of Buckingham Palace and set course for Farnborough again. It was found that she could make no headway against the wind while flying due south and the flight ended, somewhat ignominiously, when she landed in the grounds of the cycle track at Crystal Palace. She had been in the air for three and a half hours.

Cody's aircraft reached its final stages of construction during the summer of 1908 and he made a number of tentative hops in it. On May 16th, it left the ground and achieved a flight of 50 yards at a height of between 5–8 feet. Cody brought his aircraft safely to the ground but, on turning round to taxi back for another flight, he caught one wing against a horse trough. This postponed operations, and then the Antoinette engine, which had been borrowed from the *Nulli Secundus*, had to be returned to the airship for further trials and Cody's work was further delayed.

He resumed work in September and, on October 16th, made a flight of 1,390 feet, which is now recognized as the first powered aeroplane flight in Great Britain. The landing was by no means gentle.

Meanwhile, Dunne was also enjoying success on the Duke of

Atholl's estate at Blair Atholl, where keepers and gillies of the Duke's private army kept inquisitive visitors at bay. His first satisfactory effort was a swept-wing glider which made some successful flights until it was crashed by Capper during one of his visits. From this glider Dunne evolved a swept-wing biplane powered by a 20–25 h.p. REP engine. In Dunne's own words, it was "more of a hopper than flier", but some short, successful flights were achieved during the summer of 1908.

Thus, thanks to the efforts of Capper in overcoming the continued War Office reluctance to flying, aeroplane flight in England was started. But the puny grants made by the War Office prevented any real progress and it was fortunate for Great Britain that there was a number of enthusiastic, talented and, above all, monied young men who were anxious to achieve success in flying. Men like A. V. Roe, Thomas Sopwith and Frederick Handley-Page, whose aircraft were later to form the back bone of the R.F.C. and R.A.F., received no encouragement from either the War Office or the Government. Theirs were purely private ventures, often carried on in the face of official interference.

In 1909 there emerged one man who was to do much to overcome War Office prevarication—Richard Burdon Haldane, Secretary of State for Air. During this year he underwent a dramatic conversion in his attitude towards airpower, and the man generally credited with bringing this about was Lieutenant Dunne. Haldane's conversion is well illustrated by his answers to two questions in the House of Commons. In March, in reply to the Earl of Ronaldshay, he stated that there would be no advantage in forming a body to advise in military aeronautics. Then, on May 5th, he made a statement to the House which ended with the following words:

"For the superintendence of the investigations of the National Physical Laboratory, and for general advice on scientific problems arising in connection with the work of the Admiralty and War Office in aerial construction and navigation, I have appointed a special committee."

This decision, which was made after conversations with Dunne, led to the formation of the Advisory Committee for Aeronautics, which was presided over by Lord Raleigh of the National Physics Laboratory. This important step forward in British military aviation provided an opportunity for the Navy, which was conducting tentative experiments as well, and the Army to pool their knowledge of aviation, and it made available to these experimenting officers some of the best scientific brains in the country. It was a well-conceived idea; that it did not have a marked success was attributable to the continued scepticism of the Services, whose attitude was still: "We have done very well without aeroplanes so far, we can do without them today."

In 1909, also, Captain J. D. B. Fulton became the first serving officer of His Majesty's Forces to obtain an Aero Club certificate of ability to fly. Fulton was a skilled engineer with a yen for flying. That he succeeded owed no thanks to official support. During the summer of 1909 he tried to build a Blériot-type monoplane himself, but found the task beyond him. A little earlier, he had won a monetary award from the War Office for a suggestion which had led to the improvement of field guns. With this money be bought a Blériot monoplane and taught himself to fly. Two other officers, Captain Bertram Dickson and Lieutenant L. D. L. Gibbs, had learned to fly in France, and all three did their best to demonstrate the usefulness of the aeroplane. In the autumn of 1910, Dickson and Gibbs arranged to make trial reconnaissance flights during army manoeuvres. They did not meet with much success. Commanding officers were unwilling to make use of aerial reconnaissance because they feared that the sound of aero engines would frighten their horses. Then, when a flight was eventually arranged but had to be cancelled because of bad weather, the view of the sceptics was strengthened.

The press continued to report military aviation developments in Germany, France, and other European countries, and this brought about constant public agitation which, very slowly, began to take some effect. On October 10th, 1910, the War Office announced that the scope of the Balloon Factory at Farnborough should be enlarged to include opportunities for "aeroplaning" as well as ballooning. "The object to be kept in view," the statement went on, "will be to create a body of expert airmen, both officers and other ranks, from which units capable of acting with troops operating in the field can be drawn." It was the first sensible step taken by the War Office in the whole history of British military aeronautics. Yet another was to follow. On February 28th, 1911, an Army Order announced: "It has been decided to organize an Air Battalion to which will be entrusted the duty of creating a body of expert airmen, organized in such a way as to facilitate the formation of units ready to take the field with troops, and capable of expansion."

The Air Battalion came into being on April 1st, and was placed under the command of Major Sir Alexander Bannerman. The Balloon Factory became a separate, but co-related, unit of the Air Battalion and, with Mr. Mervyn O'Gorman as its Superintendent, had its name changed to the Army Aircraft Factory. The formation of the Air Battalion now meant that the development of military aviation was part of the duty of the War Office and should no longer be left to individual officers. That there was no lassitude in the Army itself as regards flying was amply proved when, by the summer of 1911, no fewer than forty volunteers had applied to join the Battalion.

The Air Battalion was not well off for equipment. The "mounts" were a strange collection of what were looked upon, even in those early days, as antiques. Nor were there sufficient of them. Nevertheless, the Air Battalion set about the task of discovering how the Army should adopt air power with great gusto. Officers of No. 2 Company of the Air Battalion, who were stationed at Larkhill, were ordered to take part with their aircraft in army manoeuvres to be held in Cambridgeshire. An abnormally dry summer and a drought caused the manoeuvres to be cancelled, but No. 2 Company decided that the flight to Cambridge in itself would be excellent training, and set off on the first cross country flight of any distance to be performed by a military unit. Five officers started and two eventually reached their destination. All had a series of adventures and crashes, the retelling of which was to lighten many a subsequent evening in the messes at Larkhill or Salisbury Plain, where the rest of the Air Battalion was stationed.

Without any doubt, the most remarkable adventure was that which befell Lieutenant H. R. P. Reynolds. He had completed his first stage to Oxford without incident and took off for Cambridge at seven o'clock one evening. He was pleased to find the air extremely still, although there was an uneasy suggestion of thunder. Reynolds put the worry of a possible thunderstorm out of his mind and gloried in a particularly smooth flight as far as Bletchley. After that, the air became steadily more bumpy. Then it suddenly became *very* bumpy and Reynolds decided that it was high time he descended from 1,700 feet to the safety of the ground. A large, black thunder-cloud, looming up on his starboard bow, clinched the decision.

As Reynolds switched off his engine and pointed the aircraft downwards, a sudden, violent gust caught his tail and he witnessed the alarming sight of his elevator, which was fixed out on booms in front of the machine, swinging down beyond the perpendicular. He was not strapped in and did not have a very clear recollection of the following few seconds. "I suppose I caught hold of the uprights at my side," he recalled, later, "for the next thing I realized was that I was lying in a heap on what was normally the under-surface of the top plane. The machine, in fact, was upside down."

A worrying reminder of the laws of gravity, which he was trying, not very successfully, to defy at that time, came when he saw his suitcase, which must have slipped, as he had, from the lower wing to the top wing, slide off and go whistling earthwards. Feeling a little like an animal trapped in a swinging, swaying cage, Reynolds struggled to his feet, holding on tightly to the struts between the two wings. For a while, the aircraft swung from side to side like a piece of falling paper. Then it swung too far to one side and went straight down sideways, turned right way up, flipped on to its back, then reverted to its original imitation of a falling leaf.

All this time Reynolds had been grimly clutching the struts and observing the motions of his machine in awed fascination. He had also watched the ground coming nearer. Worried as he was, Reynolds still had the presence of mind to realize that much depended on whether the aircraft reached the ground in the middle of a swing or at the end, when it would be moving comparatively slowly. Deciding not to gamble on the aircraft's choice, he resolved to jump just before the aircraft hit the ground.

The final swing came at a height of some thirty feet and the aircraft hit the ground hard. Reynolds jumped from an estimated height of ten feet—and landed safely. He lay down on the ground and closed his eyes for a few moments to regain his composure and his breath.

His alarming descent had been watched in horror by two men bathing in a nearby river. Both were stark naked but, as this was obviously a dire emergency, they ran towards the crash without bothering over the formality of dressing. What Reynolds saw when he opened his eyes was two naked men standing over him. Understandably, he closed his eyes again to ponder this new conundrum. His crash had been witnessed, also, by people in a nearby village and a group of them arrived at the scene a few seconds after the bathers. Seeing the naked men, they reasoned that these must be the brave aviators who had escaped from the crash, literally with their skin. During the subsequent hilarious misunderstanding and explanations, Reynolds was allowed to rest undisturbed on the grass, a fact for which he was most thankful.

Although the Air Battalion was having its share of aerial adventure, and was steadily learning from its mistakes, its efforts were childish compared with what was going on across the Channel in France. While the military aviators of England were fully occupied, both in keeping their flimsy and outdated machines in the air and persuading their superior officers that the aeroplane could be a boon to the Army, the French Air Corps were already practising co-operation with other arms on a large scale. France had two hundred or more serviceable aircraft. Great Britain had twelve which could, with a little imagination, be called seviceable.

The writing on the wall was now plain enough even for the War Office. In November, 1911, it was anounced that a scheme for officers to join the Air Battalion in the event of mobilization would be drawn up. Then, on March 4th, 1912, when Colonel Seely, Under-Secretary of State for War, rose to present the Army Estimates, he announced that he had appointed a committee, of which Lord Haldane was chairman. This committee was to set up a Royal Flying Corps to embrace "soldiers, sailors and civilians". No-one would hold executive rank unless he were an expert flyer. The present Air Battalion would cease to exist and would be absorbed into the new corps. The headquarters would be at Netherton, on Salisbury Plain, and a large tract of land had been purchased for this purpose for the sum of £90,000.

To join the Royal Flying Corps, officers would first have to have the consent of the military authorities, be medically fit, and then obtain a Royal Aero Club Aviators certificate. The cost of this, some £75, would have to be borne by the officer, but would be refunded if he passed and was accepted into the R.F.C.

The Royal Flying Corps was constituted by Royal Warrant on May 13th, 1912. At long last, Britain was in the military aviation business—but war with Germany was only a little over two years off.

CHAPTER TWO

Trials—and Tribulations!

ON PAPER Britain was the proud possessor of an air force. It was to have two units called Wings—a Military Wing and, because the Royal Navy had been conducting aviation experiments as well as the Army, a Naval Wing. At this time the air force was seen as a homogeneous arm in which both sailors and soldiers would serve, although in different units. This idea was to prove hopelessly optimistic. A Central Flying School for both the Military and Naval Wings was also proposed. The purpose of the C.F.S. was not to teach officers to fly, but to take qualified pilots and turn them into fighting airmen.

The constitution of a flying school to serve both sailors and soldiers required special thought. It was decided that it should be run along military lines, but that its commandant should be a sailor. So the choice of commandant fell to Winston Churchill, then First Lord of the Admiralty. In mid-April, 1912, Churchill sent for Captain Godfrey Paine and bluntly informed him that he was to learn to fly before May 1st, because he was to be appointed Commandant of the C.F.S. The choice of a man who did not even know how to fly might seem somewhat short-sighted, but time was to prove Churchill's wisdom. Indeed, a quick investigation of Paine's career is sufficient to show the main reasons behind this choice.

Paine had entered the Royal Navy in 1885 and had risen to the rank of Captain by 1907. He had been given command of H.M.S. *Actaeon*, a torpedo ship at Sheerness, and shortly received on the strength of this ship a few of the Navy's pioneer pilots who had been trained at Eastchurch. He was later given command of the Naval Flying School at Eastchurch which the Admiralty had established before the formation of the R.F.C. Thus, although he could not fly at the time of his appointment, he was well acquainted with the problems of running a flying school. Among Paine's many assets was a mastery of invective which could startle even his naval colleagues. A little later, when the C.F.S. was in full operation, the effect of Paine's language on young army officers who deviated from R.F.C. discipline could be most salutary.

While Paine was selecting his staff from the lists of those with experience of flying in both the Navy and Army, the War Office was concerning itself with the equally important task of deciding a site for the new school. Its choice of some 2,400 acres of land on Salisbury Plain, two miles from the village of Upavon, did not meet with unanimous approval. Those who had to work in this remote spot soon christened it "Siberia". They also complained that, because the airfield itself was on a fairly high plateau while all buildings were scattered around on a lower level, they had to walk uphill wherever they went. *The Aeroplane* magazine was puzzled why the school should be "located on the top of a mountain where it is open to every wind that blows"—a salient point when one remembers the frailty of early aircraft and the fact that flying was only safe in calm conditions.

The Central Flying School was not ready for its official opening until June 19th, and even then it could hardly be called fully operational. As planned, its aircraft strength was twenty-five: at mid-June it had only seven—two French and the rest British. One realistic touch was the provision of a medical detachment comprising one sergeant and one man of the Royal Army Medical Corps. One of these was to be always on duty when flying was in progress. The sergeant spent some time teaching himself to ride a motor-cycle over rough ground so that he could reach the scene of any crash in the shortest possible time.

The task of finding pupils was not as difficult as that of setting up and constructing the school. There was already a nucleus of naval aviators and pilots from the Air Battalion and further recruitment from the Regiments was quite satisfactory once the formation of the R.F.C. had been announced—despite the fact that the parsimonious War Office still expected a man to learn to fly in his own time and at his own expense. It still cost £75 to become an airman, although this money was refunded once the officer had earned his brevet and had been accepted for the R.F.C. Fortunately for Britain, there was no undue pressure to join the Flying Corps; those who did join were officers who could foresee the difference which flying could make to fighting, or those with an unadulterated love of adventure. Britain was to be in sore need of both types in the R.F.C. when war came.

There was, of course, a distinct glamour in being a pilot. Aeroplanes and aviators were so rarely seen in those days that a pilot was regarded with open wonderment and as a man apart. Because of some odd quirk in the British character, neither the War Office (and much later on, the Air Ministry) nor the pilots were anxious to cultivate this. Instead, they did their best to minimize their own achievements and to direct all interest towards the aircraft and the tasks which they had to do. They were not entirely successful in this and a soldier with R.F.C. wings on his breast would often be pointed out with undisguised awe in the street.

Although the recruiting situation was reasonably satisfactory, that of aircraft was not. Because the War Office's head had been firmly in the sand as regards aviation since the beginning of the century, the British aircraft industry was virtually non-existent. This was keenly felt when the R.F.C. began looking around for aeroplanes. The ultimate strength was to be 131 aircraft, Colonel Seely had announced when outlining the formation of the R.F.C. to Parliament in March. He said that 71 aircraft had been sanctioned at that date but, unfortunately, not all orders could go to British firms. French aircraft had been proved better.

"The Government cannot buy British machines at the cost of human life," said the Colonel. These might seem hard words, but they were true. The fault, however, did not lie with the British industry, but with the Government, which had stunted its growth from the start. Only a few British companies were building fairly reliable aircraft—and none of these had been designed solely for military use, nor could they be produced in large numbers. But they did provide the R.F.C. with a nucleus of machines in which they could get some type of practice.

The problem of selecting suitable aircraft for the R.F.C. was tackled by organizing trials, which were held on Salisbury Plain during August, 1912. These were not an outstanding success. Twenty-five aircraft took part, almost one third of them French. The tests called for a series of flights to demonstrate climbing ability, top speed, load-carrying potentialities and operation from rough ground. The last mentioned test involved a landing and take-off in a ploughed field.

Entirely at the whim of the weather, the aircraft staggered through the tests with varying degrees of success. Among the contenders was the inimitable Cody, who had entered a huge aircraft nicknamed "The Cathedral". This was powered by an equally huge 120 horse-power Daimler engine. Cody soon established himself as favourite, so much so, that on August 8th, when a large Parliamentary party paid an official visit to see the trials, Cody refused to take off for their benefit. A fairly stiff wind was blowing across the Plain, and although a few aircraft managed to take off for a demonstration, Cody refused. "I have only one aircraft entered," he explained. "Why should I risk it in this weather, especially as it is already doing so well in the trials?"

Cody's optimism was justified for, under the terms of the competition, the judges, who included Paine and Mr. Mervyn O'Gorman, Superintendent of the Royal Aircraft Factory, had to agree that Cody had won. At the sime time, it was quite obvious that Cody's huge biplane was not a suitable military machine. This Cody himself admitted. The secret of its success was its large engine which had pushed it doggedly through the performance sections of the trials.

Paradoxically, there was one other aircraft present which should obviously have been declared outright winner. This was a B.E.2, designed by Geoffrey De Havilland and built at the Royal Aircraft Factory. But the factory had no authority to construct aircraft as it was purely an experimental establishment. It overcame this by "re-furbishing" crashed aircraft. "Refurbishing" usually meant a completely new design by the gifted De Havilland. The designations applied to the aircraft continued this fiction. The letters "B.E.", for instance, stood for "Blériot Experimental" because the machine was, ostensibly, a reconstructed Blériot.

Flown by its designer, the B.E.2 won the highest marks in most sections of the competition, despite the fact that, during one flight when Major F. H. Sykes, Commander of the R.F.C. Military Wing, was passenger, De Havilland reached a height of 9,500 feet and, flying above the clouds, got lost and had to find his way home, somewhat ignominiously, by coming down low to read the names on railway stations.

Despite the outright success of the B.E.2, it could not be declared the winner because, officially, the Royal Aircraft Factory could not build aircraft, and because the Superintendent of the Royal Aircraft Factory was among the judges. Thus, an unsuitable aircraft became the winner and the machine which would have served the R.F.C. best had to be flown *hors de combat*. The Salisbury Plain Trials had provided an interesting and often exciting interlude, but brought Britain no nearer to obtaining suitable military aircraft.

The frustrations of the new Royal Flying Corps might have been laughable except for the news which came from the Continent. The French Air Corps was a flourishing concern and had taken part in several large scale manoeuvres with the Army. During the very time that flimsy machines had been hopping around Salisbury Plain so that the R.F.C. could choose a suitable aircraft, the French had been holding a bombarding competition with theirs.

In Germany, the Zeppelin force continued to expand and experiments using wireless telegraphy between ground and air were being made. A build-up of conventional aircraft was also taking place. The way in which Britain was lagging behind the rest of Europe in air power seemed to concern everyone except the Government. In an attempt to help the R.F.C., the chairman of the Aerial League of the British Empire, Major-General H. T. Arbuthnot, launched a public appeal for one million shillings. This, he hoped, would provide £50,000 with which to buy machines for the R.F.C., but the British public, quite willing to grumble against the Government's lack of foresight, was not so willing to step in and pay for aircraft itself. The appeal was not a success.

During the late summer of 1912 a decision was taken which was to have far-reaching effects on aerial development, not only in Britain, but throughout Europe. On August 3rd, Lindsay Campbell, a 50-year-old Australian who was taking an advanced flying course at the Brooklands Flying School, crashed while flying a Bristol monoplane. Campbell's tuition was being paid for by the Australian Government so that he could be appointed chief organizer of an Australian flying service at a later date. Campbell was rather old to learn to fly and his instructors found him heavy-handed on the controls. In the opinion of one of them, he was not a suitable pilot to be flying a monoplane as these aircraft were more sensitive to the controls than the biplanes. Nevertheless, Campbell managed to make a flight in a monoplane. He was seen to nose up into a sudden stall and died in the crash which followed the subsequent nose-dive to the ground. There was no doubt in anyone's mind that his death was due to pilot error and this was the verdict at the inquest.

A little later, during the Salisbury Plain Trials, Mr. R. C. Fenwick, who had built and entered an aircraft called the Mersey Monoplane, took off for a flight. His take-off was seen to be unsteady, but this was not unusual with any aircraft, and spectators were convinced that the monoplane would stabilize once it was in the air. But it had reached 300 feet, and was still in difficulties, when it suddenly turned on its back and disappeared behind a clump of trees. When it did not re-appear, a party of rescuers rushed off. They found the crumpled remains of the monoplane and, in the middle of the wreckage, Fenwick's mangled body.

These two accidents, following so closely upon each other, were enough to convince the military authorities that the monoplane was dangerous. It was decided that no more monoplanes would be used by the R.F.C. and this general distrust was felt in Europe as well. Its effect was to retard aviation development considerably, for the monoplane was, aerodynamically, the better design, and therefore, more effective in performance. This decision cannot be classified as another Government blunder. The War Office did, in fact, set up a body, generally known as the "Monoplane Committee", to review the series of accidents to this type of aircraft. In February, 1913, the committee pronounced that the accidents had not been caused by any fault inherent in the monoplane. But, although this type of aeroplane was exonerated, the feeling of revulsion remained. The monoplane had been given a bad name and the early pilot was a superstitious fellow.

These many problems which dogged the development of Britain's air arm did not deter the Royal Flying Corps from throwing itself whole-heartedly into the task of becoming as efficient as its equipment would allow. The pilots were anxious to try out their skill under the most realistic conditions obtainable during peace-time. The chance came during the autumn manoeuvres of 1912, which were held in the Buckinghamshire-Northamptonshire area. Two mythical armies—the Red Army and the Blue Army—were set in opposition. The original suggestion was that the two armies should have eight aeroplanes each, while the Director of Manoeuvres should have four at his disposal. The ban on monoplanes knocked these plans awry and, when the two armies were eventually lined up for battle, they had only seven aircraft each and the Director had none.

The first really useful task ever given to the R.F.C. was a request from the Red Army commander who, on September 16th, at the start of the manoeuvres, wanted to know whether "enemy" concentrations were complete, and whether their advance had started. Aircraft were sent out to see, and by 9.30 a.m. the same morning, the commander had received the information he required and was suitably impressed.

Both sides, in fact, found the aircraft very useful and the R.F.C. did a good job. The unreliability of engines was, as always, a menace, and one Blue Army aircraft was forced to land in Red territory where its pilot suffered the ignominy of being taken prisoner by cavalry. A Red Army aeroplane also was forced down in "enemy" territory through engine failure, but the pilot managed to start the engine and take off just before he was reached by Blue Army troops. The umpires ruled, however, that in a real war, with live ammunition, he would have been shot or captured, so the pilot, who was feeling pleased with his escape, was thwarted when told that the reconnaissance information he had obtained during this flight could not be passed on to his army commander.

The good work performed by the R.F.C. during these manoeuvres was achieved in spite of crowds of sightseers. The aeroplane was still a rare sight and the airmen's business was severely hampered by neck-craning crushes of humanity which collected wherever the aircraft were working.

These 1912 manoeuvres taught the R.F.C. much. They learned that there was urgent need for quick communication methods between the air and the ground, that landing grounds should be established as near as possible to headquarters units, that none but trained personnel were of use as observers and that aircrew, aeroplanes and engines were unlikely to stand the strain of all-out war for more than two months without relief.

The Army, in turn, learned that it would have to teach itself the art of concealment very quickly, if it was to survive in the air age. It was quite obvious that no large body of troops or cavalry could be moved without detection unless artfully camouflaged. The Army should have been grateful for this knowledge but some officers, at least, were not. "The aeroplanes completely spoiled the war," grumbled Lieutenant-General J. M. Grierson, C.B., C.M.G., C.V.O. That the Army did eventually take note of this lesson was borne out the following year when great stress was laid on concealment. "If you cannot find a hedge, hide yourselves under your blankets and make a noise like a mushroom," one officer told his men during the 1913 manoeuvres.

While the R.F.C. was having its first taste of operational conditions in the Home Counties, the aeroplane was being tried out, yet again, in live conflict. In September, 1912, the newly formed Balkan League of Nations declared war on Turkey. The Bulgarian Army had one Blériot aeroplane and two pilots, Lieutenants Petrov and Terakchiev. After the war started, Bulgaria immediately set about purchasing more aircraft from Germany, France and Britain, and sent Petrov and Terakchiev to Russia to see if they could buy any other machines. The two young pilots set about their task with much vigour, but little foresight. They bought the first aircraft they saw, recruited other officers and started to teach them to fly. Their training was as haphazard as their purchasing had been, and within a short time three Albatros aircraft had been wrecked, the Bristol which had been bought from England crashed, and the whole scheme came to an end when a Lieutenant Toprakchiev was burned to death in a crashing Blériot.

Somewhat shaken by the results of this attempt to build up an air arm, but still convinced of the usefulness of aeroplanes, Bulgaria hired the services of a man called Shchetinin, who was part proprietor of a private concern known as "The First Russian Aeronaut Company". With four Farman biplanes and four Russian pilots, Shchetinin took his "air force" to Mustapha Pasha, which became his main base. There the weather was so cold that the aircraft had to spend the night in tents, while the men relied on old packing cases for protection. Most flights were made around the Adrianople area and were for the purpose of training Bulgarian personnel in the art of flying, observing and bomb-throwing. The bombs were primitive missiles weighing about 10 kilogrammes. They were hung from the feet of the pilot and dropped with a smart kick which released a slip knot. During one of these flights, Kostin, a Russian pilot, became lost and was taken prisoner by the Turks, an event which caused a minor international incident when his nationality was discovered.

Thanks largely to a Slavic tendency to experiment rather than get on with a practical job, Bulgaria's use of aircraft in this short-lived conflict was not entirely successful. The most useful job performed by Shchetinin's aeroplanes was to establish contact between Bulgaria's Second Army and her Third Army. This task was entrusted to the Russian pilots, Kolchin and Esiukov, flying Farmans, and to Bulgaria's original pilot, Lieutenant Petrov, who, quite undeterred by his previous exploits, accompanied the Russians on the 94-mile flight over rugged territory to Chatalja in a Blériot. The flight took two hours. It was estimated that it would have taken a week to pass a message that distance by road. While at Chatalja, Kolchin achieved undesirable fame by becoming the first military aviator to be shot down and killed in war. He was found dead beside his aircraft, which had been hit by rifle fire.

The Turks also had aircraft at their disposal and, on at least one occasion, found them extremely useful. Unconfirmed reports were received that Derkos on the Chatalja Front had fallen to the Bulgarians. This could have been serious as the way would then have been open for the Bulgarians to march into Constantinople. Before weakening the Adrianople garrison to defend Constantinople, however, the Turks had the sense to send an aircraft along the Chatalja Front. It returned with the report that the Bulgarians had been repulsed at Derkos, and the situation was saved, for Turkey was able to avoid a serious tactical error.

The Balkan League's three-month war against Turkey was hardly an outstanding example of how aircraft could be used in future conflicts, but it did show that even minor nations were now thinking in terms of aerial warfare. The knowledge did little to egg on the people responsible for building up the Royal Flying Corps. The impetus which was expected to follow the formation of the Corps did not materialize. The number of aircraft grew only spasmodically and continued to be of a diversity of types, mainly French. Confirmation that Britain continued to lag—if such confirmation was needed—came on the evening of October 14th, 1914. At about seven o'clock the drone of aero-engines was heard over Sheerness. It did not sound like an aeroplane and some people who saw lights in the sky swore that they belonged to an airship. When the Admiralty later stated categorically that "the unknown airship heard over Sheerness . . . was not one of our ships", the British nation was alarmed. If the ship was not British then, without any doubt, it was German. Was Britain to be attacked from the skies by an unfriendly nation? If she was, then what protection did she have?

These worries were voiced for the British people by Mr. W. Joynson-Hicks, a member of the Opposition Party in the Commons. He asked the First Lord of the Admiralty how many aircraft Britain had capable of intercepting the alien airship, and how many pilots were capable of flying these aeroplanes. The only answer he got from Winston Churchill was that Britain had no airships capable of intercepting the intruder.

Neither the country nor Joynson-Hicks was satisfied. Early in December, the outspoken M.P. asked Colonel Seely for a progress report on Britain's new air arm. "Fourteen aeroplanes are in use in the Military Wing," replied the Secretary of State for War. "Three of these are at present under repair. Sixteen machines are on order. No machines have been ordered since September 30th, but tenders for eighteen have been provided."

When announcing the formation of the R.F.C., just nine months earlier, Seely had stated that the ultimate strength of the R.F.C. was to be 131 aircraft and that, of these, 71 had been sanctioned. It was more than obvious that there was something very wrong with Britain's Royal Flying Corps.

CHAPTER THREE

"Master of Your Own Air"

THE YEAR 1913 dawned with more mystery lights off the south coast. Newspapers reported that the lights belonged to the German Zeppelin *Hansa* of the German Airship Transport Company, but, said the papers, on these flights she was manned by a crew of naval officers and ratings. These statements were vehemently denied in the German press but disclaimers carried little weight with the British public. People were not particularly concerned about what the airship was doing off the south coast. They just wanted to know how they could be defended against such craft if war came. The War Office would not announce that it had guns capable of shooting the Zeppelin down, because there were none, and what the public read in the press about the R.F.C. was far from reassuring. Practical jokers added to the scare by releasing fire balloons at night in many different places.

Joynson-Hicks continued his campaign against the Government. On January 8th, 1913, he asked Seely whether he was aware that 400 aircraft had been bought by France during the past year, in addition to the 218 aircraft already in possession of the French Army in 1911. He also wanted to know how many aircraft the R.F.C. had available. Seely, in a written reply, stated that the R.F.C. Military Wing had twenty-nine aircraft, and the C.F.S. twenty-six. Of these, twenty-six and nineteen respectively were in flying order.

A total of fifty-five aircraft, forty-five of which were serviceable, was an improvement on the figures Seely had given the previous month—such an improvement, in fact, that Joynson-Hicks and other M.P.s were suspicious. Joynson-Hicks did some checking of his own. It must be remembered that Joynson-Hicks was looking for aircraft not only capable of flying, but capable of being usefully used in wartime. Seely, on the other hand, was anxious to include anything with wings to help swell the total. The difference between the two sets of figures was startling.

"Would the Secretary of State confirm," Joynson-Hicks asked, early in March, "that the total effective strength of the R.F.C. is as follows? No. 2 Squadron has two 'B' biplanes and three Maurice Farmans at Montrose, No. 3 Squadron has one 'B' biplane and two Maurice Farmans at Larkhill and No. 4 Squadron has two Breguet biplanes and two 'B' biplanes at Farnborough."

Seely replied that this was not so. He would not comment at that time because he would soon be making a statement about the R.F.C. when he presented the Army Estimates for 1913–14. These Estimates were presented to the House on March 19th. Seely had obviously been given the task of quietening the tremendous agitation which had sprung up about Britain's lagging air arm. His first announcement, that the sum of £500,000 had been set aside for the War Office to spend on aviation, did little to quell the disquiet which many Members felt. Even in those days, aviation was a comparatively expensive hobby, and £500,000 would not go very far. Seely's next announcement, that a squadron was planned to consist of three flights each with four aircraft and two reserve aircraft, to make a total of eighteen, brought many wry smiles. It was obvious that this planned strength was nowhere near achievement.

So far, the House had been content to listen to Seely's explanations. Then he said, "We have in the possession of the War Office 101 (aeroplanes) capable of flying as far as we can decide . . . We have 101 at this moment and, if there is no further delay, we shall have on May 31st, 148. Of these 101 a great many are machines of the newest type."

These figures were so obviously misleading, if not inaccurate, that questions poured forth immediately.

"How many of these aeroplanes are ready for war?"

"How many are monoplanes, forbidden even for practice?"

"How many are capable of flying?"

Seely's evasive answers did not impress the House. As far as he could remember, some eleven or twelve aircraft were monoplanes and all the 101 were capable of flying. Of efficiency he said, "It all depends on what you mean by efficient. They are all efficient for one purpose or another. Practically all the aircraft would be available for the purpose of manoeuvre but I hasten to add that those most useful for instructional purposes would be of less use in time of war when they might be encountered by hostile aircraft."

The animosity of the House must have been apparent to Seely as he went on with his Estimate speech. He revealed, no doubt in the hope of showing that there were far better things to come in the near future, that a new type of high-speed aeroplane had been tested and flown successfully against very high winds, but, after questioning, admitted that this aeroplane—it was presumably the B.S.1, a single-seat biplane which never entered service—had crashed recently and wrecked its engine. Seely was a little more successful with his announcements that remarkable progress had been made with anti-aircraft guns, although he would not reveal details, and with the revelation that a competition was to be held to discover an efficient British aero engine.

The debate wrangled on for several days. The overall impression gained was that the Government had been almost criminally lax in building up the R.F.C. "The blame must be placed fairly and squarely on the King's Ministers," pronounced *The Times* newspaper. "As long as money is not stinted . . . we shall be fairly well found in the course of a year or so."

For the Opposition, Joynson-Hicks summed up by saying: "The right hon. gentleman might have 101 aeroplanes which can fly: so he might have 101 tom-tits that can fly. What the country is concerned about is how many of these aircraft are efficient for military purposes. I do not care how many the right hon. gentleman has in school for training."

A little later, Winston Churchill announced the Naval Estimates. For aviation in the Naval Wing, R.F.C., the sum of £350,000 had been set aside. Britain's grand total for military aviation was thus £850,000. With a nice sense of timing, the German Government immediately revealed that they were to spend the equivalent of £7,000,000 on the immediate development of aviation.

This latest development seemed to panic Seely into some action at last. He instructed the Directorate of Military Training, the War Office department then dealing with aeronautics, to buy immediately eight aeroplanes from British companies. The aircraft were, of course, all of different types and none of them suitable for military purposes.

Joynson-Hicks, in the meantime, was still puzzled, as were many others, by the figure of 101 aircraft which Seely had given. He took the trouble of visiting every military aerodrome to make a personal count of the number of aircraft. He did, in fact, count 101, but the majority of these, he said, were unserviceable and most of those which could be safely flown were unsuitable for military use. Many sceptics still refused to believe this figure. They swore that the R.F.C. had been instructed to fly the aircraft round, ahead of Joynson-Hicks's visiting commission, and that, therefore, the M.P.s had counted the same aircraft each time at a different airfield. There is no proof of this. In the words of one officer of that time, the Government were not usually so ingenious as this in covering up their mistakes!

All these troubles rose, not only from the lack of money made available for aviation, but from the War Office's policy of refusing to buy from British manufacturers. Most orders went to French firms and the English companies were given only spasmodic orders for one or two aircraft at a time. This meant that they were unable to set up production facilities and, in consequence, were hard-pressed to keep delivery dates for the few aircraft which were ordered. The same conditions applied to aero-engines. The Royal Aircraft Factory bought all that it needed from France and ignored British manufacturers, who might otherwise have been encouraged to spend time and money developing suitable engines. This latter deficiency Seely hoped to overcome with his announcement of the aero-engine competition.

Meanwhile, what of the men of the Royal Flying Corps? To a large extent they were not troubled by the political storms raging over their heads. They were sorry that they could not get better aircraft and more of them, but made do quite cheerfully with those they had. Their primary task was reconnaissance but, unlike the War Office, most R.F.C. officers had the foresight to realize that the aeroplane opened up many possibilities in future wars. The majority of training had to be devoted to reconnaissance but, whenever the opportunity was presented, the squadron commanders, and even the pilots themselves, would experiment in other duties. Most of the year 1912 had been taken up with mastering the new element in which they were working but, from 1913 onwards, the R.F.C. began to realize the full potential of an air force, and experiment was rife.

Perhaps the most obvious extra role was the extension of pure reconnaissance to artillery spotting. Long-distance artillery has always been just as good as its forward observers—the men who watch the bursting of the shells and signal back the necessary corrections to the guns. The aeroplane offered an excellent observation platform, but it also created the problem of relaying the necessary information back to the guns, for wireless telegraphy was an infant science at that time. The R.F.C. tried to overcome this difficulty in a variety of ways, with varying degrees of success. Some aircraft were fitted with Klaxon horns under the fuselage and, after observing artillery fire, would turn towards the gun positions and give corrections in booming morse code. If the R.F.C. had persevered with this method they might have chilled the hearts of enemy troops with these mysterious bellows from the heavens, but it is unlikely that the guns would have received their corrections efficiently. Aiming the Klaxon horn directly at the guns did not ensure that the message would get through, because the bellow was entirely at the mercy of the winds, and this method was discarded. Coloured flags were also tried but these taxed the eyesight of the gunners too much. Coloured lights and Very lights, on the other hand, were found satisfactory. A lesson had been learned from these experiments and the R.F.C. had another role in which it could fight if the need arose.

Not quite so successful were experiments with bombing. There were no aerial bombs in existence in England but 2 lb bags of flour proved a reasonably realistic substitute for practice—especially if these had achieved rock-like hardness while stored under army conditions. No difficulty was experienced in throwing these missiles out of the cockpit against the slipstream, but the pilots soon found that extremely accurate judgement was needed if they were to fall anywhere near a target. It was, in fact, almost impossible to aim with an acceptable degree of accuracy while looking over the side of the cockpit.

A more ambitious experiment was made by No. 3 Squadron. Flying in a Henri Farman biplane, the C.O., Major (later Air Vice-Marshal Sir Robert) Brooke-Popham, and his second-in-command, Major "Josh" Higgins, practised firing a rifle at kites. The success which they achieved has not been recorded but the pastime was reckoned to be so hazardous—not so much for those in the air, but for those on the ground watching—that this form of practice was reserved for senior officers.

The limitations of the aircraft meant that, at this time, the R.F.C. was strictly a fair-weather air force, although the pilots themselves were always willing to fly, whatever the conditions. There were, however, several attempts to spread the sphere of operations into the hours of darkness. This was not easy. Few of the aircraft had any instruments except a petrol gauge, and the pilots relied on the horizon to keep their aircraft level. In April, 1913, Lieutenant Cholmondeley of 3 Squadron, demonstrated that, given a little luck, a little moonlight and a lot of nerve, night flights could be made. He proved this by flying at night from Larkhill to Upavon and back. During the landing he discovered the value of cool nerves because, although the moon had provided sufficient horizon while he was airborne, the last few hundred feet of his landing approach proved rather exciting as he found himself too low to get a good horizon and the moon too weak to illuminate the airfield sufficiently. In later experiments he tried landing by the light streaming from open hangar doors.

A slightly more scientific approach to this problem was made by Lieutenant G. I. Carmichael who, in June, asked Major Brooke-Popham whether he might use petrol flares to light the landing ground. Permission was granted and, with commendable foresight, Carmichael asked his mechanic to make a "night flying control". This was a simple switch which enabled him to illuminate his compass and tachometer, together or separately. When Carmichael made his flight, he discovered that tree tops provided sufficient horizon while flying. During the landing the petrol flares proved their worth by giving the pilot depth perception, that is, the ability to judge height accurately during the last few vital feet of a landing. Following this success, the petrol flarepath was used for night landings until well into 1917.

Experiments of this nature were most valuable to the R.F.C., although not very exciting to the public in general. The press, however, were able to keep the R.F.C. in the limelight by reporting notable flights which were made from time to time. Perhaps one of the most dramatic was made by Captain C. A. H. Longcroft who was attached to Number 2 Squadron stationed at Montrose. At 5.25 a.m. on Wednesday, May 21st, Longcroft set out from Farnborough to fly to Montrose. He landed at the Scottish base at 4.20 p.m., a fearful sight with his face torn and bleeding, but triumphant at his success. The flight had been remarkably free from trouble. Longcroft had completed it in three stages and not until the last stage, as he was nearing St. Andrews, did he run into difficulties. He met a rain storm which soon changed to hail. Determined to complete the flight at all costs, he ignored the terrible punishment which the exposed parts of his anatomy were taking from the hailstones and pressed on. He covered the 550 miles in 5 hours 45 minutes of flying time, often travelling at over 100 miles an hour, and maintaining a height of between 5,000 and 6,000 feet throughout.

In August, Longcroft made another flight over the same route, this time landing only once, and in November, while flying a B.E. type aircraft with a long-range petrol tank of his own design, he flew from Montrose to Portsmouth, and from there to Farnborough, without landing once. The flight took 7 hours 20 minutes.

That achievements of this type were rare was no fault of the pilots. They had to contend with notoriously cantankerous aircraft. The majority of machines were either Henri Farmans or Maurice Farmans and the R.F.C. soon learned, from hard experience, some of the things which could go wrong. In the Henri Farman a lack of balance of the 50 h.p. Gnome rotary engine was the main source of trouble. This could cause fractured petrol pipes, broken rocker bars and push-rods flying loose, cracked engine bearers, petrol tank leaks and the shearing of petrol tank bolts—any one of which troubles would usually result in a pilot hurriedly selecting a place for a crash landing.

The Maurice Farman was generally more reliable, as its 70 h.p. Renault engine gave less trouble, but engine failures were still no rarity. One engine, which was shut down after giving severe vibration, was dismantled and the mechanics were astonished to see two big-end pins broken and the crankshaft twisted out of shape.

Other troubles, common to nearly all aircraft, included perished petrol pipes, which caused fuel blockage, fraying of control cables, icing up of carburettors with consequent loss of power and, perhaps the most dangerous defect of all, the seizing-up of magnetoes through dampness.

Many of the aircraft in use carried their elevator in front of the wings and tended not to pull out of a dive if this were entered too steeply. The answer was to keep clear of dives, but this was not easy, especially when pilots found themselves flying in cloud with no air speed indicator to warn them of an unexpected increase in velocity. The R.F.C. pilots even found an answer to this difficulty—although the safety drill was probably more alarming than the emergency itself.

Lieutenant Randall of the C.F.S. was one of those who lived to recount his experience. He was flying a Maurice Farman Longhorn, one day, when he entered a cloud and became disorientated. When, unexpectedly, he flew out of the cloud, he was alarmed to see a huge hill directly ahead. He thought he knew every inch of Salisbury Plain, over which he was flying, but he could not recognize the hill. It took him some seconds to realize that it was not a hill before him but the earth below. His aircraft was pointing vertically downwards. He tried to pull back on the stick but the machine refused to come out of the dive. As a last-minute, desperate experiment, he tried pushing the stick forward. The aircraft answered and turned right over so that it came out of the dive but in an inverted position. Randall managed to get right way up once again and, rather shaken, flew back to Upavon. During his return flight he began to think of the negative load which he had placed on the wings by his manoeuvre and shuddered at a vivid picture which formed in his mind. Would the wings of his aeroplane fall off before he reached the airfield? Nevertheless, he reached Upavon safely and this alarming method of recovering from a steep dive was later to save the lives of other pilots in similar difficulties.

Aspects of airmanship such as this were passed on from pilot to pilot over drinks in the mess and not during training. Very little thought had been given to flying training when the R.F.C. was set up and, although most instructors were capable pilots, few if any were good instructors. The result was that pilots qualified with the ability to make take-offs, simple turns and landings, and very little else. Aerobatics were forbidden during training and pupils rarely flew above 4,000 feet, as this was considered to be the maximum height at which reconnaissance should be made. After training, any added skills which the pilot achieved were solely the result of his own determination and inventiveness. That many pilots did achieve high standards, despite the general lack of aerodynamic knowledge and the built-in hazards of the aircraft they flew, was a testimonial to the

War Office's selection methods—methods which were based purely on guess-work but which were more than justified by the performance of the Royal Flying Corps in the war which was soon to follow. The type of officer selected for training as a pilot had to be a good horseman and a good soldier. So, unwittingly, the War Office was selecting the right type of man. Good horsemanship meant, of course, that a man had a good sense of balance, could gauge distances accurately and had good and quick judgement of a situation—all attributes of a successful pilot. That he was a good soldier meant that he was keen and so contributed to the remarkable *esprit de corps* which developed in the R.F.C.

The way in which this latter attribute worked is, perhaps, best demonstrated by one, Second Lieutenant G. B. Rickards, who was selected for training at the C.F.S. He was just over forty years of age and a little old for the R.F.C. but, nevertheless, keen. One day he crashed a Maurice Farman while landing, was treated to a virtuoso display of invective by the Commandant, Godfrey Paine, and forbidden to fly again. Crestfallen but still determined, Rickards sat down that night and made out a new will in which he left to the State sufficient money to replace the wrecked machine. This document he sent to Paine, together with a request that the ban on flying should be lifted. Paine could not resist this appeal. Rickards continued his training and served with distinction in the R.F.C., and later the R.A.F., until 1921.

Over the period 1913–1914, some thought was given to the possibility of arming aircraft with guns. Officers of the Military Wing, R.F.C., well aware of continual experiments, in both France and Germany, in firing machine guns from aircraft, pressed for action. They had little support. On War Office instructions, the Royal Aircraft Factory fitted a Hotchkiss machine gun in a Henri Farman but, although some success in hitting ground targets was achieved, the gun was not suitable for aerial use. Then, in November of that year, an American-designed Lewis gun was brought to England. A civilian pilot, Mr. Marcus Manton, suspended a basket between the undercarriage struts of a Grahame-White biplane and, with Lieutenant Stellingwerf of the Belgian Army nursing the gun in the basket, took off. Shots were aimed at ground targets with some degree of success. News of this test reached the War Office, who ordered trials to find the machine gun most suited to aerial needs. The weapon chosen was the air-cooled Lewis gun, but no action was taken until September, 1914. The belief was that the role of the R.F.C. was purely reconnaissance. The War Office and the Government did not realize that, if war came, enemy forces were unlikely to allow British aircraft freedom of flight over their troops to report on movements—even when this was pointed out by no less an astute person than Winston Churchill, First Lord of the Admiralty. "The only real security upon which sound military principles will rely," he said in the House of Commons, "is that you should be master of your own air." In other words, he was stressing the importance of air supremacy—an importance which the R.F.C. was later to realize after costly and dangerous lessons in war.

However, the Government was unable to remain totally immune from the pressure of opinion inside the R.F.C. and the public outcry against its policies during the early part of 1913. When the Army Estimates for 1914 were presented, the sum set aside for aeronautics was almost doubled, from £520,000 in 1913 to £1,000,000. This meant that the Directorate of Military Aeronautics was able to pursue a definite policy in ordering machines and, at last, the struggling, starved, British aviation industry found that ten, and sometimes as many as twelve, aircraft of the same type were being ordered from one factory. These orders were spread throughout the industry to keep as many firms alive as possible. This it succeeded in doing, but it was still little more than a starvation diet.

Meanwhile, the political scene in Europe was clouding over at an alarming rate. With one eye on this political situation, Lieutenant-Colonel Sykes, Commander of the Military Wing, persuaded the War Office to hold a mock mobilization of the Royal Flying Corps. This was to be combined with a month's combined training and general exchange of ideas on the art of flying and fighting in war. During June, the whole of the Military Wing found itself gathered at Netheravon, on Salisbury Plain. The move to Netheravon proved excellent practice for what was to follow later that summer, and the programme of training, drawn up with typical thought and care by Sykes himself, was to iron out many problems which individual squadrons had been facing.

Tactical exercises, such as reconnaissance flights searching for troops and motor vehicles, were combined with purely technical practice, like achieving the best climb rate to specified heights and landing short after passing a tape in a cross-wind. On the ground, committees worked out establishments for stores and personnel and there were regular lectures. One, on the use of machine guns in aircraft, though negative in that it dealt mainly with the difficulties of this type of armament, excited a few of the more lively imaginations in the R.F.C., among them that of Lieutenant Penn-Gaskell of No. 5 Squadron. Filled with a vision of the power which could be wielded by a properly-armed aeroplane, he would speak of little else for weeks afterwards. It was to prove fortunate for the R.F.C. that his, and other, imaginations were so fired.

On June 22nd, the day of the King's Birthday Parade at Aldershot, four Sopwiths, led by Major Higgins of 5 Squadron, four B.E.s, led by Major J. H. Becke of 6 Squadron, and four Blériots from 3 Squadron, led by Captain A. G. Fox, flew at 200 feet past the saluting base on Laffan's Plain and dipped their wings in salute. On June 26th, the whole of the Military Wing was reviewed at Netheravon by the Prime Minister, Mr. Asquith.

The Royal Flying Corps was still inadequate; Britain still lagged behind Germany and France; but patriotism was running high. The spirits of the men of the R.F.C. were higher than ever after the combined training. The last few days of June, 1914, were certainly proud ones for the men of Britain's military air arm.

Notably absent from the Camp were the squadrons of the Naval Wing, the other half of the Royal Flying Corps as it had been established in 1912. From the start, the Naval Wing had gone its own way. The ultimate reason for the Royal Navy's existence is home defence and its aircraft had vastly different tasks from those of the Military Wing. While the latter had been giving most of their attention to the problems of reconnaissance, the Naval Wing had been experimenting with floatplanes, operating aircraft in conjunction with ships, and giving far more thought to aerial defence than their soldier comrades. Apart from training at the Central Flying School, the men of the Military Wing rarely came into contact with those of the Naval Wing. Service differences and pride were, in any case, far too strong for any combined force to survive for long.

The inevitable schism came on June 23rd, 1914. The Admiralty announced a series of organization changes and among them was the formation of the Royal Naval Air Service. With perfectly straight faces, the Board of Admiralty stated that this was "to form part of the Naval Wing". This was the equivalent of saying that such-and-such Supermarket Company had been floated to become part of a particular local grocery store. No-one was taken in by this statement. The Admiralty were cutting themselves off completely from the Royal Flying Corps. The new Royal Naval Air Service was a separate body, analogous with the Royal Marines. Within it, officers would be promoted independently of their rank in the Royal Navy.

Without a doubt, this was a high-handed action by the Admiralty. The Naval Wing had been formed as part of the R.F.C. by decision of the Government of the day, when the plans for an air arm were being made. The decision to divorce it from the R.F.C. was made by the Admiralty alone, yet it was never questioned in the House of Lords, in the Commons or in the press, such was the political strength of the Admiralty.

News of this partition only served to strengthen the high morale of the Royal Flying Corps as the squadrons packed their gear and prepared to return to their stations at the completion of the Camp. Five Squadrons had attended, Nos. 2, 3, 4, 5 and 6. No. 1 Squadron had been operating airships since its Air Battalion days and was in the process of converting to aeroplanes, and another squadron, No. 7, was still in the formation stage at Farnborough. This was the force, puny by any standards, to which the Army had to look for help in the event of war.

Even to the most optimistic, war could not now be very far away. On June 28th, Archduke Franz Ferdinand, nephew and heir to the Emperor of Austria, and his wife were assassinated in the streets of Sarajevo, the capital of Bosnia. Germany, by this time bubbling with restless ambition, took advantage of these killings to push Austria into making unreasonable demands on Serbia who, it was alleged, engineered the attack. Serbia turned towards Russia for help and advice; Russia was tied by Treaty with France—and thus to England. Obviously the peace in England was nearing an explosive end.

The pilots of the Royal Flying Corps realized that their days of experiment and practice were almost over. Soon, they would be flying and fighting in earnest. This fact was driven home to the pilots of No.

2 Squadron when their C.O., Major C. J. Burke, told them that, if they met a Zeppelin after war was declared, they would obviously have to do their utmost to shoot it down. If they failed, they were to take other measures—in other words to ram it. None of the pilots questioned this order.

In the Directorate of Military Aeronautics at the War Office, the department chief, Major Sefton-Brancker, a young officer whose enthusiasm and foresight did so much to overcome Government blundering over aviation, worked his staff and himself day and night to bring the squadrons up to strength. Every suitable civil aeroplane in the country was commandeered and Brancker ordered his officers to scour France, as well, to buy up all available aviation equipment.

The £1,000,000 which had been voted for aviation during the year 1914–1915 was soon overspent. There was no authorization for this. Until general mobilization was ordered no unusual expenditure was permitted. Luckily for Britain, this did not deter Brancker. Backed by General Henderson, he continued to build up the R.F.C. Henderson, in turn, was backed by the Treasury. He explained the vital need for the purchases to Sir Charles Harris, Assistant Financial Secretary of the War Office. "Well," said Harris, "it's hell with the lid off now! Go and order what you think necessary."

Within the Cabinet there was a strong "peace at any price" contingent and, during the last few days of July and the start of August, there seemed every possibility that England was going to sit on the fence and watch France being attacked. This was contrary to popular feeling, and certainly contrary to the feelings of most officers in the Army.

"We knew that the French Army relied on us absolutely," says one officer who was on the Staff of the War Office at the time. "Some of us could hardly contain our rage and shame. There were several officers of the General Staff who were seriously thinking of resigning their commissions and joining the French Army, and pilots in the Royal Flying Corps who were talking of flying quietly across the Channel, without orders, to help our French friends in the air."

But such drastic action was not necessary. On August 4th, German troops crossed into Belgium. The British Government sent an ultimatum that, if the German forces had not withdrawn by midnight, a

Above, the Maurice Farman Longhorn and, *below*, the Maurice Farman Shorthorn—the skids beside the wheels gave the aircraft its name—were used for training in the R.F.C. during its early years

Above, a Lewis gun mounted experimentally in a Maurice Farman biplane. The addition of a heavy gun on a frame barely stout enough to carry both crew and fuel was the main handicap of pre-war aeroplane armament. *Below*, Sergeant Ridd, of the R.F.C., seen here in a Maurice Farman biplane, was the first N.C.O. in the British Army to gain a pilot's certificate

state of war would exist between Britain and Germany. Germany did not withdraw her troops and Britain was officially at war.

Dotted around British airfields, the Royal Flying Corps awaited the orders which would tell them what part they would play in this conflict. Sceptics were wondering just what effect 63 aeroplanes, 105 Officers and 95 motor-transport vehicles—the force which the R.F.C. had available to send to France—could have on the fighting.

Thanks to the spirit of this small force, the sceptical ones were in for a surprise.

CHAPTER FOUR

Into Battle

THE ROYAL FLYING CORPS was not noted for the frequency of its parades. It was, above all, a practical unit of the Army, and the still air of the early mornings was far too valuable for flying to be used for ceremony. So it was apparent that something out of the ordinary was afoot when No. 4 Squadron, busily engaged in normal training procedure at Netheravon, was assembled for a special parade on the morning of July 31st, 1914.

The Commander of the Squadron, Major G. H. Raleigh, roughed out the European situation as it existed at that time, and then broke the news that the Squadron would be taking up its war station at Eastchurch to defend the Chatham area in the event of war. The men were left in little doubt about the seriousness of the situation when Raleigh ended his short speech with the orders to return to their huts at once, pack overnight bags and be ready to take off for Eastchurch within half an hour.

Thus, No. 4 Squadron was the only unit of the R.F.C. to be at its war station when Britain finally declared war on Germany at 11 p.m. on August 4th, and to them fell the honour of making the first operational flights. On the following day, while the news of Britain's entry into the war was being discussed in hushed, rather awed voices in millions of British homes, the pilots and observers of 4 Squadron were droning over the Chatham dockyards, on the look-out for Zeppelins—the one type of German aircraft which was thought to be capable of attacking Great Britain.

It was a duty which was boring. It was neither glamorous nor exciting. The observers were issued with service rifles, two rifle grenades and fifty rounds of ammunition which they wore in a canvas bandolier. Their orders were to attack and destroy any Zeppelins which approached their patrol area. These orders were the subject for much musing by the airmen. They knew that Zeppelins usually flew at heights far beyond the reach of their flimsy B.E.2a aircraft but, just supposing that by a miracle they could reach the airships, what use would their ineffective armament be? This question was never answered because they saw no Zeppelins.

But the War Office had no intention that its aerial arm should spend the war defending the Royal Navy. By August 9th, the British Expeditionary Force, under Field Marshal Sir John French, had begun to embark for France and soon began to take up positions in a roughly triangular area between Mauberge and Le Cateau. A handful of R.F.C. officers, under the Deputy Assistant Quartermaster-General, Major H. R. M. Brooke-Popham, sailed with the B.E.F. Their task was to select landing grounds for the squadrons which would soon be in France helping the Army.

The task of mobilizing the R.F.C. had, in fact, started on the day before Britain declared war. No. 2 Squadron, somewhat isolated up in Montrose, began the long move southwards on August 3rd. That the pilots did not expect the situation to be as serious as it was is evidenced by the fact that they left the majority of their belongings in their huts, locked the doors and issued instructions that nothing was to be touched until their return.

News that at last they would be flying and fighting in a war was greeted with mixed feelings by the Royal Flying Corps who numbered some one thousand men all-told. Discussions in the various messes centred around the expected war casualty rate, which, combined with the known accident rate, was expected by some authorities to give the R.F.C. a 100 per cent loss of pilots and observers within a few weeks. But the majority of officers refused to believe in these ratther gloomy official forecasts and the general feeling was of enthusiasm and exaggerated exuberance. In 5 Squadron's mess at Gosport the irrepressible Penn-Gaskell, the machine gun enthusiast, gave noisy and vivid impressions of how he would range up alongside enemy aircraft and loose off his heavy Vickers machine gun, to the consternation of the Hun. Another 5 Squadron "character", Lieutenant Robert Smith-Barry, who, seemingly, did not take his training seriously (the time was to come when he took training very seriously, indeed) and delighted to frighten others with his hair-raising aerial antics, seemed suddenly to realize the gravity of the situation and insisted on donating his own Rolls-Royce car to the Squadron's motor section, despite the fact that this had already been considerably enhanced by a colourful mixture of impressed civilian vehicles, including the pride of the Squadron, a large red van clearly labelled "H.P. SAUCE".

But it was soon to become apparent that the R.F.C. had more to fear from "acts of God" than the German Air Force. Incomplete understanding of the medium in which they flew, inadequate training and the unreliability of their machines combined to make the movement of Nos. 2, 3, 4 and 5 Squadrons to France a hazardous affair. Second Lieutenant R. R. Skene, one of 3 Squadron's most experienced pilots, and his mechanic were killed when their aircraft crashed soon after they took off from Netheravon for Dover. The remaining aircraft of this squadron reached Dover safely and were there joined by the aircraft and personnel of Nos. 2 and 4 Squadrons on August 12th.

Lieutenant-Colonel Sykes arrived at midnight with orders for the move to France to start at dawn the next day. He issued the pilots with maps of Belgium and France, to a scale of 6 miles to 1 inch, and, for the first time, the airmen had some idea of their destination. Each man was issued an inner tube, which was expected to be an airman's salvation in the event of a forced landing in the Channel. There followed a few hours' rest and then, at 6.25 a.m., Lieutenant H. D. Harvey-Kelly of 2 Squadron took off for France. Miraculously, Harvey-Kelly and all the aircraft which followed made the Channel crossing in safety.

One formation of aircraft from 4 Squadron, led by Captain F. Cogan, also crossed the coast safely. Then Cogan's engine cut out. This type of occurrence was regarded as an occupational hazard in the R.F.C. and so Cogan was not unduly perturbed. After a few mild curses, he set about looking for a likely field in which to make a forced landing. What did perturb him, as he circled, was to see the rest of his formation circling with him. He waved energetically to signal to them that they should fly on without him. The other pilots, reasoning that if their flight leader was landing then they must have arrived at their destination, interpreted the wave as confirmation of this and followed their leader down. The incident might have been conveniently forgotten if the field which Cogan had chosen had not proved to be ploughed. Several aircraft were damaged in the landing.

Meanwhile, back in England, No. 5 Squadron were having trouble getting started. Not until August 14th did aircraft start leaving Gosport for Dover. One aircraft landed with engine trouble on the way and two others crashed, although no-one was badly hurt. "A" Flight Commander, Captain G. I. Carmichael, was taxiing across the airfield for take-off in his Henri Farman when the inter-plane struts collapsed and he had to wait for another aircraft. Thus, after a series of adventures, the Royal Flying Corps arrived at Amiens, where Sir David Henderson had earlier set up his headquarters. Because they had been flying off to war, the pilots and observers had naturally expected they would be roughing it and few of them had bothered to take pyjamas. It was with some consternation—mixed with relief—that they discovered that many of the billets were in quite high class hotels, and French shopkeepers in the district did a brisk trade in pyjamas.

For a few days nothing happened and the squadrons had an opportunity to patch up some of the damage caused to aircraft by the move to France. The Aircraft Park, under Major A. D. Carden, had also started its move to France. With it came twenty-four crated aircraft which were soon being assembled to replace those lost through accidents. Captain Carmichael and two other pilots of 5 Squadron were sent to Buc to collect three Henri Farmans on August 16th. One of the pilots did not return to Amiens with the others. The missing pilot, Lieutenant R. M. Vaughan, turned up three days later. He explained that an engine failure had forced him to land near Senlis. The French had been suspicious of his identity and locked him up. When he was at last able to convince them that he was British, he was set free, and he regaled his fellow pilots with a glowing account of how the Mayor's two charming daughters had atoned for the mistake of their countrymen.

The story was not so well received by the C.O., Major "Josh" Higgins, who was annoyed that one of his pilots should go missing in this fashion. At that time, the R.F.C. aircraft had no national identity markings—except for one aircraft which bore evidence of its recent civilian use, having the word "DAILY" under one wing and

"MAIL" under the other—and he straight away instructed his pilots to sew Union Jack insignia on to their aircraft so that they would immediately be recognized. The practice was followed by other squadrons. The small flag sewn on the fuselage side was soon replaced by six-foot wide Union Jacks painted under the wings, and later, because they could be confused with the German cross, by red, white and blue roundels, which are still in use with the R.A.F.

The arrival of the B.E.F. and R.F.C. in France had been watched impassively by the German forces. It seemed to them that the British forces were settling in an area where they could quite easily be wiped out. The Germans were correct in their assumption; the British area had not been wisely chosen. But they had reckoned without the Royal Flying Corps.

As soon as a squadron was fully up to strength, it moved to Mauberge, and it was from there, on August 19th, that the R.F.C. flew on its first war task. Two aircraft, a Blériot from 3 Squadron and a B.E. from 4 Squadron, were ordered to the Nivelle-Genappe area to report if any Belgian forces were in the vicinity. The pilots were Captain Philip Joubert de la Ferté (the late Air Chief Marshal Sir Philip Joubert) in the Blériot and Lieutenant G. W. Mapplebeck in the B.E. Mapplebeck had the additional task of locating enemy cavalry in the Gembloux area. The pilots were told to stay together as far as Nivelle so that one could report back if the other were forced down.

The reconnaissance was not exactly crowned with success. The two aircraft became separated in a cloud and did not meet again in the air. Joubert, after trying to steer a compass course through cloud, landed at Tournai to inquire after the Belgian forces. Nothing was known. He left Tournai, landed at Courtrai after getting lost, and eventually got back to Mauberge at 5.30 p.m. He had left at 9.30 in the morning. On landing, he discovered that Mapplebeck had had slightly better luck. After getting lost over Brussels, he had eventually reached Gembloux, where he saw a small body of cavalry heading south-east.

That these first reconnaissance flights had little success was no fault of the pilots concerned. They were flying over strange country, with strange maps and no navigational aid other than a simple compass. But these early difficulties of the R.F.C. did not help its standing with the Army commanders in the field. Naturally suspicious of the value of aircraft, they would not attach much credence to isolated reports from pilots.

This general doubt which greeted unconfirmed reconnaissance reports was almost to cost the British Army many lives. On August 22nd, Captain Joubert, with Lieutenant D. L. Allen in the observer's cockpit of his Blériot monoplane, took off from Mauberge to report on the fighting around Charleroi where French forces under General Lanrezac were heavily engaged against the Germans. Liaison with the French in this area had not been too good.

The art of concealment from the air had not yet been born and Joubert and Allen, bumping along at some 2,000 feet, had no difficulty in locating Charleroi or the heavy fighting which was taking place. It was also patently obvious that the French were being steadily driven back. Their report was received coldly. British Intelligence Officers pointed out that they had liaison officers with the French forces and, although communications were proving difficult, they would not fail to get through news of this import. The R.F.C. must be mistaken.

That evening, the Grand Rue of Mauberge echoed to the strains of "Brian-Boru" as the Royal Munster Fusiliers marched through in style towards Mons. Both the soldiers and the local populace were in high spirits. The British First Division was marching towards Mons to launch an offensive against the enemy, completely unaware that the French on their right flank were rapidly falling back—a fact that had been reported to G.H.Q. and disbelieved.

Fortunately, from another reconnaissance flight made that day, a report was made of a long column of enemy troops, believed to be as large as an army corps, moving westward on the Brussels–Ninove road. It was in fact, General von Kluck's Second Corps, and the advancing British First Division was marching straight into a trap. Brigadier-General Sir David Henderson, himself, took this report to G.H.Q., where it provided much food for thought.

That night, Sir John French held a conference at Le Cateau. There he considered the R.F.C. reports. They were still not trusted implicitly but French believed in them sufficiently to call off the offensive he had planned. He agreed, however, to keep his forces in position for a further twenty-four hours to help General Lanrezac's hard-pressed army. The Royal Flying Corps had prevented Mons from becoming a major disaster, as the British forces were now fully prepared for the retreat which started on August 24th. But, if the reports had been believed implicitly when they had first been made, many thousands of lives might have been saved.

A few days later, when R.F.C. reconnaissance aircraft flew over the same area, they were bringing in reports which were far from welcome. Flying over the British Second Corps on the Cambrai–Cateau line, Lieutenants Allen and Wadham looked down on the attempted withdrawal of British guns, the crews of which had been killed. Relief teams galloping up ran straight into enemy artillery fire. Shrapnel shells burst in the midst of them and, when the smoke had cleared, all the airmen could see were struggling, panic-stricken horses.

For the R.F.C., too, the retreat from Mons was an unpleasant memory. In the twelve days between August 24th and September 4th, R.F.C. Headquarters occupied no fewer than nine different locations. Squadron aircraft returning from a reconnaissance would find that their unit had moved. They had standing instructions in such cases to fly on southwards, until they saw their own aircraft on the ground. No. 5 Squadron found their large red H.P. Sauce lorry an invaluable landmark when trying to find their new airfields. The weather was atrocious. A move from St. Quentin to La Frere had to be made in heavy rain, the aircraft flying at no more than 300 feet above the ground. As a result of this soaking, many of the engines short-circuited and could not be switched off—and once they had been stopped they would not start again. Aircrew found that they were spending one night on a feather bed in a comfortable billet, and the next out in the open, sleeping under the wings of their aircraft. But there were no complaints from the R.F.C. Their daily flights over the fighting showed them that their lot was far, far better than that of the soldiers.

Even under these adverse conditions, the R.F.C. lost none of the resourcefulness which had marked its early training in Great Britain. An aircraft from 3 Squadron was forced down near the fighting around Cambrai. A forced landing was successfully made near a road and the pilot and observer removed the wings from the aircraft, hailed a passing French car and asked the driver to tow them back to their base. The Frenchman agreed—reluctantly, as he was in a hurry to get away from the advancing enemy. All went well until the wingless aircraft slipped sideways on a corner and fell in a ditch. Arguments and threats would not persuade the Frenchman to linger any longer and the airmen were left by their machine, which they destroyed. They then "commandeered" two bicycles and pedalled back to their base.

Nor did the mud and misery of the Mons retreat prevent the natural inventiveness of the R.F.C. having full play. Lieutenant Conran of 3 Squadron wondered what effect a hand grenade would have if dropped among enemy forces. There seemed only one way to find out and when, while on reconnaissance, Conran noticed two enemy columns converging on one road, it seemed that his chance had come. He bided his time until one column pulled into a field to wait until the other had passed. Then, flying low over the enemy forces, he tossed out several grenades. The puny explosions were not enough to do very great damage, but the sudden noise stampeded the horses, and Conran reported that several soldiers must have been severely wounded, if not killed, by the pounding hooves.

In 5 Squadron, Captain L. A. Strange had been musing on the value of petrol as a weapon. On August 28th, during a quiet period in the morning, he manufactured a number of simple petrol bombs, which he took with him on two sorties he made in a Henri Farman during the afternoon. The first two bombs were dropped with little success, but the third bomb, thrown overboard during his second sortie, hit a German lorry, which ran into a ditch and caught fire. The flaming, exploding petrol splashed a following lorry and that, too, caught fire. Strange was pleased with his afternoon's work.

So far, the Royal Flying Corps had little to fear from the attentions of the enemy. Germany had anti-aircraft guns but these were not very accurate and shells usually burst about 1,000 feet below the aircraft. Rifle fire from the ground was, at that time, far more lethal. The R.F.C.'s first casualties from enemy action came on August 22nd, when Lieutenants Bayly and Waterfall failed to return from a reconnaissance in the Soisnies region. Their aircraft was hit by rifle fire, crashed, and both men were killed. On the same day, Lieutenant M. Noel of 2 Squadron returned from a reconnaissance and reported heavy rifle fire over Ollignies. His observer, Sergeant-Major D. S. Jillings, had been wounded in the leg.

But of far more interest to the pilots and observers of the R.F.C. was the fact that enemy aircraft were now being encountered. The first one to make its presence known appeared over Mauberge before the retreat had started on August 22nd. It was nearing lunch-time when those on the airfield became aware of an unfamiliar shape in the sky. It was certainly no British aircraft and was identified by some pilots as a Taube, by others as an Albatros. But, whatever its name, it was a German, and that was enough for machine gun enthusiast Penn-Gaskell, who saw his chance of proving his theories of aerial combat. Calling for Strange to start the engine of his Henri Farman, Penn-Gaskell heaved his massive Vickers gun and three hundred rounds of ammunition into the cockpit. As the British aircraft took off, the German climbed to 5,000 feet. Strange nursed his aircraft slowly up to 3,000 feet, but it seemed reluctant to climb into the sky. Almost inch by inch, he coaxed it to 3,500 feet, at which height it refused to climb any higher. The weight of Penn-Gaskell, his gun and his ammunition was too much for the aircraft. Penn-Gaskell hopefully shot off some rounds, but the German aircraft remained unchallenged at 5,000 feet for some time before flying off towards the west, chased by two other enthusiasts in B.E. aircraft who had eagerly taken off armed with bombs and hand grenades with which to make the interception.

Better luck came the way of Lieutenants C. W. Wilson and C. E. C. Rabagliati on August 25th. Flying on a reconnaissance from Le Cateau, they ran across a German Taube monoplane. Wilson gave chase, while Rabagliati stood up in the rear cockpit and fired his rifle over Wilson's head. The German pilot, disconcerted by the bullets whistling about his ears, landed beside a British column near Le Quesnoy.

On the same day, three aircraft from No. 2 Squadron gave chase to a German aircraft and forced it to land. One of the three British aircraft, that piloted by Lieutenant Harvey-Kelly with Lieutenant W. H. C. Mansfield as observer, also landed near-by and, anxious not to let their quarry escape, the Britons chased the German air crew on foot. The Germans escaped into a wood. Harvey-Kelly and his observer returned to the German aircraft and, after loading themselves with several souvenirs, set fire to it, returned to their own aircraft and flew back to Le Cateau.

No thought had ever been given to arming the R.F.C.'s aircraft and the Henri Farman used by Strange and Penn-Gaskell was the only British aircraft to carry a machine gun. Both pilots and observers carried rifles and revolvers for their own protection and, sometimes, grenades to drop on any target which might present itself on the ground, and it was with these weapons that they launched themselves into battle against German aircraft. They did, however, have a naturally aggressive spirit and this worked very much in their favour. Soon after the first two German aircraft had been forced down by rifle fire, Lieutenant N. C. Spratt, who had come over to France with the Aircraft Park, met a German aircraft while flying a single-seat Sopwith Tabloid. By flying around the German machine in what he termed "an aggressive manner", he forced it to land. Neither Spratt nor his aircraft carried any weapons or ammunition.

A few days later, Spratt took off to attack a German machine over Serris. This time, he was armed with a revolver and managed to manoeuvre his aircraft close to the German and fire 30 rounds at close range. This had no apparent success. The German showed no signs of flying away so Spratt landed again and, in desperation, tried to tie a hand grenade to a length of control cable. He intended to fly above the German aircraft, with the grenade trailing behind, and smash the bomb against the German propeller. Luckily, other British pilots managed to persuade him that this might well prove more dangerous to himself than the German as the cable could easily wrap round his own elevator or rudder.

But these spasmodic flings against the opposing air force could not disguise the fact that the R.F.C.'s only *raison d'etre* in France was to be the eyes of the Army. Reconnaissance had to come before all things—although the Army was still inclined to think twice before accepting unconfirmed aeroplane reports. Even when the retreat from Mons was nearing its end, the R.F.C. pilots often had a hard time convincing army officers who were very much their seniors, that their reports were factual.

Towards the end of the retreat Lieutenant "Kipper" Atkinson of 4 Squadron had been given the task of reporting on a bridge at Compiègne which had been shelled by British artillery. He located the bridge and saw that it had been destroyed. As informality was the keynote in those somewhat disorganized early days, Atkinson landed at G.H.Q. to make his report in person before returning to his airfield. He sought out a staff officer and made his report. The staff officer replied, with obviously forced patience, that there must be some mistake because the bridge had not been destroyed.

Atkinson was at a disadvantage in both age and rank, but he stood his ground and stressed that he had seen the bridge and it had been destroyed. This only seemed to convince the staff officer that Atkinson was the typical R.F.C. man as envisaged by the Army at that time—young, brash, over-enthusiastic and with too little military knowledge to be of value to an experienced man like himself. He explained how British engineers had reported on the bridge and said that its construction was too strong to make damage by artillery shells feasible. The British artillery had, therefore, stopped shelling it.

At this point, a French Army officer bustled up and broke into the argument to ask whether the British staff officer had heard the good news—the bridge at Compiègne had been destroyed! This time, the statement that British engineers had reported the bridge too strong was uttered with less conviction. The Frenchman listened impassively. "Ah, yes," he said at last, "that was too strong for your artillery, but not for ours." Atkinson beat a strategic retreat to his aircraft. It was just one more feather in the R.F.C. cap and the fact that one more staff officer would attach more credence to reconnaissance reports in the future made it a worthwhile achievement.

As the retreat drew to a close, reconnaissance became of more and more importance as the British aircraft plotted the daily movements of the German forces, showing Sir John French how von Kluck was attempting to envelop the British Expeditionary Force, and enabling him to keep his hard-pressed army continually just out of reach. When, at the end of August, von Kluck wheeled his army towards the south-east, the R.F.C. spotted it at once. A few days later, when the pressure on the British forces had begun to ease a little, French became anxious because von Kluck's cavalry had been unaccounted for over two days. On the evening of September 3rd several reconnaissance flights were sent out to clear up the mystery. Among them was a B.E.2a crewed by Joubert and Allen.

On the B.E.F.'s right front they spotted groups of German infantry moving southwards, but these seemed far too few in numbers for the numerous divisions believed to be behind them. There were none of the ranks of infantry, horse-drawn artillery or endless supply trains which the airmen expected to see.

Towards the east the sky was sombre with the approaching dusk and, in the near-darkness, both Joubert and Allen gradually made out thousands of twinkling bivouac fires. They both realized that the main German advance had swung towards the east and not towards the British forces in the south. They flew eastwards while Allen marked off the fires on his map. Then, around a series of ponds, they saw horses being watered. The more they searched the ground, the more horses they saw. Flying low over the area, they saw horses at every pond and stream and horse lines around every farmhouse. This was certainly von Kluck's cavalry. That night, the accuracy of the R.F.C. was not doubted. French made his plans to fall on the back of von Kluck's army and thus the British forces were able to make their first contribution to "The Miracle of the Marne".

The Royal Flying Corps had undoubtedly proved its worth in Sir John French's eyes and, on September 7th, with his forces on the advance once again and the Battle of the Marne nearing its successful climax for the Allied forces, he sent the following despatch to London.

I wish particularly to bring to your Lordship's notice the admirable work done by the Royal Flying Corps under Sir David Henderson. Their skill, energy and perseverance have been beyond all praise. They have furnished me with complete and accurate information which has been of incalculable value in the conduct of operations. Fired at constantly by friend and foe, not hesitating to work in every kind of weather, they have remained undaunted throughout. Further, by actually fighting in the air they have succeeded in destroying five of the enemy's machines.

The men of the R.F.C. were still tired from the retreat from Mons. Their machines were showing obvious signs of too long a time spent in the open: the fabric sagged on wings and fuselages; engines were damp and short-circuiting often made them difficult to switch off and even more difficult to start; performances, never very impressive deteriorated. To add to this, the weather suddenly broke. The R.F.C.

squadrons had just arrived with their tired aircraft at Saponay aerodrome when, on the night of September 12th, a gale sprang up. Four aircraft of No. 5 Squadron were completely wrecked. A Henri Farman of No. 3 Squadron was lifted thirty feet into the air and smashed down on top of another. B.E.s of No. 2 Squadron were blown across the field like so many autumn leaves. Hangars had not yet been issued and the frail aircraft were entirely at the mercy of the weather. The next morning there were not more than ten serviceable aircraft belonging to the R.F.C. in France.

But pilots, observers and ground crews were in high spirits. They knew now that they had been finally accepted as a useful, indeed, invaluable part of the British Forces. This meant much to them.

CHAPTER FIVE

Choose Your Weapons

OFFICIAL acceptance by the Army did not make the R.F.C. complacent about their wartime role—far from it. The eager, thrusting pursuit of knowledge and the love of experiment which had been so important a part of the Corp's early life did not suddenly cease. Nor did the airmen stop looking beyond pure reconnaissance flights for their future work. Early clashes betweeen British and German aircraft had begun to make it obvious that, the better protected an aircraft was, the less chance it stood of being deflected from its main reconnaissance task by enemy aircraft. Less than one month of fighting had been sufficient to prove this to Henderson and, on September 4th, he sent the following signal to Brancker, who was looking after the R.F.C.'s interests in London:

There are no aeroplanes with the Royal Flying Corps really suitable for carrying machine guns; grenades and bombs are, therefore, at present more suitable. If suitable aeroplanes are available, machine guns are better undoubtedly. Request you endeavour to supply sufficient fighting machines as soon as possible.

Henderson could have had little hope of any early response to this request. He was only too well aware that nearly all the trained men in the R.F.C. and virtually all the airworthy aeroplanes had been taken to France. Brancker and Trenchard certainly had no organization back in England to deal with a request of this kind, and the short-sighted politicians of the day had already made sure that the British aircraft industry had never reached fruition. And so, for the time being, the men in France had to make do with the equipment on hand.

To people like Penn-Gaskell this was a challenge too good to miss.

Everyone agreed that a machine gun was the best weapon for shooting down enemy aircraft but Penn-Gaskell was among the few intent on proving that one could be carried on aircraft with limited performances like those in France. For some time, he insisted on carrying his Vickers gun on reconnaissance flights but Strange, who was usually his pilot, complained quite justifiably that the danger caused by being limited to a height of some 3,000 feet by the weight of the gun far outweighed the extra protection which the gun was alleged to give. Higgins, C.O. of 5 Squadron, told Penn-Gaskell that he would have to be content with a rifle when flying in a Henri Farman.

At the end of September several new aircraft arrived from England and among those received by 5 Squadron was an Avro 504 and a Bristol Scout, which had been christened "The Bullet" because of its vaunted speed of 100 m.p.h. This aircraft had obvious possibilities as a fighter and the pooled ingenuity of 5 Squadron concocted a mounting for a rifle with a sawn off stock clamped to shoot diagonally forwards, thus missing the propeller. The aircraft was normally flown by Higgins, the C.O. The problems in aiming the off-set gun were naturally considerable and this, combined with Higgins's eyesight, which was such that any enemy aircraft always saw him and made off long before he saw it (there was no medical examination for those who wanted to join the R.F.C. at that time), meant that this aircraft enjoyed little success. Additional armament carried for good measure was a rack of rifle grenades with the rods sawn off, and streamers attached to make them fall upright. The detonators had to be withdrawn from these by the pilots' teeth.

The Avro 504, on the other hand, came in for the attentions of the enthusiastic team of Strange and Penn-Gaskell. The latter had by this time abandoned the heavy Vickers gun in favour of a Lewis and Strange and he soon devised a simple gun mounting for the Avro. This consisted of a crossbar between the centre struts over which a rope was slung to haul up the Lewis so that it could be fired backwards over the head of the pilot. The technique worked out by Penn-Gaskell was for the pilot to place his aircraft below and in front of the enemy, while the observer fired backwards. It might sound a dangerous practice nowadays but, at that time, when propellers proved an impenetrable barrier to forward firing, it was a sensible course to take.

Above, the Vickers Gun Bus was originally produced as a private venture by the Vickers Company. The Royal Naval Air Service, recognizing its value as a warplane with a machine gun which could be fired directly forwards, ordered it, but the War Office were slow in awakening to its virtues. *Below*, the B.E.2c was a product of the Royal Aircraft Factory. It had great stability, which made it ideal for bombing and reconnaissance, but this same quality rendered it easy prey for enemy fighters

Above, air-to-air shots of First World War aircraft are rare. This one shows an F.E.2b in flight. *Below*, the F.E.2b, designed by the Royal Aircraft Factory, proved its worth in combating the Fokker menace

This device was first tested by Strange and Lieutenant R. O. Abercrombie on October 21st. Their luck was in and they soon found an Albatros aircraft. Strange manouevred his machine into the correct position, Abercrombie lined the enemy up in his sights and opened fire. He had fired only a few rounds when the gun jammed. Nothing Abercrombie could do would free it. Reluctantly, the engagement was broken off and the Avro returned to its airfield, where Penn-Gaskell was anxiously awaiting news of his contraption. The inquest became rather heated. Abercrombie was convinced that the Lewis gun was at fault, while Penn-Gaskell was equally sure that Abercrombie had maltreated his beloved weapon. The last words in the argument came from Abercrombie. "Well, you can go up and use your bally old gun yourself!" he said.

Penn-Gaskell had every intention of doing so. With Strange once again at the controls, they searched for enemy aircraft—but without luck. Determined not to land without firing his gun in anger, Penn-Gaskell turned round and began to shout instructions at Strange. At last with the use of much gesticulation and bellowed monosyllables, Strange was given to understand that they were to go down and fire at enemy forces on the ground. This they did. They found a train and a party of troops. Both targets were liberally dosed with Penn-Gaskell's bullets but the actual damage caused was never recorded.

It was not until November 22nd that the Lewis-armed Avro met with true success and, ironically, it was not Penn-Gaskell in the observer's seat but Lieutenant F. G. Small. Strange was once again the pilot. They came across a German Aviatik. As Strange flew past the enemy to take up his attack position in front, he was treated to fire from a Mauser pistol and also a salvo of Very lights. These did nothing to dim the enthusiasm of the two Englishmen. Standing up at his gun and taking careful aim, Small sent bullet after bullet whistling through the Aviatik. It took less than a drum of ammunition to persuade the Germans that the Lewis gun was more than a match for a Mauser and the Aviatik landed near Bailleul, where the crew were taken prisoner. They were unharmed but their aircraft was liberally riddled by bullets.

This machine gun armament was, however, in advance of its time. Too few aircraft were physically capable of carrying the load and a workable mounting was difficult to achieve. The rifle and the pistol remained the stock protection against enemy aircraft for some months. And despite this somewhat ineffective armament, some amazing results were achieved. On the morning of February 5th, 1915, Second Lieutenant V. H. N. Wadham was piloting a Morane of No. 3 Squadron, with Lieutenant A. D. Borton as his observer. They were engaged on reconnaissance duties near Merville when a German Aviatik flew up. The German pilot opened fire from a rather ineffectual distance with a pistol, while his observer looked more lethal with a rifle. Shouting to Borton to hold his fire, Wadham concentrated on manoeuvring his aircraft nearer to the Aviatik to give his observer a better chance of scoring hits. Borton opened fire at a range of 100 yards. The Morane was faster than the Aviatik and, ignoring the return fire from the German, Wadham moved closer still, until Borton was blazing away from a mere fifty feet. He could clearly see his bullets ripping through the Aviatik, which soon broke off the engagement and landed, somewhat abruptly, two miles from a German airfield at Lille. The Morane had received one bullet through its propeller, another had lodged in the fuselage and two had ripped through the wings, but its flying ability was unimpaired.

A more spectacular success attended Captain R. M. Vaughan and Second Lieutenant J. F. Lascelles who were flying in a B.E.2c of 4 Squadron on a reconnaissance to Bruges, on April 15th. They met an Aviatik and Vaughan was able to bring his aircraft within 80 yards of the German from which distance Lascelles fired twenty-four shots. The Aviatik then began to make some abrupt aerial manoeuvres and landed heavily in the French lines near Elverdinghe. Vaughan and Lascelles watched it hit the ground and then proceeded on their reconnaissance. When they returned to base, they learned that the German pilot had been killed by Lascelles's bullets. The enemy observer, who was unwounded, had been taken prisoner.

Generally speaking, there were few opportunities for combats of this type. The sky was a large place and there were very few aircraft. When opposing air forces did meet, it required a considerable amount of luck to bring the other aircraft down with rifle or pistol fire. There was, moreover, a camaraderie among the early pilots. Lord Douglas of Kirtleside, then Lieutenant W. S. Douglas, has recalled how he met a German two-seater while on reconnaissance duties with Harvey-Kelly: "The two-seater was about 100 yards away and just below us," he said. "The German observer did not appear to be shooting at us and we were completely unarmed. There was nothing to be done. We waved a hand to the enemy and proceeded with our task. The enemy did likewise. At the time this did not appear to be in any way ridiculous—there is a bond of sympathy between all who fly, even between enemies."

Sometimes this camaraderie of the air produced a somewhat bizarre aspect to the war. Among the zany pranks which adorned this period a notable one was the brainchild of Louis Strange. On Christmas Day, 1914, while most of the R.F.C. were enjoying the Air Committee's Christmas hampers and Princess Mary's gift of gilt boxes of chocolates, this most individualistic of officers decided to celebrate the occasion by taking off for the German airfield at Lille where he dropped footballs which went bouncing among the Germans, who were at first alarmed at this new aerial weapon, and then merely astonished.

Even the fighting in the air was occasionally touched by humour. A German pilot, Hauptmann von Leutzer, has recorded how he was carrying out a reconnaissance flight around Dunkirk, St. Omer and Amiens when he met a British aircraft. The observers in both aircraft blazed away in patriotic fashion with rifles and pistols for some time, without result. Then both ran out of ammunition. The German observer, not to be outdone, brought out his Very pistol and tried to attack with this. The British crew replied in kind. Both pilots realized that they would have to get at close quarters for the Very lights to be effective, and this they did. None of the shots looked as if it could be lethal. Von Leutzer was the first to see the joke and was soon shaking with mirth. The British observer was near enough to see the effect of the combat on the German pilot and he, too, joined in the merriment. Soon, all four men were enjoying the joke. The last few shots in this strange battle were fired with no thought of achieving a victory but merely to add to the fun.

Because of this general inability to carry out effective air-to-air firing at this time, pilots were almost immune to attack from above. Their biggest worry was attack from the ground. Machine gun fire from the ground could be very disconcerting, and most casualties came from this source.

The Germans had anti-aircraft guns from the start, but their gunners usually under-estimated the height of their targets. They also displayed their field artillery upbringing by ranging on an aircraft as if they were ranging on a target on the ground—that is to say, the first shot might be some way out to the right, the next well to the left, the third would be to the right again but not so far . . . and so on. The trajectories of the shells could, therefore, be forecast with some accuracy, and this led to the deliberate practice of teasing anti-aircraft guns.

In this connection, on September 19th, 1914, there occurred a flight which, although its tactical importance might have been negligible, was to produce a word that passed into history. Lieutenant A. E. ("Biffy") Borton, a dapper, monocled pilot with a reputation for being something of a dare-devil, was detailed to carry out a reconnaissance of troop movements in the Soisson area. With him went Lieutenant Thompson, as observer. There was a strong wind blowing and Borton carried out his mission downwind so that his speed over the ground should be as high as possible. On the return flight, he passed over the location of a four-gun anti-aircraft unit which was quite well known to the R.F.C. and had the reputation of being one of the better gun units in the German Army. Feeling in the mood for gun-baiting, Borton turned into wind as he approached the site. Flying in this manner, his speed over the ground was quite slow but he was able to turn and move sideways relatively quickly.

The engagement started, in foreseeable fashion, with the ranging shots, but even when the gunners were on target, Borton was able to estimate when the next shot would be fired. He then turned smartly to the left or right and watched the white puff appear where his aircraft should have been. Borton enjoyed this somewhat precarious pastime for some little while before flying back to his airfield. On the way back, both he and his observer were so elated with their success at confounding the gunners that they burst into song. The song was one popular on the music halls at that time, "Archibald, certainly NOT!" "We sang it," Borton explained later, "because it seemed to sum up our attitude towards the anti-aircraft guns at that time."

The story was told with relish in the mess that night, and soon every anti-aircraft gun used by the Germans was christened "Archibald". This name was soon abbreviated to "Archie" and, before many weeks had elapsed, was in general use throughout the R.F.C. It remained in common use until 1918, but most of those who referred to "Archie"—which was soon to be respected, however light-hearted its nickname—had little idea of who had christened it, or how.

Whatever diversions the pilots might find for themselves, whether it was trying to shoot down German aircraft, baiting anti-aircraft guns or dropping footballs on the Germans, the sole purpose for the Royal Flying Corps was still to be the eyes of the army. By the end of October, 1914, all the squadrons had settled down in the area of the British Army, which held a line running from Givenchy to Zonnebeke. Up to this time, reconnaissances had usually been arranged with General Headquarters but this soon became cumbersome. Henderson then worked out a scheme in which his squadrons were divided into groups which he called "Wings". It was a scheme which involved several postings and promotions. When it was put into operation during November, the First Wing, which comprised Nos. 2 and 3 Squadrons under Trenchard, who had been brought out to France to take command of it, concentrated on work with the Indian Corps and the Fourth Army. The Second Wing, under Lieutenant-Colonel C. J. Burke, who had been promoted from command of No. 2 Squadron, consisted of Nos. 5 and 6 Squadrons and operated with the Second and Third Army Corps. At this time, wireless telegraphy was in its infancy as regards its use in aircraft and No. 4 Squadron was kept, under the control of R.F.C. HQ, as a specialist unit whose duties could be called upon when required.

This reorganization was a great step forward for the Royal Flying Corps. It made Britain's air arm much more flexible in its use and, as the Army commanders began to realize the potentialities of aircraft, so the R.F.C. found themselves contributing more and more to the war—and their contributions soon became far more effective and exciting than the daily run of reconnaissance had been so far.

CHAPTER SIX

Death from the Skies

IT WAS soon after lunch on the afternoon of March 10th, 1915, that a handful of men made their way from a hut, graced by the name "Officers' Mess", on the airfield of Poperinghe, Belgium. One of them, easily recognized by the bulk of his flying jacket, was a pilot. Slowly, without much conversation, the men made their way to one of a collection of B.E.2c biplanes.

While the pilot peered into his cockpit, an engineering officer crouched in front of the aircraft and squinted up at three small streamlined shapes clamped one under each wing and another under the fuselage. He called the pilot down and, for the final time, ran over the functioning of the crude apparatus which had been rigged up on the aeroplane. For this B.E.2c, designed as all R.F.C. aircraft were at that time as a reconnaissance aeroplane, was on this day to be used purely as a bomber.

The pilot, Captain L. A. Strange of No. 6 Squadron, indicated his understanding of the mechanism and clambered into the rear cockpit. The front cockpit, which usually housed an observer, was left empty. It would be easier to cope with the extra weight of the bombs without another body. Besides, as this was something new in air warfare, perhaps it was best not to risk a life unnecessarily.

There followed the usual drill of priming the engine and passing the signal to a mechanic to swing the propeller. A few splutters and the 90 h.p. Royal Aircraft Factory 1a engine burst into life with its characteristic throaty roar. A quick look at the very few instruments in his cockpit, and Strange waved for the chocks to be taken away. Those who had come to see him off on this new venture stood back and the B.E.2c bumped slowly over the uneven field, turned into wind and, with black exhaust smoke trailing, took off over the trees at the far end of the airfield.

Strange had first heard about this special mission only the day before. Intelligence had reported that German reinforcements, urgently needed to counteract attacks by British infantry, were passing through Courtrai station by the trainload. They had to be stopped. The target was too far away for an effective attack by artillery, so the R.F.C. had been asked to drop bombs. Until this day, no-one in the R.F.C. had used an aircraft to bomb a specified target. Strange, like many other pilots, had lobbed occasional, assorted missiles at any collection of troops or vehicles which had presented itself during a routine reconnaissance, but he was breaking new ground on this flight. As he nursed his B.E.2c up to a safe altitude, he reflected, somewhat grimly, on the reception which could be waiting for him at Courtrai.

He also reflected on the weather. It was by no means the ideal day for carrying out this unfamiliar task. The sky was almost covered with heavy cloud at 3,000 feet and below this were scuds of smaller clouds. Rain seemed imminent. Strange knew that he would have to stay below cloud for accurate navigation, and this he did. But, as he neared the German lines, bright flashes on the ground, followed by dark puffs in the sky not far from his aircraft, warned him that the German anti-aircraft guns were not going to let him pass unmolested. Strange had braved the "Archie" many times before, but the German gunners were improving. He reasoned that he stood more chance of reaching Courtrai if he disappeared into the clouds and tried to navigate with occasional glimpses of the ground.

The half-hour flight seemed to take an age. Strange was not completely certain of his navigation until a cluster of roof-tops to the south resolved unmistakably into his target. He eased down out of the clouds and put his aircraft into a diving left-hand turn through a flimsy lower layer of cloud towards the eastern outskirt of the town, where he could just see the railway line running towards the centre.

Flattening out at 200 feet above the railway, he headed along it. His B.E.2c could fly at a little more than 80 m.p.h., but, even at this comparatively slow speed, things seemed to be happening with startling rapidity at such low altitude.

The station appeared in the distance. At the end of one platform stood a solitary German sentry. Panicking at the sight of the aeroplane racing towards him, the German opened fire with his rifle far too early. Warned by the whistle of bullets, Strange saw the man with a few seconds to spare. He knew the answer to this problem.

From the pocket of his flying jacket he produced an ordinary infantry hand-grenade, whipped out the pin with his teeth—for at this level he dare not let go of the control stick—and, with a nice sense of timing, pitched it overboard at the sentry. The German was effectively silenced as the grenade burst almost at his feet, but Strange's preoccupation with this unimportant opposition almost cost a collision with the station roof.

The next few seconds were far too hectic for Strange to notice the small-arms fire now coming at him from all directions. He hauled back on his stick to avoid the roof, and yanked a make-shift bomb release lever just before reaching a train standing in the station. He could not resist the temptation to squirm round in his cockpit to see the results of his attack.

It nearly proved his last movement. Only blind instinct caused him to whip round again, just in time to see a row of telegraph poles apparently approaching him at break-neck speed. He pulled back on the stick once more and, as he made a wide, climbing turn around the station, caught a brief, satisfying glimpse of the chaos he had wrought. He returned to his airfield safely and discovered that twelve enemy bullets had passed through his aircraft during the attack. Later, reports indicated that two coaches had been hit at Courtrai, 75 German soldiers had been killed or injured, and traffic would be delayed for three days. The first serious attempt at bombing by the Royal Flying Corps had undoubtedly met with success.

The R.F.C. had always realized the possibilities of this type of attack from the air but there had been no official need for it. Neither had they suitable weapons. The more inventive pilots such as Strange, himself, had concocted their own explosive devices which they had heaved overboard at any target which presented itself during reconnaissance sorties, or on privately-planned individual attacks. A little later, the airmen had been issued with solid steel darts known as *Flechettes* with which to shower the Germans. Someone started a rumour that these weapons were illegal under the Geneva Conventions, although few stopped to puzzle out why a non-explosive device should be illegal while an explosive one was permissible. They were used very little and eventually discarded, mainly because they were completely ineffectual. Much more effective were the modified rifle grenades. All these missiles had been dropped over the side of the cockpit and not carried on bomb racks; such refinements did not exist.

It was not until late February, 1915, that serious thought was given to using aircraft purely as bombers against specified targets. Sir John French's spring offensive called for an attack to be made on German forces at Neuve Chapelle. The final details of the attack, worked out by Sir Douglas Haig, seemed promising—except for one difficulty: a spy had reported that the Germans would probably be able to rush in more than forty battalions as reinforcements some thirty hours after the British onslaught had started.

Reconnaissance flights by the R.F.C. had already provided valuable sketches and photographs which built up a detailed map on which the whole attack was to be based, so it was decided to entrust the fliers with the additional task of harassing the movements of German forces behind the lines. No. 1 Wing was to carry out the normal reconnaissance work, while Nos. 2 and 3 Wings began laying plans to attack strategic transport points beyond the front line. A few minor attacks were made in the early morning of March 10th, but the real punch started with Strange's effort at Courtrai in the afternoon.

As Strange took off, No. 5 Squadron were preparing for their part in the bombing. This unit, now commanded by Major A. C. H. Maclean, had been briefed to have one aircraft available to bomb a railway fork just north of Menin. Maclean decided that the best aircraft would be the new Martinsyde S.1, a single-seater scout aircraft, one of the first to arrive in France. Choice of this aircraft immediately narrowed the choice of pilot to one of the three who had flown it—Lieutenant C. W. Wilson, Captain G. I. Carmichael and Lieutenant C. E. C. Rabagliati. It was hoped that the aircraft would be able to carry 80 lbs of bombs, and so "Daddy" Wilson was ruled out because, said the Squadron wit, "he already carries 100 lbs more than anyone else." The remaining two pilots tossed for the honour and Carmichael won from a disappointed Rabagliati.

Pre-war "bombing practice" with bags of flour had taught Carmichael one lesson above all else—aiming was difficult to the point of being impossible. With this in mind, he had a hole cut in the cockpit floor, immediately below his feet, so that he could look vertically downwards. In store the Squadron had some 20 lb bombs, and racks were fitted under the Martinsyde's wings to carry these. What little there was left of the cockpit floor was taken up by a plug, fitted to a bowden cable, to work the bomb release.

When Carmichael went across to 3 Corps to receive his final briefing on the target, he was left in no doubt about its importance in the coming battle. On the day before the attack, a 100 lb bomb was delivered to the Squadron and the racks on the Martinsyde were hastily converted to carry it. Carmichael regarded this huge new weapon with mixed feelings: with the 20 lb bombs he could have more than one go at the target if the first attack failed; now, he would have to be right first time.

The first part of his flight passed off uneventfully, apart from some "Archie" which sent shrapnel through his tailplane as he crossed the trenches, but this was no new experience. Carmichael had reasoned that his attack stood much more chance of success if he could achieve surprise and so, when he was approaching Menin, he switched off his engine, hoping that he would be able to swoop silently on to his target. This hope was rudely dashed when the chatter of a solitary machine gun cut across the background whistle of wind in struts and wires. The bullets caused Carmichael little immediate danger, but he realized that all hope of surprise had been lost and opened up his engine. He did not realize, then, just how much the sharp-eyed German on the ground was to cost him.

He picked up the railway line leading to Menin with little difficulty and brought his aircraft down to 300 feet. Through the hole in the cockpit floor, he could now see the railway lines centrally placed below, the sleepers blurring together with the speed of his movement. One drawback of this primitive bomb-aiming device was that Carmichael could not see ahead but he had already worked out an answer to this. He knew that he would first pass Menin station and that the junction he had to bomb was just a little way beyond this. If he waited until he saw the junction between his feet, his bomb would overshoot, and so he resolved to release his missile a few seconds after passing the station, relying on his "bomb-sight" merely to keep him on course.

The station flashed past below. Carmichael held his breath, counted to himself and then pulled the release plug. He was prepared for his aircraft to surge upwards as it lost its 100 lb cargo, but nothing happened. Carmichael was mortified. "It's failed!" was the only thought in his mind.

Then came a mighty "crump" and a great push from below and behind. Looking back, he saw a boiling cloud of black smoke swelling from a point only ten yards short of the junction. His heart began beating again, but his elation was to be short-lived.

Turning east, away from the railway line, he was suddenly aware that the ground below was swarming with German soldiers. Obviously, there was a barracks at Menin, a point which had not been mentioned at his briefing. The machine gun fire which had greeted Carmichael before his attack had alerted the Germans and he found himself in the centre of a storm of bullets. Vainly he tried waving to the Germans to make them think him a friend, but the attack on the railway had left little doubt of his aggressive intentions and the Germans were not deceived.

Carmichael next tried to unnerve the opposition by diving down and heaving a couple of rifle-grenades overboard. These caused some local consternation but did little to stem the flow of bullets, and the British pilot pulled out of his dive painfully aware that his engine was spluttering in an alarming manner.

The problem of getting back safely then became uppermost in his mind. This was not just worry about his own skin but the thought that, if he did not return, no-one would know whether his attack was successful or not, and another officer might have to risk his neck finding out or making another, and unnecessary, attempt.

The crackling of the rifles died away in the distance as Carmichael set course for his base. The immediate danger was over but he was far from happy. The control stick had a peculiar floppy feeling and a brief experiment in controlling his aircraft soon showed that a lateral movement of the stick had no effect of the ailerons. The engine was vibrating as well as spluttering.

Had Carmichael known then that, fifty years later, he would still be around to show the cause of the misbehaving engine to any interested party, he would have been a happy man. As it was, he could coax the Martinsyde no higher than 200 feet and was completely dependent on the aircraft's inherent stability to maintain the wings in a level attitude. The Martinsyde never had much aileron control, anyway, but a little would have been better than none at all.

Carmichael reached his airfield safely. The erratic sound of his engine warned those on the ground that he had run into trouble and, by the time that his landing run had ended, a sizeable crowd had gathered. The force of the air passing round the ailerons had kept them straight during the flight and during the landing but, as the aircraft stopped, suddenly they flopped down. "It looked completely tired out and forlorn," Carmichael says of the machine, "and maybe it was because of this that I was told I could spend the next day in bed." Investigation showed that the engine had been hit by a bullet, which had passed through a cylinder and lodged in a plug. Carmichael still has the plug.

So far, the R.F.C.'s first attempts at tactical bombing had met with great success but those who took part in these attacks would be the first to admit that an element of good luck had entered the proceedings. It deserted them now, for the raids continued next day with poor results.

Once again, the pilots were fighting the weather as well as the Germans. Three pilots of No. 4. Squadron had earlier been briefed to attack the station at Lille at first light. This sortie imposed several problems, not the least of which was that of taking off and flying to the target at night, and, in order to cut down the distance flown in darkness, the three pilots, Captain R. J. F. Barton and Lieutenants A. St. J. Warrand and G. W. Mapplebeck, took off from their own airfield, near Amiens, and landed at Bailleul the previous evening.

Take-off was scheduled for 4.45 a.m. the next morning. To cut down the risk of collision and to help formation-keeping, "navigation" lights were hurriedly rigged up for the aircraft. These were ordinary hand torches strapped to the pilots' backs. The risky take-off was accomplished without incident, then Barton's engine suddenly stopped. This was no uncommon experience in those days but it left Barton in the tricky situation of carrying out a crash-landing in total darkness. He survived this completely blind and bumpy landing with no injuries, but his aircraft was wrecked and he was badly shaken.

Warrand and Mapplebeck managed to reach Lille station but were met with an extremely fiery welcome. Both aircraft were shot down and Warrand subsequently died of his injuries. Mapplebeck managed to bring off a reasonably successful crash-landing near a wood south of the town and eluded German search parties, to become one of the first to establish the R.F.C. and, later, the R.A.F. tradition of escaping from enemy territory. He laid low until the evening and then found sympathizers in Lille who were willing to hide him. While in hiding, he had the satisfaction of reading a notice offering an award for his capture dead or alive. He was eventually smuggled into Holland and from there walked back to his unit.

And so the second day of the R.F.C.'s attempt at tactical bombing passed with a marked lack of success. The third day, March 12th, was little better. Four B.E.8s of No. 1 Squadron, newly arrived from England, took off to bomb a railway bridge north-east of Douai and a junction at Don. Two aircraft reached their targets but the pilots reported that the bombs seemed to have little effect. Another pilot hit a railway line at Wavrin, mistaking it for the Don junction, and the fourth was shot down and taken prisoner.

Worse was to follow later in the day. An aircraft of No. 3 Squadron was detailed to make another attack on Don and the pilot, Captain R. Cholmondeley, was supervising the bombing-up of his aeroplane, a French Morane Parasol. The bombs, also of French origin, were converted artillery shells, with no safety device except a lead shearing-pin. A mechanic dropped one while offering it up to the wing and it fell on its nose. There was an immediate and violent explosion and the aircraft disappeared in flames. Cholmondeley and eleven others were killed outright and four more seriously injured.

Not all the bombs detonated in this explosion and there was an immediate offer of volunteers from both pilots and ground crew to carry the unexploded bombs to a safe distance, but Major Salmond, the Squadron Commander, issued strict instructions that the wreckage was not to be approached until the following morning. Early risers on the morning of the 13th were surprised to see that the wreckage had already been partly cleared and the remaining bombs taken away. Had someone disobeyed orders? Finally, Salmond admitted that he had got up at first light and removed the bombs, himself, rather than risk the lives of his men.

The target of Don was finally attacked successfully later in the morning of March 13th. Captain Pretyman of No. 3. Squadron, who had witnessed the tragedy of the day before, managed to blow up the centre carriages of a train standing in the station. This proved to be the final aerial blow of the battle of Neuve Chapelle for, on that same morning, the Duke of Westminster, a Lieutenant-Commander in charge of an R.N.A.S. Armoured Car Squadron being used in the fighting, took two three-pounder armoured cars to the front-line trenches at Fauquissart and silenced a few remaining enemy snipers and machine gun posts in the village of Trivelet. The battle of Neuve Chapelle was virtually over.

Sir John French was delighted with the results and gave full marks to the Royal Flying Corps for their part in bombing behind the lines. Without a doubt, the earlier attacks had done much damage to the enemy, but the R.F.C. was not satisfied: the cost in men and aircraft had been considerable. There was no thought of calling off bombing attacks, however.

One of the many difficulties the R.F.C. faced in those early days of bombing was that of assessing the results of an attack. If a pilot did not return from a mission, his Wing Headquarters had no way of confirming whether the attack had been successful or not. Spy reports might not come in for weeks and it would not be known whether to send another aircraft to make sure of the target or not. All pilots were impressed with the need to return to British lines, somehow, after a bombing sortie.

With the Battle of Neuve Chapelle over, the urgency of bombing attacks diminished, but there was still the occasional target demanding R.F.C. attention—and still the need to get back safely with information. The importance which pilots gave to this factor is best illustrated by the actions of a 27-year-old pilot of No. 2 Squadron.

Second Lieutenant W. B. Rhodes-Moorhouse was, despite his comparatively young years, a British aviation pioneer. He first flew in 1909 and gained his Aero Club Certificate in 1911. The next year he came into public view by finishing third in the Aerial Derby and, a few weeks later, established a record by being the first pilot to carry two passengers across the English Channel.

When war started, Rhodes-Moorhouse lost no time in joining the R.F.C. and soon found himself in France with No. 2 Squadron. His chance for action came on the afternoon of April 16th, 1915. Concentrations of German troops had been spotted in the Ghent area and the R.F.C. were asked to mount bombing attacks. Aircraft from Nos. 7 and 8 Squadrons enjoyed mixed success with their attacks, so a back-up effort was made by four pilots from No. 2 Squadron. One of them was Rhodes-Moorhouse.

He was briefed to bomb the railway line just west of Courtrai station and told to use his own discretion on the height from which to make the attack. Taking off from Merville at five minutes past three, Rhodes-Moorhouse reached Courtrai safely but then encountered considerable small-arms fire from the Germans, who were beginning to learn how to deal with bombers.

Rhodes-Moorhouse knew that Intelligence had reported some 40,000 German troops being rushed through Courtrai to the front. Obviously, it was vital that they should be delayed, so he ignored the stream of bullets and brought his aircraft down to 300 feet for his attack.

A battery of guns on the belfry of Courtrai church was now firing at him from point-blank range and almost on his own level. Just before Rhodes-Moorhouse reached the station, a bullet entered his abdomen but he managed to release his bomb on target.

With his senses hazed by shock and pain, Rhodes-Moorhouse struggled to urge his aircraft higher, away from the punishing stream of bullets which now came at him from all directions. Another bullet smashed into his thigh, and yet another ripped open his hand.

Fighting unconsciousness with all his will power, Rhodes-Moorhouse turned his aircraft back towards the British lines. Through his mind ran the constant thought that somehow he had to get back and report. For forty-five minutes and thirty-five miles of intense pain and near-unconsciousness, he urged himself on to his own airfield at Merville. Despite his injuries, he managed to pull off a perfect landing and reported his mission successful. He was rushed to hospital but next day died from his injuries.

So Rhodes-Moorhouse did not live to see his action described in an official despatch as "the most important bomb dropped in this war so far". Nor did he live to learn that he was to be awarded his country's highest decoration for bravery—the Victoria Cross. Rhodes-Moorhouse was the first of many R.F.C. men to be accorded this honour.

But extreme bravery by such men as this could not disguise the fact that bombing sorties by the R.F.C. were far too expensive in men and aircraft. Even the results were far from promising. Of 141 bombing attacks made between March 1st and June 20th, only three had been definitely successful. On July 24th, there came an order that, in future, only bombing attacks carried out on the direct orders of General Headquarters should be made.

It was not so much German opposition which caused this decision but the actual technical difficulty of dropping a bomb. Pilots were misled by the fact that when they watched one of their bombs fall it seemed first to fall straight down then to flatten out and shoot forward, whereas an observer on the ground saw the line curve as the bomb's initial velocity diminished and gravity took over. This simple phenomenon was easy to understand but it did make aiming extremely difficult without proper bombsights. It also encouraged pilots to make their attacks from very low levels, rendering them more vulnerable to enemy fire.

Luckily for the R.F.C., a young staff officer, Second Lieutenant R. B. Bourdillon, was intensely interested in this problem of the falling bomb. Although his work did not normally bring him in touch with aircraft, he lost no opportunities of visiting the squadrons and discussing bombing problems with the pilots. Being of an inventive frame of mind, by early 1915 he had evolved a small, crude bombsight, and this was in limited use during the first organized attacks.

Bourdillon's work came to the notice of his superiors and he was immediately shipped back to England and posted to the Experimental flight of the Central Flying School. There, with the help of a meteorological officer, Second Lieutenant G. M. B. Dobson, he had ample opportunity to design and perfect a more sophisticated bombsight which enabled pilots to gauge their speed over the ground with some certainty—one of the first requirements in accurate bomb-aiming, and one not previously available to pilots, who had had to work solely on air-speed, which was not the same thing.

Bourdillon's bombsight was sent out to the squadrons in France and enjoyed its first real tests during the autumn offensive of 1915. Between September 23rd and 25th many successful bombing attacks were made on targets behind enemy lines. Railway bridges, goods yards and even moving trains were hit with commendable accuracy from moderate levels.

Then, on September 26th, Lieutenants M. G. Christie (No. 7

Squadron) and Second Lieutenant G. G. A. Williams (No. 5 Squadron) took off to bomb locomotive sheds at Valenciennes. Christie, carrying a 112 lb bomb, was first over the target, at 2 p.m. He was flying at 4,800 feet but had no difficulty in aiming for the sheds. He watched his bomb fall and explode among some locomotives standing just outside the sheds, which was by no means a bad aim, from that height, at that date.

Ten minutes later, Williams arrived, flying at 6,000 feet. His 112 lb bomb hit the sheds centrally and the bomb explosion was immediately followed by other violent eruptions. Williams had made a direct hit on an ammunition train. Spies later reported that twenty trucks of ammunition had exploded and train traffic was disrupted for a considerable period.

Between September 23rd and 28th, the R.F.C. dropped a total of eighty-two 100 lb bombs, a hundred and sixty-three 20 lb bombs and twenty-six incendiaries. It had wrecked railway lines in fifteen places, damaged five trains and destroyed a signal cabin, in addition to wrecking the sheds at Valenciennes. All this had been accomplished at the cost of two aircraft missing and two pilots wounded. The Royal Flying Corps had undoubtedly proved its worth as an attacking force.

CHAPTER SEVEN

Murder!

THE ABILITY to drop bombs from a reasonable height and with some degree of accuracy was not exclusive to the Royal Flying Corps. Germany, maybe because she was a more military-minded nation, had been thinking about, and experimenting with, bombing for some years before the war. This meant that she could bomb not only the British Army in the trenches in France but, with her larger, longer-range aircraft, England itself.

This was soon realized by many people living along a fifty-mile line of the south bank of the River Thames, from the Estuary up to the outskirts of London. On Christmas Day, 1914, soon after midday, the drone of aero-engines was heard over the Estuary. Many Christmas chickens and turkeys must have been in danger of burning in ovens as people flocked out of their houses to watch, for an aeroplane was still a rare sight.

The art of aircraft recognition had not been born and few civilians watching this aircraft high in the sky realized that it was German. Luckily, the course of the enemy aircraft took it over several military airfields and its shape was sufficiently unfamiliar to warrant closer investigation. Aircraft were dispatched from Eastchurch and Grain airfields and began the long climb to intercept. By this time, the crews of the British aircraft, and some of those on the ground, were certain that they were looking at an enemy aircraft and excitement mounted.

Only one of the aircraft could have been of any use against the German seaplane. This was a Vickers F.B.5, a new fighter aeroplane owned by the Royal Naval Air Service. It carried a pusher airscrew at the rear of a fuselage nacelle, and a gunner, complete with Lewis

Gun, was placed in front of the pilot with an uninterrupted field of fire. It was an extremely draughty position for the gunner who, on this cold Christmas Day, was going to regret the icy blast which battered him a little more than he realized.

The F.B.5 did, in fact, get near enough to threaten the enemy but, no sooner was it within firing distance of the seaplane, than trouble started. The engine began to misfire and the pilot found it almost impossible to maintain his altitude. In front of him the gunner had opened fire but, after one short, strangled burst, the Lewis Gun jammed. There was a drill laid down for clearing these stoppages but the gunner found it impossible to carry out his drill. In the excitement of the unexpected take-off he had forgotten his gloves. The first, painful symptoms of frost-bite were making their appearance and the gunner's hands were useless. Reluctantly, the F.B.5 had to head back to base.

This abortive interception was not quite as ineffective as it appeared. The pilot of the German seaplane, realizing that he was not going to be entirely free of attention, banked into a turn over Erith, on the outskirts of London, and headed back down river. For a few minutes he must have wrestled with his conscience about what to do with the bomb his aircraft carried. Undoubtedly it had been intended for London, but perhaps it was better to drop it somewhere on England than to take it back to Germany—or was it? He reached a decision over Cliffe in Kent and released the bomb. It fell, and exploded harmlessly, a little way from the railway station.

For all concerned this sortie had been something of a storm in a teacup. Neither side gained any capital from it but the raid threw Britain's anti-aircraft defences into a rather disturbing limelight. England was completely unequipped to deal with attack from the air.

The fact that England could be attacked had been realized very early on—in fact, Blériot's cross-channel flight in 1909 had been the starting point for a whole host of dismal prophecies concerning aerial armadas attacking England from the skies. The first official step to guard against this likelihood was taken in November, 1913, when discussions which were to lead to the divorce of the R.N.A.S. and R.F.C. were taking place. It was decided that the War Office—that is to say, the R.F.C.—were responsible for aerial supremacy over the

British Isles, while the Admiralty would have the responsibility of defending the Fleet and ports. Then, just before the war started, the War Office increased its responsibility by announcing that it would also take over aerial defence of ports—graciously adding that the R.N.A.S. could help if it had aircraft stationed nearby.

This was a pipe dream of alarming proportions on the part of the War Office. Sir David Henderson realized that, in order to carry out these commitments, he would need six squadrons comprising 162 aircraft—more than the R.F.C. possessed at that time. The dream was completely shattered in August, 1914, when virtually the entire R.F.C. was sent to France.

And so the Admiralty found itself the only ministry capable of playing the home defence role. Winston Churchill, as First Lord of the Admiralty, laid down orders that all hostile aircraft approaching or over British shores were to be attacked. His orders did not specify the means because, generally speaking, there were none. Three one-pounder pom-pom guns were mounted for the direct protection of government buildings in Whitehall and, for a few weeks, this was Britain's anti-aircraft defence No complete blackout was thought to be necessary, although some of the longer roads in London had their street lighting broken up. These were difficult times, for not only was England battling against the new art of aerial warfare, but she was still trying to assimilate rapidly increasing numbers of automobiles into outdated streets. Traffic conditions were bad enough without having to cope with a blackout as well!

The first air attack against Britain was made at a little after 1 p.m. on December 21st, 1914, when a German seaplane made a surprise attack on Dover and dropped two bombs into the sea, making off again entirely unmolested. Three days later, another German aircraft appeared, very high over Dover, and dropped the first enemy bomb to fall on British soil. It exploded near Dover Castle, broke a few windows but caused no other damage or casualties. On the following day came the daring flight up the Thames to Erith and the bomb near Cliffe station. It was fairly obvious that England was wide open to aerial attack.

The Admiralty cannot be blamed for their lack of readiness. Unrealistic War Office plans had foisted home defence on to the Navy at the very last minute. Moreover, the War Office made it quite plain that they *still* considered home defence a job for the R.F.C. The Admiralty were merely filling the gap until the Flying Corps had sufficient aircraft available. Understandably, the Admiralty took no strenuous steps to gear themselves to this problem.

The general lack of readiness was enhanced by the unexpectedness of the method of German attack—by aeroplane. Count Zeppelin had flown the first of his lighter-than-air ships in 1899 and the Germans had experimented with bomb-dropping from these machines at an early stage. When the War started, the German Army had a fleet of six Zeppelins and it seemed obvious that these would be used to attack Britain. Luckily for Britain, the German Army was obsessed with the desire to prove the Zeppelin as a tactical bomber and used it to bomb Allied front line positions. Attacks of this type had to be very accurate and could not be made from the great altitudes of which the Zeppelins were capable. The huge gas-bags were easy targets for gunners on the ground and the Germans quickly lost three Zeppelins. If Germany had used Zeppelins to attack Britain from the outset of war, she could have bombed practically at will for almost three months. As it was, she did not use Zeppelins until 1915, by which time the Admiralty had organized many more guns and searchlights and was resigned to the fact that the Navy was going to be the sole Service engaged in defending England for quite some time to come.

Zeppelin attacks on England began in May, 1915, and it was immediately apparent that these lighter-than-air craft were almost invincible, despite the increased numbers of guns and searchlights in use on the ground. Aircraft were practically useless against the Zeppelins, which flew over at heights of around 10,000 feet. Defending aircraft took some forty-five minutes to reach this height—by which time the Zeppelin was over another part of England. It was futile, anyway, shooting bullets at the airships. They merely passed in one side and out the other. With luck, they might puncture a gas-bag, but the slow leak caused would be no more than an irritant to the German crew. Anti-aircraft guns were not accurate at such a range and it would have to be a very lucky shot to burst close enough to a Zeppelin for hot shrapnel to pass through the gas-bags.

And so the Zeppelins were able to wander over Britain with impunity. Towns on Tyneside and in East Anglia suffered from their attentions but it was not until the end of May, 1915, that Britain's lack of aerial defences was forcibly brought home to the Londoner. On the night of the 31st of that month, Zeppelins appeared over London. They dropped high explosive and incendiary bombs, the physical effect of which was almost negligible: seven people were killed, thirty-five injured and damage to property was estimated at £18,596.

The effect, however, was that of a far more serious attack. The Government had imposed a censorship on reports of air raids, for the sensible reason that Zeppelin navigation was by no means accurate. Detailed information of where bombs had fallen would have been invaluable to the Germans for planning future attacks. But the censorship of the time also precluded published lists of casualties and damage: most Londoners knew that there had been a raid but were entirely dependent upon hearsay to know the extent of casualties and damage. The rumours, naturally enough, exaggerated the truth.

Anti-German feelings, which had run high at the start of the war but which had later diminished to more reasonable proportions, blossomed forth again, causing mob-reactions. Angry crowds congregated threateningly outside the houses of anyone suspected of having German nationality. One unfortunate individual, who suffered from a distant Prussian background, was pursued by an infuriated, insult-throwing mob along the Hoxton Road. Some shopkeepers with Germanic names had taken the precaution of barricading their premises. The barricades were hauled down.

A few days later, these feelings were exacerbated when reports of the inquests on the victims were published. Henry Good, aged 49, and his wife, Caroline, 46, had been killed when their house was hit by incendiary bombs. The newspapers spared few details of the gruesome story told to the coroner. The couple had been found kneeling by their bed "in an attitude of prayer". Both were naked as their clothes had been burned off. In her hand the woman clutched a bundle of her own hair and a medical witness testified that she had probably torn her hair out in her pain. The man's arm was around his wife's waist.

News such as this did little to calm the public. Nor did the verdict at this particular inquest, which was murder—"murder by some agent of a hostile force".

Opportunists were soon playing on the public's nerves. "Buy Anti-Zepp," urged the advertisements. "Anti-Zepp Grenades," the public read, contained a "new compound" which counteracted the "thermit" believed to be the chemical used in German incendiary bombs. The advertisements lost no opportunity of further alarming a worried community. "Thermit," according to the copywriter, was "a terrible compound which upon ignition immediately generates enormous heat of 5,000 degrees Fahrenheit, which can best be realized when it is stated that at this heat steel runs like melted tallow."

During the Second World War Londoners won an enviable reputation for their fortitude. If the parents of those who endured Hitler's attentions appeared to show little resilience, it should be remembered that they were enduring something completely new, something for which they had been neither educated nor prepared. Official advice on air raid precautions was not forthcoming until more than two weeks after the attack of May 31st—and, even then, it was of a negative nature: do not go out on the streets during an attack, do not turn gas-meters off at the main. There was great public concern, too, about the possible use of poison gas and, once again, official advice was not too helpful. "Gas can be detected by a peculiar and irritating smell following on dropping of a bomb," ran a statement issued by the Commissioner of the Metropolitan Police and intended to be helpful.

The Zeppelin attack did have one beneficial effect. Compulsory national service was still a matter for stormy debate in the Commons and the armed services still depended upon volunteers. Recruiting boomed reassuringly in the weeks following the raid.

The more thoughtful Londoners were not caught up in the high feelings which were running, but they were tremendously concerned about the future. It was realized that this attack on London had been carried out with such impunity that others, much more serious, were bound to follow. What, if anything, was being done to defend the capital city and, indeed, the rest of England? The answer, as most suspected, was very little.

The Admiralty were still doing their poor best. An anti-Zeppelin bomb, a narrow missile filled with petrol, had been designed for the defending aircraft. In theory, the aeroplane flew above the Zeppelin and the pilot pushed the bomb through a narrow opening in the floor of the cockpit. As the missile fell, an electrical contact lit the petrol and a number of hooks sprang out from the bomb. The whole flaming assembly then fell downwards, to lodge in the fabric of the airship and ignite the gas-bags. It was an ingenious idea and one which had some success soon after the attack on London.

At 3 a.m. on the morning of June 7th, Flight Sub-Lieutenant R. A. J. Warneford was flying between Ghent and Brussels when he spotted a Zeppelin flying at 6,000 feet. He manoeuvred his Morane monoplane over the airship, released six anti-Zeppelin bombs, and was immediately blown upside down as the Zeppelin disappeared inside a blinding fireball. His engine stopped and he was forced to land in enemy territory, where he tinkered with his engine, got it going once again and took off for an uneventful flight back to his base.

He had been a qualified pilot for a little over three months and this 22-year old naval aviator became a public hero, was awarded the Victoria Cross and did much to rescue the rapidly tarnishing picture of the military flyer in the minds of many of the public. But, without detracting anything from Warneford's achievement, anyone with some knowledge of military flying and defence problems knew that attacking a Zeppelin at 6,000 feet was vastly different from trying to intercept a raider flying at 10,000 feet or more. It was practically impossible for a British aeroplane to reach that height in time to make an interception, let alone fly even higher to release the fish-hook anti-Zeppelin bombs.

The War Office was still insisting that home defence was inside its province, but it still had no more than a handful of aircraft to spare. The Navy still tried to cope in the face of increasing criticism, both in Parliament and the press, as other attacks on London followed. Lord Kitchener, the Secretary of State for War, was forced to take a close interest in the problem. He examined the sorry history of home defence and had to place the blame squarely on Sir David Henderson's shoulders. Henderson, still heavily committed in France, slowly began to appreciate the War Office's folly in insisting that the Royal Flying Corps would be responsible for home defence and, through Kitchener's insistence, had to take some concrete action towards organizing a home defence policy.

Since January, 1915, all R.F.C. airfields had been warned to keep two aircraft ready at night for use against Zeppelins. Special lighting was arranged so that aircraft could land and take off in the dark. But, because the R.F.C. airfields did not lie in the Zeppelin's general route, these aircraft did not see much action.

The R.F.C. sorted their many difficulties into two main problems. The first was the physical difficulty of flying at night. A primitive flarepath was sufficient to give the pilot a horizontal reference during take-off. This was vital, for there were no instruments to tell the flyer if his wings were level or not. Once airborne, the pilot was dependent on lights from towns or villages in order to keep his wings level and, even then, a horizon was difficult to see. If a ground mist suddenly formed on a dark night, the only sense the pilot had left was the seat of his pants—a sense which, even in those days, was recognized as thoroughly unreliable. Once visual reference was gone, vertigo surely followed—and, almost as certainly, a crash.

The second problem was to get the aircraft up to the Zeppelins despite the slow climb rates of the current machines.

The decision was taken to use outstanding pilots, specially trained in night flying, for home defence duties, thus minimizing the risk from pure flying accidents. The War Office also planned to maintain aircraft on continuous patrols along Zeppelin routes and at Zeppelin heights. The chances of meeting one of the airships would then be very much enhanced. But all this was for the future when more men and machines were available.

The first forward step in home defence was in the nature of an experiment. In collaboration with the Admiralty, the War Office organized what might be termed the embryonic forms of the Royal Observer Corps, Fighter Command and Anti-Aircraft Command. Cordons of ground observers were set up around London and were in direct telephone communication with Home Defence Headquarters. Six aircraft were specially allotted to carefully sited landing grounds; two at Joyce Green, two at Hainault Farm and two at Sutton's Farm at Hornchurch in Essex. A ring of 13-pounder anti-aircraft guns was also set up around north-eastern London.

The weather forecast for the second week in October suggested fine Zeppelin weather, and so it was decided to put the experiment into action from October 5th–12th. It was spoilt by the Germans, who refused to attack. Rightly suspecting that an enemy agent had passed details of these plans to Germany, the War Office sent a message for the 13-pounders to return to Woolwich. This was followed by a top secret order giving new positions for the guns. It seems that the ruse worked, for six Zeppelins, including L.15 under the command of Kapitan-Leutnant Breithaupt, set course for England in the late afternoon of October 13th. Breithaupt's plans were to reach London, where he would bomb the Admiralty and the Bank of England.

The Zeppelins had been spotted by the ground observers well before reaching London and the Home Defence Headquarters had ordered the defending aircraft into the air. At the Sutton's Farm landing ground the duty pilot was Second Lieutenant John Slessor who, thirty-five years later, was to become Marshal of the Royal Air Force, Sir John Slessor, Chief of Air Staff. A telephone call from London roused him from an uncomfortable camp bed alongside his aircraft in the hangar. Because of the time it would take to reach operational height, orders had to be a little woolly. He was told to climb to 10,000 feet and patrol for as long as fuel would allow, keeping a sharp look-out for Zeppelins.

Take-off was accomplished without incident. Breithaupt, in the meantime, had reached London, but missed his specified target; his bombs fell in a line from the Strand to Limehouse. Slessor was soon fortunate to see, far above him, the gently gleaming shape of Breithaupt's Zeppelin—lit up by the blaze of light from an unblacked-out London. To describe what followed as a chase would be quite wrong. When first sighted by Slessor, Breithaupt was floating along with the wind and with his engine idling. He had dropped most of his bombs and was then listening for the sound of aeroplane engines, to find out whether or not he could safely stay in the vicinity of London.

The roar of Slessor's 90 h.p. R.A.F. engine carried clearly through the night air as the B.E.2c climbed as hard as it could to get above the Zeppelin and drop its fish-hook bombs. The British pilot was unaware that he was advertising his approach quite so blatantly, but the fact became obvious when he was about a thousand feet from the Zeppelin. Then, Slessor witnessed the galling of showers of sparks shooting out as Breithaupt opened up his engines, off-loaded ballast and climbed away at full throttle.

Gamely, Slessor continued the unequal chase. As the B.E.2c flew higher, so the rarified air increased its stalling speed. There came the inevitable point when the top speed attainable from the engine only just equalled the stalling speed. Slessor found his aeroplane floundering about rather alarmingly in the dark sky. The Zeppelin, away from the lights of London, was now a dim sight in the distance and thousands of feet higher than the biplane.

Obviously it was time to call off the chase, and Slessor spent a few anxious minutes rescuing his aircraft from some rather ungainly flying attitudes and trying to find his position over England. Eventually, he picked up the Thames and continued to patrol between Tilbury and Chingford. After one and three-quarter hours in the air, shortage of fuel forced him to seek out the distinctive flares of Sutton's Farm and to land.

But the night's adventures were not yet over for Slessor. While he had been airborne, fog from the Thames had crept up and blanketed the airfield. The flares illuminating the airfield were just visible as he began his final approach, somewhat keyed up for what would certainly be a difficult landing. Then, the searchlight crew stationed at the landing ground decided to come to his aid. Unfortunately, they had little idea of the effect their help would have. They decided to illuminate the airfield from one end as Slessor was about to land at the other. He had just dipped into the fog level when the dazzling light from the searchlight flashed on, to turn everywhere into a dense white blanket! The landing was successfully accomplished at the cost of a wing-tip, an aileron and part of the undercarriage.

The statistics for the night's operations were not very encouraging. Six Zeppelins had attacked England and five aircraft were sent up to intercept. Of these, only that flown by Slessor had made contact, and even that had been without results. The fog had caused three of the five aircraft to crash on landing but there were no injuries.

However, it was a start. For the first time, a Zeppelin had been challenged over British soil. The Royal Flying Corps went ahead with its plans to train pilots in night flying and to maintain a constant patrol over Zeppelin routes. By December 1915, when the R.F.C. officially took over home defence from the long-suffering Admiralty, a ring of ten airfields, each with two aircraft, and the constant patrol principle were beginning to take shape. The days of the Zeppelin seemed to be numbered or, at least, they would be if sufficient aircraft could be produced, not only for France, but for home defence as well.

CHAPTER EIGHT

Producing the Goods

ONLY a few more minutes of useful flying time were left of the late afternoon of November 5th, 1914, and Geoffrey de Havilland was turning his B.E. aircraft into wind to land on Laffan's Plain at the Royal Aircraft Factory, Farnborough. He was concentrating on lining up for the landing, when his attention was suddenly taken by an awesome sight on the far side of the airfield—a meteor-like trail of flames and sparks curving ever more steeply towards the ground. It seemed an age before the fireball finally hit the ground, to dissolve into one vaporizing holocaust.

It was a shaken de Havilland who brought his own aircraft in to land a few minutes later, for there was no doubt in his mind who was flying the other aircraft. Ted Busk had taken off at the same time as himself and they were due to land at the same time. No one could have lived through the accident and Geoffrey de Havilland grieved at the loss of a gay and gifted colleague.

What did not immediately enter his mind was that the accident he had witnessed was a vitality-sapping blow to the development of British military aircraft—and it had occurred at a time when Britain could least afford the loss. Over in France, the pilots of the R.F.C. were trying their machines in action and finding them wanting. The call was for more, and still more, aircraft with better performances. It was the responsibility of the Royal Aircraft Factory to design these aircraft and Busk was playing a vital part in the organization.

Second Lieutenant Edward T. Busk was, without doubt, unique in aviation at that time. He was a trained scientist *and* a gifted pilot —the only scientific test pilot in Britain. In those early days even the men who designed aircraft were, for the most part, not scientists but gifted engineers. The pilots entrusted with the risky task of discovering the flying abilities of the aircraft in their care had even less scientific background, for flying an aircraft was regarded as an art and not as a science. But, by this time, Mervyn O'Gorman, Superintendent of the R.A.F., had gathered around him some brilliant scientific minds to help on the design side. They were anxious for firm figures which told of an aircraft's behaviour in the air under different conditions. Only Ted Busk could tell them exactly what they wanted to know in their own language. Now he was dead.

Nor was this the only immediate loss caused by the crash. The B.E. aircraft which Busk had been flying was fitted with the R.A.F.'s only "factory-designed" engine. In the past, Britain had relied on French engines, but now France was in urgent need of every aero-engine she could get for her own aircraft. Because there was no suitable British-designed engine, the R.A.F. had made one. This eight-cylinder air-cooled engine produced 90 h.p. and showed great promise. The first prototype was destroyed with Busk.

There was little doubt about the cause of the accident. The B.E. had been fitted with two petrol tanks and it was standard practice for fuel to be pumped from the reserve tank to the main tank, periodically, while the aircraft was flying. There were no petrol gauges to show when the main tank was full, so a pilot kept pumping until the petrol overflowed. De Havilland, himself, recalled that he once landed with more than an inch of petrol lapping around his feet on the cockpit floor. The inherent danger of this practice had never been fully realized—except, possibly, by Busk himself. Among his effects was found a collection of newspaper cuttings all relating to aircraft accidents caused by fire.

Busk was 28 when he died. "But for his experiments, mathematicians would still be writing treatises on stability and pilots would still be relying on unstable machines," wrote one of his colleagues. The Aeronautical Society made Busk the posthumous award of its Gold Medal, the highest British honour of its kind.

Just how little the R.A.F. could afford to lose a man like Busk, especially at that time, may be realized from the fact that, in France during 1914, squadron aircraft had to be completely replaced every three months. There was no British aircraft industry to supply this need and so the onus fell on the Royal Aircraft Factory. The Government was now paying dearly for the folly of ordering aircraft from France instead of encouraging home designs.

Nor, as has already been stated, was there a British aero-engine. The need for this had been realized early in 1914, when the Government offered a prize of £5,000 for an indigenous engine. The competition was won by a man called Green, who submitted a six-cylinder engine delivering 100 h.p. Orders were actually placed before it was realized that the engine was far too heavy to be practical. It was this fiasco which had led to the R.A.F. producing its own engine.

Engine difficulties were not helped by the uncomfortable fact that, at the outbreak of war, Germany was the only country producing the all-important magneto. All existing British stocks of aero-engine magnetos were impressed for Government use in August, 1914, and an attempt to organize British production was made. This was no easy task because most of the essential materials had to be imported. Some magnetos were bought from the U.S.A. but these had been designed for motor transport and, understandably, did not endure the rigours of aerial use too well. It was not until the autumn of 1916 that British production of magnetos was able to supply all needs.

This lack of suitable engines was keenly felt at the Front. Lieutenant-Colonel H. R. M. Brooke-Popham told, in April, 1915, of one pilot who had made thirty flights in one aircraft. On no fewer than twenty-two occasions had this unfortunate pilot been forced into an untimely landing because of engine trouble. The general inefficiency of these early engines can be appreciated when it is remembered that, in 1914, engines weighed up to 23 lb for every unit of horsepower they produced. By 1918, this figure had decreased to 7 lb per unit of h.p.

The whole burden of meeting this drastic shortage of aircraft and engines lay on the Royal Aircraft Factory. The solid background of aeronautical science built up under O'Gorman proved a tremendous asset and was responsible for the series of inherently stable aircraft, which had started with the "rebuilt" R.E.1 and R.E.2, and had progressed through to the B.E. series which were on the strength of most squadrons by the outbreak of war. The great difficulty for the R.A.F., however, was production. O'Gorman soon found that the problem of producing a few sample aircraft was very different from that of mass production needed to meet the insistent calls from France.

There were few facilities for production on any scale at Farnborough and few of the starved British aircraft companies could help. Vickers and Handley Page produced a few B.E.s apiece, but O'Gorman had to look elsewhere for further production facilities.

This difficulty had been created by the Factory's pre-war policy of demanding that it should have sole control over aircraft design. The manner in which the R.A.F. sought to overcome this self-induced deficiency was, paradoxically, far-sighted, and helped swell the British aircraft industry to proportions which not only enabled it to cope with the demands of the First World War but with those of the 1939–45 conflict as well. It was decided to entrust production of R.A.F. designed aircraft to firms with no aviation experience. Furniture factories, piano works and agricultural implement makers were all called in to help. The system meant that extremely simple, yet detailed, drawings had to be supplied and a close watch kept on production. Managers and foremen were given concentrated courses on aeronautics and then left to get on with their work. Surprisingly, the scheme worked. From it grew firms like the Gloster Aircraft Company which, during the first half of 1914, produced only furniture. By the end of that year it was manufacturing aircraft and remained in this business until 1961, when governmental policy forced it to close down. During World War Two, the Gloster Gladiator stemmed the gap in R.A.F. Fighter Command's equipment for the first few weeks, until the Spitfires and Hurricanes began to arrive in greater numbers.

With this scheme in operation, the Royal Aircraft Factory was able to concentrate on problems of design. The aircraft which had accompanied the R.F.C. to France had, by design, been just adequate to carry fuel and crew. In no time at all, they were being loaded with small-arms, bombs, heavy cameras and even cumbersome wireless sets. It was not surprising that their performances in the field were far short of those envisaged.

The squadrons in France were not slow in letting the R.A.F. know what they wanted but, because the fighting pilots were not scientists, their requests required some sifting before action could be taken. If some untoward accident occurred to an aircraft, back would go a suggestion for some impracticable modification which would, supposedly, overcome the imagined defect. Thus, when the first R.F.C. machine was shot down by ground fire, there was a request for armour-plated aeroplanes—clearly impossible with the then current state of aero-engine construction. A little later, during the retreat from Mons, bad flying weather and the approach of darkness often threatened that aircraft could not be flown away and might have to be left behind. Back went the request for aircraft which could be speedily dismantled and packed for towing along roads.

Luckily, the R.A.F. staff were able to sort out the practical requests from those that would be purely time-wasting. They were misled on only one subject. The inherently stable aircraft which they were proudly producing at the start of the war were found to be lacking in the manoeuvrability needed to escape ground fire and enemy aircraft. Pilots were convinced that, because their machines had too much stability, it was difficult to divert them from their course. The Royal Aircraft Factory wasted valuable time designing aircraft which were *not* inherently stable, in the hope that this would make them more manoeuvrable—until it was realized that the basic trouble was merely inefficient control surfaces on the stable aircraft. Better ailerons, elevators and rudders were the simple answer.

One of O'Gorman's great difficulties during the first few months of the war was getting the right type of test pilot. Busk's untimely death came soon after most of the other pilots who had been employed at Farnborough had suddenly left to busy themselves with a job which they regarded as far more important—fighting. The Superintendent regarded himself as fortunate, therefore, when he managed to secure the services of one, Frank Gooden. Gooden, twenty-four years old, was an easy-going, good-looking and friendly young man who had won the admiration of a large part of the British public through a series of daring air displays, which even critical fellow pilots regarded with awe. There was no doubt about Gooden's ability to fly, but he still had the failing which had frustrated the scientists when dealing with earlier test-pilots—he found great difficulty in rendering his findings down to figures. "The inherent stability is so perfect," he wrote of one aircraft he tested, "that once you have reached the desired altitude you can cuddle up comfortably inside your cockpit and read a book." Such graphic descriptions did not help the scientists.

At this time, one of the great problems besetting these men was the task of working out what stresses an aircraft was likely to incur at any particular point in its framework. They calculated the strain which the wings could take by the simple method of turning an aircraft upside down and loading the wings with sand-bags of known weight, but they found it almost impossible to discover whether an aircraft was likely to receive this loading in the air or not. Later in the war, this vacuum in scientific knowledge began to fill and aircraft could be designed and built with far more confidence that they would stay in one piece during the stresses of aerial combat or flying in bad weather.

The problem of armament was also perplexing. Experience in France was already showing that swivel-mounted Lewis guns in aircraft like the B.E.2c were difficult to aim at other aircraft, and that the home-made mountings for forward firing guns used by some squadrons caused similar problems because, in each case, it was necessary to aim the aircraft in one direction and the gun in another, a very difficult feat. Obviously what was needed was a gun which would fire directly forwards—but the propeller appeared to be an insurmountable obstacle. While the Farnborough scientists were deliberating on this problem, a partial answer was forthcoming from one of the few private firms to have reasonable aircraft production facilities in England, Vickers Ltd.

At the Aero Show of 1913 they had exhibited a small biplane with a pusher-type propeller at the rear. The front cockpit was occupied by an observer with a gun and an uninterrupted field of fire forwards. The aircraft was purely a private venture and owed nothing to government foresight but from this machine the Vickers F.B.5 was evolved in 1914. Christened the "Gun Bus", it was to provide a useful intermediate answer to some of the problems of aerial fighting. It was also to frighten some pilots and observers with a few of its undesirable antics.

CHAPTER NINE

Overwhelming Odds

ON MAY 10th, 1915, a Vickers Gun Bus took off from No. 5 Squadron's airfield to patrol the Ypres salient. Lieutenant W. H. D. Acland, who was the pilot, and 1st Air Mechanic J. N. Rogers, his observer, had endured not a little leg-pulling from their comrades just before setting out, for the record of this aircraft in France at that time was not good. It was in a Gun Bus that the pilot mentioned by Brooke-Popham crash-landed because of engine failure on twenty-two occasions. Acland and Rogers, however, were not particularly perturbed as the small, pusher-type biplane bounced across the grass, teetered somewhat uncertainly into the air and set course for the front. Rogers busied himself checking the Lewis gun in the nose of the aircraft.

Acland had not been in the Ypres area for long when he spotted a small dot some three or four miles away and high up in the sky. The chances were that it was a German machine and, after gesticulating to Rogers to indicate that they were going to investigate, Acland put his aircraft into a climb so that, if necessary, he could attack from above.

It was a painfully slow business to coax his aircraft up to 10,000 feet, but Acland managed to achieve this without, apparently, being spotted. "We then gave chase," he recorded later. "The enemy aircraft did not appear to see us and was apparently making for Lille. We caught him up and opened fire from above and behind at about fifty yards."

Rogers had been itching to let fly at the aircraft as soon as they had come within range but was disciplined enough to hold his fire. He was thus able to achieve complete surprise, and ensure that his first bursts would have results. And very gratifying results they were. After a few short bursts the enemy pilot was apparently hit, for he first slumped, and then struggled feebly, in his cockpit. Small pieces of German aeroplane broke loose, seemed to float in mid-air for an instant and then came flashing past the Gun Bus.

As Rogers was lining up for more bursts, the German machine dived earthwards. Acland could not tell whether this was intentional or not, but he was taking no chances and followed the German down. So far, the conflict had been one-sided but, as the two machines careered downwards, the German observer pulled out a pistol and began firing back. Rogers replied with interest and saw the German observer's pistol arm drop suddenly to his side.

At 2,000 feet Acland began to level out but the German continued a little further and then, without warning, turned over on its back and fell to the ground not far from Lille. As they circled over the spot, Acland and Rogers could see that their adversary was completely wrecked.

It was, of course, to take more than just one victory of this nature to erase the impression made by the Gun Bus when it first came over to France in February, 1915. But more victories were to follow and the Gun Bus was to prove itself a sturdy and redoubtable fighter aircraft at a time when the R.F.C. were in sore need of fighters.

It was not until the Battle of Loos was almost over that Royal Flying Corps H.Q. began to realize that, unless some form of aerial protection could be afforded the reconnaissance aircraft, the vital information would not be brought back, so insistent were the Germans becoming in trying to stop these flights. There was no aircraft in the R.F.C. really suitable as a fighter, nor had the Royal Aircraft Factory back in England anything ready for the Front.

Vickers, convinced that when inevitably war came, their F.B.5 machine would prove its usefulness, had had the foresight to order a batch of fifty into production despite the fact that no official order had been placed. Still the R.F.C. did not order the aircraft and the first F.B.5s went to the R.N.A.S. Not until February, 1915, did the squadrons in France start to receive a few examples. The spate of engine failures experienced with the 100 h.p. Gnome Monosoupape engines fitted to the Gun Bus were largely attributable to inadequate servicing instructions. When this problem was overcome, the Gun Bus became a very useful aeroplane.

The airborne antics of the early machine gun pioneers such as Penn-Gaskell and Strange were also to stand the R.F.C. in good stead until such time as fighter aircraft came from the Royal Aircraft Factory. From their early efforts two reasonably successful machine gun mountings were evolved for the single-seat Martinsyde Scout biplane. In one of these a Lewis gun was mounted to fire obliquely forwards so as to miss the propeller arc. This meant, as I have explained, that the pilot had to fly his aircraft in one direction and aim the gun in another. A better method was a mounting designed for the upper wing which allowed the gun to fire directly forward over the propeller. This arrangement worked quite well, but operating a single-seat fighter during 1915 did impose problems—somewhat frightening problems, of which Strange was to get first-hand experience.

On the same day that Acland and Rogers were proving the worth of the Gun Bus over Ypres, and in the same area, Strange met an enemy aircraft at 8,000 feet while flying a Martinsyde with a wing-mounted Lewis gun. The German aircraft was also armed with a machine gun and the pilot was not loath to do battle. For some minutes the two machines dived and fired at each other, but with no results. Then, almost by mutual consent, they broke off the fight to change ammunition drums. Strange reached up with one hand to remove his drum but it would not come free. Cursing its obstinacy, he loosened his seat straps and half stood up to get both hands on the drum. Even then it remained jammed.

While Strange was struggling, an unruly air bump took a hand in the proceedings. It was not much of a disturbance but it was sufficient to upset the Martinsyde's equilibrium. Never a very stable aeroplane, the biplane flipped upside down, and Strange was thrown from the cockpit. As the aircraft settled into a jerky spin, Strange found himself with his legs entangled in the seat strap and both hands firmly clasping the ammunition drum. The centrifugal force of the spin was trying to throw his body away from the aircraft.

Praying that the drum would remain in position as fervently as he had cursed it for not coming loose only a few seconds earlier, Strange refused to believe that this was the end. His first thought was to anchor himself to something a little more reliable than the ammunition drum. The centre strut which supported the wing was within reach but, to get at this, he would have to take one hand off the drum. Time seemed to stand still during the split second that he let go of the drum with one hand and made a grab for the strut. He was now anchored more firmly to his aircraft but not much nearer to regaining his cockpit. This he would have to do if he were to save his life, for the R.F.C. used no parachutes.

This drama had been witnessed by the German pilot. Luckily for Strange, the German thought, quite logically, that if his opponent was thrown from his cockpit the battle had ended in a German victory. He did not bother to attack again. Meanwhile, Strange was kicking to free his feet from the seat straps. He had been thrown out at 8,000 feet. By this time he was approaching 3,000 feet and there was not much time left. First one foot and then the other reached the welcome firmness of the cockpit lip and Strange literally threw himself back into the aircraft. He landed heavily on the wooden seat because his cushions had been thrown out as soon as the spin had started. The seat collapsed under him.

Seated almost on the floor, Strange tried to right the aircraft, but it would not answer the controls. He had the presence of mind to realize that this was because he was sitting on the control lines, forced himself up a little and regained control. He managed to complete the flight back to his airfield without further incident. In those days, it was asking much of one man to handle the foibles of both a wayward aeroplane and an equally wayward machine gun.

Pilots on both sides soon began to realize that what was needed was a device which would allow them to fire a machine gun *through* the propeller disc without any danger of shearing off the blades. None of them realized that such devices had been invented and proved before the war started, but that neither the British nor German governments had sufficient vision to foresee the aeroplane being used purely as a fighter. It was left to a French pilot, Roland Garros, to prod both sides into action on this vital point. Unfortunately, through no fault of his own, Garros awoke the German Air Force first.

Early in 1915, Garros found himself serving with Escadrille M.S.23 in the French Air Force and flying a somewhat outdated Morane-Saulnier monoplane. He had met German aircraft and soon realized the many difficulties of trying to shoot them down with a machine gun which could not be aimed straight ahead. Garros lacked the technical knowledge to fit a mechanical interrupter gear to his aircraft so that his gun would only fire when there was no propeller blade ahead, but he did have the resourcefulness to fix heavy metal plates around the propeller blades where they crossed the line of fire from the machine gun which he mounted.

It was literally a hit or miss method. Fortunately for both sides, an aerial combat in those days was likely to be a private affair between only a few aircraft. If Garros and his aeroplane had taken part in some of the packed dog-fights of 1917–18 his ricochetting bullets would have been a menace for friend and foe alike. But sufficient bullets went straight through to have a very gratifying effect, in 1915. Within the short space of sixteen days, he had shot down five German aircraft, a staggering total for those early days of aerial combat.

Garros was fêted as a national hero but no-one in authority seemed to realize that he owed his success to the fact that he was the only pilot on the Western Front who could fire through his propeller disc. Yet Garros's success was short-lived. On April 19th, 1915, he took part in a bombing attack on the railway marshalling yards at Courtrai. Garros came down in a shallow dive, with his engine switched off and propeller windmilling so that he might achieve some measure of surprise. In the exhilaration of the moment, he forgot that his sparking plugs would oil up if he allowed the propeller to windmill for any length of time without occasionally blipping the throttle.

Garros hurled his small explosive darts overboard and switched on his engine with high hopes of continuing his flight and surprising more Germans with his machine gun. But his engine refused to start. His forgetfulness was to bring about his downfall—and to cost the Allies dear. The French pilot managed to bring off a forced landing in a field near Ingelmunster and, anxious that the secret of his success should not fall into enemy hands, tried to set fire to his aeroplane. The linen covering was damp and refused to light.

Within a few hours, both Garros and his monoplane were in German hands. The aircraft which could shoot through its propeller had already become a legend with the German pilots and it was not long before the Morane-Saulnier had been dismantled and transported to Berlin, where the secret of the steel deflector plates was laid bare. The aircraft was shown to young Anthony Fokker, a gifted pilot and aircraft designer, who was a great advocate of the small, fast and manoeuvrable single-seat fighter.

Earlier historians have recorded how Fokker was shown the crude deflector device and, straight away, evolved a sophisticated interrupter gear for his monoplanes. But here, history has been distorted. The German war department had been made uncomfortably aware of the effect of the deflector blades by Garros's successes. They were not aware that they had turned down a far better device which had been patented by a Swiss engineer, Franz Schneider, in July, 1913. Any private ideas which Fokker might have had of improving on Garros's device were immediately scrapped when he returned to his factory at Shwerin with the Frenchman's propeller and machine gun. He showed the device to two of his engineers, Heinrich Lubbe and Fritz Heber, who immediately reminded him of Schneider's far better device.

Basically, Schneider's design comprised a cam ring which could be fitted behind a rotary engine. This actuated a series of cranks and rods and was adjusted to fire a machine gun every time the two-bladed propeller was horizontal and therefore, out of the line of fire. One of Fokker's M 5 K monoplanes was immediately fitted with this device and tested successfully within forty-eight hours. Thus, the advent of the synchronized machine gun owed nothing mechanically to Garros. The Frenchman's device had merely served to open the eyes of the German war department. What followed had nothing to do with Garros, but it was to come near to annihilating the Royal Flying Corps.

While Anthony Fokker was conducting his successful experiments with the synchronizing gear, the R.F.C. was beginning to find deficiencies in its make-up. It had become painfully obvious that, before any other offensive could be planned, the R.F.C. would have to make a bid for air supremacy. This would require first class fighter aircraft and these did not yet exist in England.

Meanwhile, the pilots were beginning to evolve their own methods of air fighting with the limited equipment at their disposal. The "ace" had not yet been born. There were far too many other jobs for the R.F.C. to do for any one man to concentrate solely on shooting down the enemy. But, in 6 Squadron was the officer who could be called the prototype British fighter ace, Captain Lanoe G. Hawker.

Hawker had already distinguished himself with a daring attack on the Zeppelin sheds at Gontrode but as 1915 progressed began to spend more and more of his time in pursuit of enemy aircraft. He was, perhaps, the first man to plan his attacks scientifically. He would wait on the ground until he received a report from an aircraft, or a ground observation station, that enemy aircraft were about. He would then take off in his Bristol Scout, accompanied by a B.E.2c aircraft which he would use as a decoy.

His ruse was often successful. On the evening of July 25th, 1915, Hawker managed to meet up with a German two-seater over the Ypres salient. He gave chase and loosed off a drum of ammunition but the enemy was able to dive away, apparently unharmed. Hawker continued his quest of enemy aircraft and, twenty minutes later, he found and attacked another two-seater over Houthulst Forest. In a brief combat some of his bullets stopped the enemy's engine. The aircraft was forced to the ground.

Hawker's fuel and ammunition were by no means spent and, at 11,000 feet, he continued with his patrol. Over Hooge he spotted a two-seat Albatros, busily engaged in artillery observation. Hawker did not attack at once. Gambling on the fact that the enemy would be so busy with the task in hand that they would not be keeping a sharp look out, the British pilot manoeuvred his aircraft until it came between the Albatros and the setting sun. Now, his trap was complete. If the enemy pilot or observer did happen to glance towards the Bristol Scout, he would see nothing but the blinding glare of the sun.

There was little that the Albatros crew could do to save themselves. Hawker achieved complete surprise and, with a few bursts, shot the German machine down. It burst into flames before hitting the earth in the British lines near Zillebeke, where it continued burning for fifteen minutes. British troops dragged the pilot and observer clear but both were already dead. On the observer they found a map, which not only had British gun positions clearly marked, but also showed the position of a German battery which had been particularly troublesome and which, up to that time, could not be discovered by British reconnaissance aircraft. The two aircraft which Hawker had shot down made his aggressive evening patrol more than worthwhile. The fortuitous discovery of the location of the German battery was an extremely valuable bonus. The award of the Victoria Cross followed this exploit.

It was unfortunate that the R.F.C. could not spare more men for the role played by Hawker but manpower was becoming a very thorny problem. In a Memorandum sent from France to London in August, Lieutenant-Colonel Brooke-Popham pointed out that, since 1914, the Army in France had grown from four divisions to thirty, but that the number of R.F.C. squadrons to supply the Army's needs had only grown from four to eleven. The R.F.C. was also finding itself involved in many other roles apart from the pure reconnaissance in which it was first used.

"If the enemy brings his troops over from the Eastern Front," wrote Brooke-Popham, "and if he resumes his offensive, he will doubtless make a determined effort to prevent our discovering his movements. Then will commence the real struggle for air supremacy where numbers will be one of the essentials of success."

But manpower was not the only problem facing the hard-pressed Flying Corps. The Fokker monoplanes were coming into service in increasing numbers, and each was fitted with a machine gun and synchronizing gear. In the hands of such gifted German pilots as Oswald Boelcke and Max Immelmann it was to prove a lethal fighting machine. With a pure fighter such as this the Germans were able to explore the art of air-to-air fighting far more thoroughly than Hawker could. They soon perfected the technique of diving to the attack from out of the sun and, if their first onslaught did not bear fruit, they would climb and make another dive rather than stay and tangle with the British on the same level. Immelmann also evolved the manoeuvre which bears his name to this day, the "Immelmann turn". After his first attack, Immelmann would pull up and begin a loop but, on the top of the loop, he would roll his aircraft right way up, ready to turn and dive to the attack immediately. The sudden gain of height and rapid change of direction which this gave him was to cause the downfall of many British pilots.

The Fokker monoplanes, with their nerve-shattering tactics and deadly ability to shoot through the propeller disc, should have sapped British morale alarmingly, but they did not. Even such unsuitable aircraft as the B.E.2c stood up to this menace, and this refusal of the British to knuckle under was, at first, to check the initial impetus of the Fokkers. A fight between a B.E.2c of 8 Squadron and two Fokker monoplanes, on October 22nd, demonstrates how sheer refusal to be beaten out of the skies stood the R.F.C. in good stead. Second Lieutenant D. A. Glen and his observer, Corporal E. Jones, had been briefed to provide escort for a reconnaissance aircraft over Le Cateau. They lost touch with their charge and were alone in the sky over Cambrai when they were dived on by two Fokkers. With no reconnaissance aircraft to protect, Jones and Glen had no real cause to fight such an unequal combat but, instead of turning tail and heading for the British lines, they stayed to fight.

Jones opened fire from some distance. Whether he was a good shot or a lucky one it is impossible to say. He was certainly a brave one. His first bursts hit one of the Fokkers, which reeled out of control and fell into a wood. The remaining German machine would have been more than a match for the unwieldy B.E.2c but, when Glen turned his aircraft towards this one, he saw it streaking back to the safety of its own lines, its pilot not yet sufficiently confident to trust the prowess of his machine.

But slowly it began to dawn on the Germans that their aircraft were, indeed, superior to anything which the British had. From that moment, their successes mounted alarmingly and the fortunes of the R.F.C. reached their lowest ebb. Even the Vickers Gun Bus could provide no effective answer to what was now known as the "Fokker menace". Reconnaissance flights had to be performed with "fighter" cover. Usually, the protecting aircraft were quite unsuitable for the task and the nerves of both reconnaissance and escort crews were strained to near breaking point. Hastily recruited, and even more hastily trained, pilots sent from England to replace those shot down were quite unready for combat. Often they were shot down during their first operational flights. The lucky ones survived a few weeks, by which time their knowledge of air fighting gave them a slightly better chance of winning through.

If the morale of the Royal Flying Corps had broken at this point, the Army would have been in serious trouble. Britain was probably nearer to losing the war than at any other time. But the British seem to find their true strength in adversity, and there were always crews ready to tackle the dangerous reconnaissance flights. From time to time came stories of prodigies of determination in the face of the enemy—stirring deeds which were to boost morale almost as much as more and better fighting machines would have done.

One noted morale booster was Second Lieutenant Gilbert Insall. On November 17th, 1915, Insall, with Air Mechanic Donald, took off for a patrol in a Vickers Gun Bus. They met an Aviatik single-seat aircraft. With the value of the synchronizing gear amply proved on the Fokkers, the Germans were beginning to fit it to other aircraft, among them the Aviatik. Insall did not have time to discover whether his quarry was so fitted because it immediately flew away from the Gun Bus. Flying over a landscape largely obliterated by scattered cloud, Insall entered into a determined chase. Then, through a gap in the clouds ahead, he caught sight of a German anti-aircraft gun battery and saw that the Aviatik was making straight for it. Ignoring this obvious trap, Insall maintained his pursuit and had soon urged his aircraft near enough for Donald to open fire from the front cockpit. His bullets entered the German engine and, seeing that he could no longer make for the safety of the battery, the Aviatik pilot put his aircraft into a steep dive through the cloud. Insall followed, the two aircraft broke cloud together and Donald was able to bring his gun into action once again.

The German had had enough and executed a clumsy forced landing in a ploughed field, some four miles south of Arras. As the Vickers came down to investigate, the crew saw the German pilot trying to take aim with his machine gun. Insall immediately dived to 500 feet and a few well-aimed bursts from Donald were sufficient to make the German lose interest in the combat and to take to his heels across the field. Ignoring another German anti-aircraft battery which was trying to bring its gun to bear on him, Insall made another pass over the crashed aircraft and lobbed a small incendiary bomb overboard. He scored a direct hit.

With little doubt that at least one German aircraft could trouble him no more, Insall turned back towards the front line. He still had to face the other menace which plagued British pilots and that was the "Archie" over the German trenches. He put the Gun Bus in a dive to cross at the highest speed, and Donald pointed his machine gun downwards to pump his remaining bullets into the German trenches. Insall zoomed over at 2,000 feet but this time his luck was out. A near burst sent shrapnel through his fuel tank and the engine spluttered into silence. There was insufficient height to glide to safety and Insall brought the Gun Bus down behind a small wood in no-man's-land.

The Germans watched this event with interest. While Insall and Donald were inspecting the damage to their machine, a whistle and crump announced that the Germans were trying to cement their initial success by calling up artillery fire on the aircraft. Refusing to leave his aircraft to the mercy of the German guns, Insall decided against making for the safety of the French lines, which were some distance away. As darkness set in, the two British airmen brought out torches and, keeping them carefully screened from the Germans, tried to repair the damage to their aircraft.

They worked throughout the night with the constant accompaniment of bursting artillery shells as the Germans tried to bring their guns to bear. Just before dawn their work was completed and, at first light the next day, the engine was successfully started and Insall took off, to regain his base safely. One month later, Insall was gazetted for the Victoria Cross and the story of his determination served to boost the morale of others in the R.F.C.

But no amount of morale-boosting could disguise the gloomy arithmetic of British losses. On November 11th, one reconnaissance aircraft from No. 6 Squadron was shot down by two Fokkers and two B.E.2cs failed to return from a bombing raid at Bellenglise. Three days later a No. 7 Squadron B.E.2c was forced to break off its reconnaissance when its pilot was shot in the leg. Losses continued throughout November and into December. On December 14th the Germans demonstrated their confidence by shooting down a 7 Squadron B.E.2c over Ypres, well inside British lines. On the same day, Insall, the morale booster, and Donald were shot down and taken prisoner. Insall later escaped. On the nineteenth forty-six fights in the air were recorded. Few of them went well for the R.F.C. A B.E.2c escorting a GHQ reconnaissance to Bruges was shot down near Oostcamp and both occupants were killed. The reconnaissance aircraft managed to get away, although the pilot was wounded in the arm and one cylinder of the engine was shot away. Several aircraft managed to get back although badly damaged. One crashed on landing and the observer was killed.

On the credit side, a Morane of No. 3 Squadron set off on a difficult reconnaissance to Valenciennes, accompanied by two similar aircraft. They met and tangled with one Fokker and two Albatros aircraft but managed to return with the information they had gleaned.

Perhaps the role of the R.F.C. at this time was best demonstrated by Lieutenant W. S. Douglas, on December 29th. Piloting a B.E.2c, he was protecting another B.E.2c engaged on reconnaissance, when four monoplanes appeared simultaneously. Two attacked immediately and the British reconnaissance machine was shot down. All four then turned on Douglas. Hopelessly outnumbered, and outclassed in his machine, Douglas fought his way back to the British lines under repeated attack by the four. Bullets from his machine gun accounted for one Fokker but the other three pressed their attacks home, at one point forcing the British aircraft down to fifteen feet from the ground. Douglas crossed the trenches at 800 feet and managed to execute an emergency landing in a field near Arras.

It was a brilliant and brave rearguard action fought against morale-sapping odds. Things were certainly looking grim for the R.F.C. The Germans had gained air superiority and this meant that the vital reconnaissance flights could no longer be carried out at reasonable cost. The R.F.C. were perfectly willing to carry out these flights, whatever the cost, but it had now become clear that unless they received more and better machines, soon they would not be able to carry them out at all.

CHAPTER TEN

The Mad Major's Magic

NEW machines were being assimilated into the R.F.C., albeit with difficulty, and the pilots were slowly learning the art of aerial combat in a painful and costly manner. But this did not deter the flyers from acquiring further gifts which were to play an important part in the conflict. During the winter of 1914–15, the aircraft of the R.F.C. presented a sorry sight as cold and damp wrought their worst on the aeroplanes, but one machine in particular was even more decrepit than the rest. This B.E.2 was a well-known sight to the troops in the trenches that winter. Few soldiers had any idea who the pilot was: it was sufficient to know that this was the wireless aeroplane.

In fact, there were two aircraft of this type, but to the men of the R.F.C. there was only one pilot and he was Lieutenant Swain Lewis. Sometime later, on April 10th, 1916, to be precise, a Morane Parasol aircraft flying east of Wytschaete received a direct hit from anti-aircraft fire and spun down to an annihilating crash. The pilot, a lieutenant-colonel, and his passenger were killed. The high-ranking flyer was none other than Lewis. His rapid advance in rank was a tribute to the part he had played in introducing a new science to the Royal Flying Corps. Swain, perhaps more than any other, had been responsible not only for the technical development of the apparatus but for its application to artillery spotting—a precarious pastime in which he took part whenever he could. "Lewis came in from spotting with his machine shot full of holes," one pilot wrote during the early months of the war. "I believe he likes it!" Whether he did like it or not, Lewis persevered and, by the time of his death, the art of wireless telegraphy was able to play a vital part in the battle, but it had not been an easy struggle.

Wireless, in 1912, was almost as new an art as flying and the R.F.C. had every intention of harnessing it to their aircraft. That it was possible had been proved in 1908, when successful ground to air transmissions were made to the balloon *Pegasus* some twenty miles away. A year later, Captain H. P. T. Lefroy, Royal Engineers, was put in charge of all wireless experiment in the Army. Sets were clumsy, huge and inefficient. That there was any aerial use of the science at all was due to the load-carrying abilities of lighter-than-air craft. When the R.F.C. was formed in 1912, airships were still in use in No. 1 Squadron and these continued to be used for wireless experiments. At this time, of course, the Flying Corps had only one duty and that was to be the eyes of the Army. If wireless was to be used to advantage, it was thought that it would have to be for the difficult task of sending back complicated reconnaissance reports over fairly large distances. This was a basic mistake, which was to delay the ultimate successful use of wireless. The R.F.C. wasted much valuable time and effort in trying to build large long-range sets when what was really needed was a less powerful transmitter which could be used for artillery spotting.

One year after the R.F.C. had been formed, an experimental branch was set up and the man placed in charge was Major Herbert Musgrave, Royal Engineers. Among those who remember these formative years there are two schools of thought about Major Musgrave. One is generous enough to say that, without the Major, wireless telegraphy would not have appeared until too late in the war to be of much use. The other asserts, with conviction, that success was achieved *in spite of* the Major's efforts. Perhaps the argument can be explained by the two sides to the Major's character.

He had served throughout the Boer War as a lieutenant and later passed through the Staff College. In 1909 he was one of the witnesses of Louis Blériot's arrival at Dover. The sight impressed him tremendously and, being a man given to direct action, he went as soon as possible to the War Office to draw attention to the threat to England which aviation posed—which, incidentally, many of the newspapers had immediately stressed.

Thoughts of military aviation then dominated his mind. He lectured on the subject and he drew attention to the threat coming from Germany. He learned to fly in 1912 and joined the R.F.C. Then, in March, 1913, he was given command of the experimental branch.

The choice is, perhaps, a little difficult to understand, for Major Musgrave had no scientific training. He was, however, known as a "good soldier" and was extremely keen on discipline. Among the edicts on the proper use of military aviation which continued to flow from him was the gem that new squadrons should be formed, even while aircraft were lacking, so that problems of discipline and organization could be settled in advance.

In his new task he had, in theory, responsibility for all or any kind of experiments. It is to his everlasting credit that, for some reason, he chose to concentrate on wireless. To help him he had two young lieutenants. One was Lewis, and the other Baron Trevenen James, a mathematical scholar who turned soldier and then developed an intense interest in flying. Between them, Lewis and James evolved a wireless set which weighed 75 lb. It was clumsy and took up all the observer's cockpit and even overflowed into the pilot's compartment, but it did work.

When the R.F.C. crossed to France at the outbreak of the war, Lewis and James became attached to No. 4 Squadron as a special wireless detachment. With them, still in command, went Major Musgrave. During the first few weeks of fighting, one or two experimental attempts at artillery spotting with wireless aircraft were made. They were successful and the gunners were delighted with the accurate instructions they were able to get back so quickly. Lewis and James looked like becoming the star attractions of the R.F.C., but the bulky equipment in their aircraft was allied to even more cumbersome contraptions on the ground and, when the retreat from Mons began, there was little chance of erecting the ground stations. Instead, Lewis and James took the opportunity of patching their aircraft and making still more improvements to their wireless sets.

By December, 1914, the Wireless Flight had become, on paper, No. 9 Squadron and was to take charge of all wireless work by the R.F.C. in France. Musgrave was still C.O. and the aircraft were still the two faithful B.E.s used by Lewis and James. It was around this time that Musgrave's good work in pushing the development of wireless stood in great danger of being nullified by strange ideas which filled his mind. The headquarters of the Squadron remained at St. Omer, where its job was supposed to be to supply equipment to aircraft and artillery batteries at the front and train men in the use of radio. The

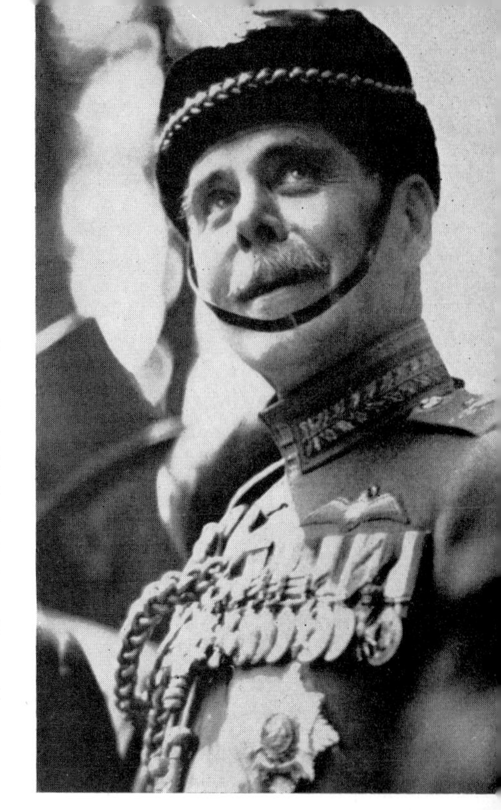

ight, Lord Trenchard's instinctive nderstanding of aerial strategy enabled ıe R.F.C. in France to overcome the okkers. *Below*, left, Frederick Lindeıann, later Lord Cherwell, was one of ıe first Experimental Pilots during the irst World War and his researches into ıe techniques of spinning were of imıense value. *Below, right,* Sir Geoffrey e Havilland served with the R.F.C. uring the war and designed some of ıe most successful aircraft while workıg for the Royal Aircraft Factory at Farnborough

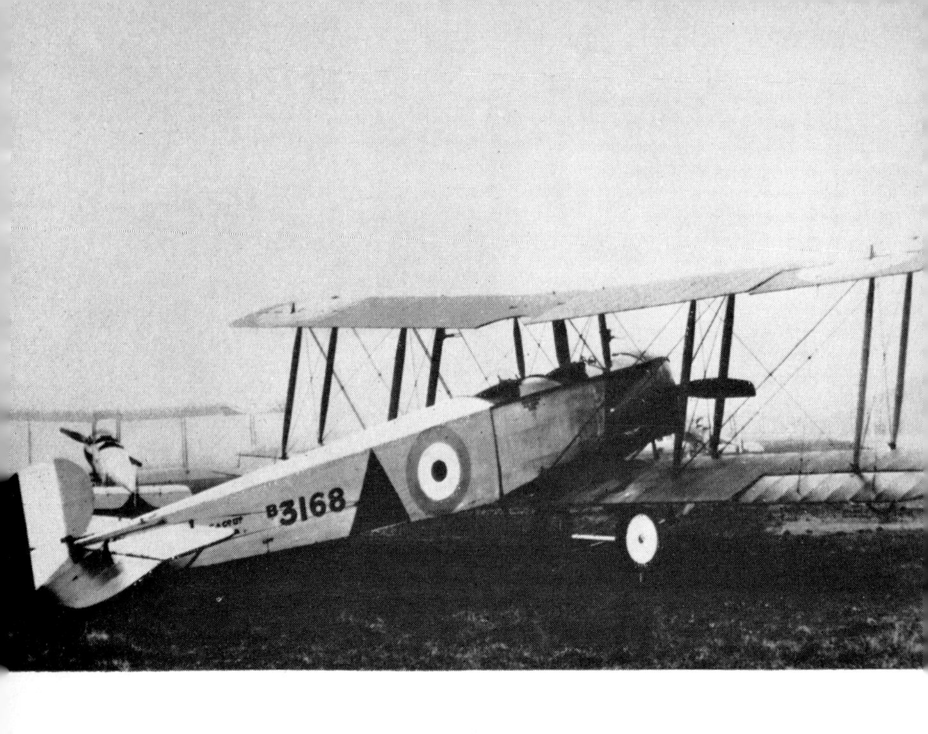

The Avro 504 which, in the hands of R. Smith-Barry, seen on the left of the picture below, revolutionized flying training during the First World War

organization was primitive in the extreme. Two radio operators and a handful of instrument repairers worked together under canvas in a gravel pit. Tools and power were supplied from a lorry which frequently broke down, and the men, only thirty miles from the front line, slept on straw palliasses in an old barn. Musgrave never lost an opportunity to impress upon them that their lot was far better than than of the infantrymen in the trenches. No-one in No. 9 Squadron disagreed with him but when the C.O. began to organize pre-dawn parades for his men—just in the interests of discipline—they were not so certain.

Musgrave had other strange ways. No. 9. Squadron came into possession of a huge German tent hangar. It was the first shelter of any kind which they had for the aircraft and the order was given that it should be erected. This was no easy task as the tent seemed to have been designed with a complicated folding mechanism expressly to baffle the R.F.C. The task fell to a young lieutenant who had just arrived at No. 9 Squadron, J. T. C. Moore-Brabazon, later Lord Brabazon of Tara. He spent much time trying to work out the secret of the hangar and finally succeeded in erecting it, with the almost superhuman efforts of fifty borrowed troops. It was well-sited in a hollow which protected it from the wind and allowed easy access for aircraft. He was pleased with the effort and stood by, expecting praise when Musgrave came along to inspect it.

The Major looked at it impassionately for some moments and then said abruptly, "Move it twelve feet to the left."

Moore-Brabazon was astounded at such a futile order. He pointed out, as politely as he could, that it would be a pointless waste of effort to move the hangar. Musgrave's reaction was that Moore-Brabazon should obey the orders of a "superior" officer. Brabazon's reply has gone down in the history of *bons mots*: "*Superior* officer? *Senior* officer if you please, sir!" Musgrave was, reportedly, not amused.

But far more serious was his attitude towards the wireless aircraft. As 1915 wore on, the demands on Lewis and James at the front increased. The artillery would ask, not just for an observation aircraft, but would specify a "wireless machine". For the same reason, Lewis and James and their aircraft were overworked. Neither man complained. Their spirit kept them going even when physical tiredness dictated that they should rest. It was not so easy with their aircraft.

After five months out in the open in all weathers, the fabric on the wings was soggy and stretched so much that at times the aeroplanes could hardly stagger into their element. Spare wings were kept in store and the pilots continually asked Musgrave for permission to fit new wings. Musgrave always refused. It was not in his nature to provide an explanation for this strange action.

A recent arrival at the Squadron had been Captain Hugh Dowding, later to be the man to lead R.A.F. Fighter Command to victory in the Battle of Britain, and now Lord Dowding. He was posted to No. 9 Squadron as Adjutant and was not impressed with the actions of his C.O. Eventually, Musgrave went back to England for a short leave. Dowding, as acting Commanding Officer, took it upon himself to give Lewis and James the new wings for which they had been waiting. These were fitted but, when Musgrave returned, he immediately ordered that they should be returned to the store and the old wings put back. Perhaps coincidentally, Musgrave was relieved of his command and returned to the Army. In June, 1918, he was killed while leading a party of men through a dangerous barrage. It was undoubtedly a brave action but, in the opinion of some, a foolhardy one. Thus departed Major Musgrave, a bristling military disciplinarian who, from the start, had seen the value of wireless telegraphy but had not, perhaps, the right phsychological make-up to lead a band of brilliant individualists.

Lewis, while doing much to further the scientific development of wireless, had not neglected its practical applications. It was normal practice in both the artillery and the R.F.C., in 1914, to give map references as "just to the left" of a topographical feature, or even as "above the 'd' in Gueudecourt". Such methods were inaccurate and also cumbersome when it came to signalling corrections to the guns. Lewis soon learned to square his maps and those of the battery commander with whom he was working. These maps came to the notice of Major W. G. H. Salmond, an ex-artillery-man who was a staff officer at R.F.C. HQ. He immediately recognized their worth and soon squared maps were being produced for the R.F.C. and the Army.

There remained the problem of signalling corrections. The normal method in use was to pass back the instructions "left", "right", "short", or "over", to signify where the shell had fallen. Again, this was not too accurate and Lewis, prompted by a suggestion trom

James, sat down and made for himself a transparent celluloid trace bearing a centre spot, twelve radial lines and eight concentric circles around the centre. The circles represented distances from the target—from 10 yards to 500 yards, and were lettered Y, Z, A, B, C, D, E, and F. The radial lines were used to signify direction and were numbered one to twelve. Lewis merely had to estimate the point of the shell burst, transfer it to the map, place the centre spot of his transparent trace over the target and read off the position of the burst. Thus "B3" would signify that the shell had burst 100 yards east of the target. The method, which became known as the clock code, and the squared map were used throughout the war.

By 1916, the cumbersome wireless sets originally used by Lewis, James and Lieutenant Winfield Smith, who joined them soon after the outbreak of the war, were being replaced by the Sterling set. This was a much lighter apparatus, built by the Sterling Telephone Company, but it had many teething troubles to overcome before it was used in service. There was a dramatic increase, too, in the number of wireless aeroplanes, which multiplied from the original two to whole squadrons. When these developments had taken place, Marconi's original invention, thanks to the efforts of a few brilliant and brave men, was all set to play a vital part in the war in the air.

The science of wireless had received attention in the R.F.C. initially because it was thought it would be invaluable in reconnaissance work. Eventually, as we have seen, it found its true employment in artillery spotting. Of much more use in reconnaissance was photography but this was a fact to which the War Office did not seem very much alive. Again, it was left to the individuals of the R.F.C. to show what could be done. Several pilots had taken somewhat shaky photographs from the air with privately-owned cameras, but it was the pilots of No. 3 Squadron who first applied themselves to getting something of military value.

No government funds were available, yet, from the beginning of 1914, the Squadron became intensely interested in the art of aerial photography and bought their own cameras. They had no photographic expert in their ranks, yet were able to modify their commercial cameras for use in the air. With the need for quick, accurate information uppermost in their minds, they also worked out a means of developing, printing and fixing prints, while still in the air, so that they could be handed over immediately after landing. But even when, in one day's flying, Squadron pilots produced a complete series of photographs of the defences of the Isle of Wight and the Solent, the War Office were not able to see the value of this science. This was a lack of foresight which was hard to explain. One of the pioneers of photography was a Frenchman, Nardar. Well before the turn of the century, he had been taking photographs from balloons. The French had immediately realized the military value of this science and asked Nardar to take photographs for the Army; the photographer, confirmed pacifist, would not agree.

When the R.F.C. moved to France, there was still no official call for photography but, fortunately, No. 3 Squadron took their adapted private cameras with them. As early as September 15th, Lieutenant G. F. Pretyman had taken five photographs of German trenches but, even then, the value of the science was not appreciated. Flyers were still expected to cruise around, often for hours, laboriously noting trenches, gun positions and concentrations of troops in pencil on their maps. It was a form of reconnaissance which was both tedious and inaccurate.

Fortunately, 3 Squadron did not lose their enthusiasm. Lieutenant C. C. Darley was, perhaps, the most enthusiastic photographer. With the help of other officers, he rigged up a dark room in the château in which the Squadron were billeted, and regularly drove to Bethune where he was able to buy the necessary chemicals. Slowly, the squadron took enough photographs to show the whole of the German trench system along their stretch of the front. Results were not always good, but Darley became adept at interpreting the prints and was able to mark in all items of military interest. The resulting photographic map which he produced was intended only for the Squadron's own use, as an aid to planning further reconnaissances, but his Commanding Officer, Major J. M. Salmond, a future Chief of Air Staff and now Marshal of the R.A.F. Sir John Salmond, was so impressed that he took it along to the Corps H.Q., where officers were immediately taken with the idea that photographic maps could be produced that were intelligible to anyone. The news spread around the squadrons and other officers began experimenting in the art.

Sykes, however, while impressed with the R.F.C.'s efforts, had seen a few examples of French aerial photographs and realized that these were vastly superior to those obtained by No. 3 Squadron. He sent Major W. G. H. Salmond to study the French photographic organization. Salmond brought back the obvious answer that the French results were so much better because they had realized the value of the science some time ago and had set up many photographic experts in units which dealt with nothing else but aerial photo-reconnaissance. The lesson had been learned and an experimental photographic branch was set up in France early in 1915. Its instructions were to report on the best form of organization and camera for aerial photography. This section came under No. 1 Wing, and Trenchard, who was then commanding the Wing, was extremely impressed with the potentialities of photography and gave the unit every encouragement.

Responsibility for the section was given to the young Moore-Brabazon, who was not a photographic expert. With him, however, was Lieutenant C. D. M. Campbell, who was. Flight Sergeant Laws was another with considerable knowledge of the science and 2nd Air Mechanic W. D. Corse completed the team. Brabazon's useful flair of mastering a subject completely came to his aid, and his zest and guidance, allied with the technical knowledge and willingness of the others, soon produced results, although problems were many. Not least of these was the difficulty of vibration from the aircraft. It was soon realized that the best results should, in theory, be obtained from a camera fixed to the aeroplane to shoot vertically downwards but vibrations of the fuselage gave blurred results.

Meanwhile, the amateurs in No. 3 Squadron were unceasing in their efforts at photography. Early in February, Darley went up with Lieutenant V. H. N. Wadham to photograph some stacks of bricks just south of the La Bassee Canal, where the French and British were planning a joint attack. The weather was clear and the results surprisingly good. Moreover, they provided a bonus by revealing a new German trench.

Soon after this, Moore-Brabazon suggested that the R.F.C. in France should set up a special unit which would print and co-ordinate all photographs produced by all squadrons. This scheme was adopted and proved its worth, a few weeks later, when the spring offensive was being planned. Haig's immediate objective was the village of Neuve Chapelle. The pioneer work of No. 3 Squadron, and the later efforts of No. 2 Squadron, had already provided him with a picture of most of the area and, during the last few days of February, many more photographs were taken, so that the whole of the German trench system in front of the First Army was covered to a depth of between 700 and 1,000 yards. The resulting maps played a vital part in the battle and Neuve Chapelle will go down in history perhaps as the first battle to be fought and won by the science of aerial photographic reconnaissance.

Shortly afterwards, Moore-Brabazon and Campbell produced their first aerial camera with the help of the Thornton-Pickard Manufacturing Company in Britain. Known as the "A" camera, it was hand-held to reduce the blurring from vibration. Two brass handles were fitted, and these were gripped by the observer while he leant over the side of the fuselage to take the photographs. It had its snags, among them the necessity for the observer to make eleven separate operations before he could take the first photograph and, for every subsequent picture, ten operations. When it is remembered that these would have to be performed by a man leaning out into a battering gale, wearing thick, cumbersome gloves, a man, moreover, who was probably keyed up because he was under fire, its drawbacks could be appreciated. In spite of this, the results were good.

A little later, the problems of vibration were overcome by mounting cameras with their centre of gravity in the plane of support; thus, although these might be vibrated sideways or up and down, this made no difference at the heights flown. It also reduced angular vibration to the minimum and ensured that all photographs were taken vertically.

As the art of aerial photography developed, so did the science—an all-important one—of interpretation. The Army was soon to be amazed by the wealth of information which could be obtained by a skilled interpreter from a good, clear photograph. By the summer of 1915, Moore-Brabazon and his men had produced their "C" camera which, as well as being fixed to the aircraft, used a semi-automatic plate-changer. Soon, so many photographs were being produced by so many pilots that the central printing and interpretation organization set up by Moore-Brabazon was unable to cope. In April, 1916, photographic work was decentralized and each corps squadron had its own photographic staff. Reconnaissance with the help of a camera was no longer a task for interested amateurs or a few experts, but an everyday and vital service, just one of the many provided by the Royal Flying Corps.

CHAPTER ELEVEN

Aircraft Versus Jungle

THE lessons being learned by the Royal Flying Corps in France were proving expensive and the shortage of both aircraft and trained men did not make planning any easier. This was a position complicated by the fact that Europe soon became only part of the War Office's problems as far as the R.F.C. was concerned—albeit a major part. The aeroplane, despite its sometimes baffling complexities, was proving an invaluable extension to the Army. Thus, wherever the Army went, aircraft were required, and the R.F.C. soon found its efforts extending far beyond the confines of Europe.

The first R.F.C. unit to be sent outside Europe was a detachment of three Maurice Farman aircraft, which arrived at Alexandria on November 27, 1914, under the command of Captain S. D. Massey. When Great Britain had declared war on Turkey earlier that month, there was an obvious threat to the Suez Canal—a threat which these three ancient aircraft luckily did not have to meet with any form of vital action. Together with two Henri Farmans, however, this small aerial force carried out some useful reconnaissance.

The political situation in Africa and the Middle East was to remain fairly steady for a short time but, inevitably, the fighting in Europe eventually spread to German possessions in South West and South East Africa, and it was not long before military aircraft were savouring the various inhospitalities which these regions could provide. While seaplanes of the Royal Naval Air Service performed the reconnaissance and bombing operations required by ground forces in West Africa, the Royal Flying Corps found itself work in East Africa.

No. 26 (South African) Squadron, R.F.C., sailed into Mombasa on January 31st, 1916, complete with eight crated B.E.2cs and an assortment of motor vehicles. The majority of the officers were South Africans. They did not find the hot humid weather to their liking, and the immediate task of unloading the aircraft and stores and reloading them into a train did little to help.

By the late afternoon of the next day, they had arrived at their base, Mbuyuni. There, the men were shown to a large, thorn-fenced square just inside the strongly-defended perimeter of the main camp. No tents awaited them. After their long journey they were almost too tired to complain about this and spread their sleeping gear on the ground. There was little chance of catching cold, but a thriving entomological community ensured that sleep was hard to come by.

The immediate task of the aircraft was to assist the Third South African Brigade, who were engaging enemy forces at Salaita while the First Division attempted to cut off lines of retreat between Maru and Kilimanjaro. The decision to send the Squadron there had been taken at very high level, not, apparently, because of a request from ground commanders. The Squadron soon discovered that there was considerable scepticism as to their value and it became obvious that any reports which they brought back would not be believed. Events which occurred on February 2nd, when the Squadron began to unpack its aircraft, did little to dispel the suspicions of the Army commanders.

When the B.E.2cs were uncrated, the riggers discovered that someone in England had forgotten to include the propellers! Six spare propellers carried among other stores seemed to be the answer but it was found that one was broken and all were of the wrong type. An acrimonious cable sent back to England did little to help the immediate situation and the five good propellers had to be modified to fit the B.E.2cs.

The first aircraft ready for flight was finally assembled on February 9th and fuelled ready for a trial reconnaissance. The Squadron had been warned that hot air was thinner than that found in more temperate climates and that the take-off performance of their aircraft would be less than that experienced during training in England. Accordingly, it was decided to send the two lightest men on the Squadron on this initial flight. Captain G. S. Creed was the pilot and the observer was Second Lieutenant Leo Walmsley. The engine note sounded healthy and acceleration during the take-off run appeared almost normal. It seemed that the warnings had been somewhat pessimistic, but Creed let the aircraft accelerate beyond normal take-off speed before pulling back on the stick. Nothing happened. He tried again, with the same negative result.

By this time, most of the improvised flying strip had passed by and there seemed no hope of aborting the take-off without running into the bush at the end. Creed considered cutting his engine and pushing hard on the rudder bar, to ground-loop the aircraft in an attempt to stop, but decided to try, once more, to take off. This time, the aircraft staggered into the air, almost clawing for lift. It missed a line of trees, literally by inches, and, half an hour later, was still wallowing slowly upwards—having reached just 600 feet.

Made cautious by this alarming take-off, Creed refused to fly far from Mbuyuni. His wisdom was shortly justified, for the aircraft was shaken by unmistakable engine vibration. Below were the matted branches of tens of thousands of trees. This was no country for an engine failure and Creed turned back to base. A quarter of a mile from the airstrip, the engine stopped completely but, luckily, Creed had sufficient height to glide in safely. Obviously there were many problems to be licked before No. 26 Squadron could add its weight to the war.

These purely operational difficulties were not helped by internal troubles in the Squadron itself. Nominally a South African Squadron, the unit also contained some British Officers. At first, there was a tendency for the plum jobs to go to South Africans, a foolishness which reached its peak when the world-famous photographer, Cherry Kearton, agreed to act as photographic officer. He was turned down and the position given to a South African who knew nothing about photography and was too heavy to fly in any case. But, as the Squadron grew to know something of the life of the soldiers they were supposed to be supporting—soldiers who spent almost all their time floundering about in swamps or staggering across waterless velds, so a sense of unity was achieved. Local phenomena, which at first caused lengthy delays and threatened morale, were soon allowed for in all planning. The men became used to the tiresome chore of continually flattening the ant-hills which marred the landing grounds and pilots regarded a sharp look-out for ant-hills, which might have sprung up overnight, as just part of the take-off routine. Many unpleasant moments in the air were avoided by the simple expedient of flipping over the aircraft cushions, before climbing into the cockpit, to dislodge any scorpions, tarantulas or centipedes which might have made their home there.

Even the thickly-growing mimosa trees, which seemed to make a crash-landing impossible, lost their terror. Engine failures were still common and pilots discovered that a glide to the point of stall a few feet above the trees, and a sharp backwards movement of the stick to put the nose up, arrested forward speed and enabled a crash-landing on the tree-tops to be made fairly safely.

"There is a most frightful cracking of timber and tearing of fabric," recalled one man who had tried this technique, "and then a wonderful sense of stillness. Barring a few odd thorns in all sorts of indescribable regions of one's anatomy, you are not normally the worse for wear."

Reconnaissance work, however, never became easy. The hot air was always turbulent and the observer trying to sketch enemy defences under these conditions was not a happy man. But, operating over a huge area, bordered by Kilimanjaro in the north and Fort Johnson at the tip of Lake Nyasa in the south, the Squadron found their duties variable.

The Allied forces, led by General J. C. Smuts, were pushing the enemy back rapidly. No. 26 Squadron found themselves advancing from one improvised airfield to another, a fact which sometimes made navigation even more difficult than usual because pilots seldom had the opportunity to become completely familiar with one region. One pilot who fell foul of these conditions was Lieutenant W. Carey-Thomas, a fiery little Welshman. During June, 1916, he took off from an airfield at Palms for a solo reconnaissance. Dusk was approaching as he flew back and he did not see the airfield. His watch told him that he had flown too far, and he was about to turn back and start a search when he saw a clearing which he recognized as another airfield used by the Squadron a little earlier but now deserted. With his fuel getting low, he decided to land there.

During the Squadron's sojourn at this field, it had been christened "Daniel's Den" because of the large number of lions which roamed in the vicinity. Carey-Thomas found that the position had not changed and he spent a miserable night huddled up in the cockpit hoping that the lions, which he could hear, would not be able to reach him. His only rations were a tin of corned beef—and he had no tin opener. Searching aircraft found him the next day, alive and well, but not anxious to repeat the experience.

At first, there was little opposition to the aircraft, although the crews soon learned to respect machine gun fire from the ground. At Turiani, however, the Germans had mounted an old field gun to fire upwards. It was a hopelessly cumbersome piece of anti-aircraft artillery and provided the crews with some amusement because they found that they could fly near to it, follow the aiming procedures on the ground minutely and always manage to get out of the way by the time that the German gunners had it set up.

Bombing attacks were made whenever the opportunity was presented, sometimes with spectacular results. Once, during a reconnaissance of the Central Railway line, Carey-Thomas, who had Leo Walmsley as observer, saw two long trains at a small station. The number of stores and parcels lying around indicated a worthwhile target. Carey-Thomas attacked in a characteristically pugnacious manner, reaching about 100 m.p.h. in the initial dive—a risky procedure because the throttle often refused to open after such a dive. He levelled off successfully at 800 feet and made four separate attacks. His first bomb exploded with a greenish flash near the trains, which were standing on an embankment, the next blew up the track immediately behind them and the third did not explode.

Coming round for the fourth time, Carey-Thomas aimed for the station building itself, and aimed successfully. The building must have been used as some type of store because the explosion which ensued could never have come from the puny bombs being used. Walmsley turned round in his cockpit in time to see the whole roof rising, showing its rafters like the teeth of a comb, before subsiding in a heap of rubble.

The fact that one of the bombs had refused to explode was no surprise, for the heat affected the detonators. When a census was taken during December, 1916, only 200 serviceable bombs could be found among the total stock of 1,600. There was little hope of obtaining new primers from England, but Air Mechanic E. R. D'Ade applied himself to the problem and soon found a chemical antidote. He began treating all the unserviceable bombs and, by mid-January, another

500 could be used. Then, on January 25th, when D'Ade was working alone in an isolated hut, there was a sudden explosion which completely demolished the building and killed D'Ade.

Although their reconnaissance reports were, at first, inclined to be disbelieved by suspicious ground commanders, the Squadron soon proved their worth. In an area with virtually no recognized means of communications, No. 26 Squadron found that they were searching for advanced British or South African units just as frequently as they were reporting on the enemy. A success in this sphere, which did much to gain the Squadron's acceptance by the ground commanders, occurred on August 10th, 1916, when an advance column under the command of Major-General Brits completely disappeared and all hope of finding the men was lost. Captain van de Spuy, flying in one of the Maurice Farmans which had been sent out from England to bolster the Squadron strength, with Second Lieutenant G. St. V. Pawson as observer, set off on what was thought to be a fruitless search. After two and a half hours—no mean achievement under jungle conditions—the airmen located Brits's column, still pressing on resolutely towards its objective.

Engine trouble continued to be one of the main hazards. Although a technique for crash-landing in the jungle had been discovered, there was a very real survival problem to be faced if the crash occurred far from an airfield. This was a conundrum faced with no little difficulty by Lieutenant G. W. T. Garrood on 17th February, 1917. Flying solo in a B.E.2c, he had taken off from a landing ground at Tuto for a reconnaissance of the Utete region. Twenty miles from the airfield, his engine stopped and he managed to land, with no injury to himself, in a swamp. The aircraft was a write-off. Twenty miles did not seem a great distance to Garrood and he set off to walk back to his base.

Ironically, the wreckage of his aircraft was seen from the air the next day, but of Garrood there was no sign. Search parties set out on foot to try and locate him, but with no success. It was not until four days after the crash that he was found, wandering in the jungle, almost incoherent with fever, shock and sheer exhaustion. He was wearing only his helmet, vest and boots.

The full story of Garrood's trek had to wait until his recovery. He had no food and, anxious to reach base as soon as possible, had swum all rivers in his path. While crossing one he had to race a crocodile, and, a little later, while resting and drying out his clothes, his trousers, pants, shirt and revolver were stolen by a gang of baboons. He had spent one night up a tree, with a leopard prowling about below. His story did not make the minds of the airmen who had to fly over the jungle any easier.

While No. 26 Squadron had been making its acquaintance with the terrors of the jungle, another R.F.C. unit was having troubles a little further north, where conditions were very different but equally inhospitable. The State of Darfur, some 500 miles west-south-west of Khartoum, had little in its favour, either politically or economically. It consisted of flat, sandy desert covered with low scrub and odd clumps of huge tebeldi trees which held most of the country's water supply. There were several sudden, low mountain ranges, very few water holes, temperatures could be as high as 120 degrees Fahrenheit in the shade and the whole area was virtually unsurveyed. It was ruled, on behalf of the British, by Ali Dinar, a rapacious potentate who was only able to subdue his people forcibly, by the use of a slave army.

Ali Dinar was a most unworthy Sultan, but the British had neither the men nor the money to rule the state themselves. This mischief-monger soon made his anti-British tendencies known once he became Sultan, but his insults were ignored. In April, 1915, he openly declared war on the British on what he called "religious grounds" but, because of a general manpower shortage in the region, this also was ignored. Not until December, 1915, when Ali Dinar wrote to Sir Reginald Wingate, Governor-General of the Sudan and Sirdar of the Egyptian Army, stating that he was going to invade the neighbouring state of Korfordan, was action taken.

Realizing that he would be dealing with primitive people, Wingate had the foresight to ask for aerial help because he felt that such a symbol of British power would do more to quell Ali Dinar than whole armies. The task of intimidating these Arabs fell to No. 17 Squadron, which had been sent to Suez sometime earlier to meet the threat from Turkey. "C" Flight of this unit was detailed for the operation. The first 900 miles of a nightmare journey were made by train to Rahad, where there were two locomotive sheds just large enough for two B.E.2c aircraft to be assembled. The men could not work in the open because the campaign was taking place during the hottest period, between May and June.

While the aircraft were being erected, spares and stores had to be carried across some 300 miles of open desert. Few goods could be carried by motor transport because the vehicles had to carry all water and supplies for the crews. Radiators were continually boiling, tyres were torn to shreds by thorny plants, and many lorries were stuck in the sand for days on end. Camels provided a better means of transport, but a spare engine and the one-piece cover of a R.E. tent needed to protect the aircraft on forward fields were large loads. These were carried by specially selected camels, which complained loudly of their loads and often died after their efforts.

The first two aircraft eventually arrived at a forward landing ground, at El Hilla, on May 11th, 1916, having flown from Rahad. Navigation had been exceedingly difficult although the Flight Commander, Captain E. J. Bannatyne, had ordered strips of calico to be laid out at thirty-mile intervals by the ground party. The pilots saw no signs of these strips which, presumably, had been regarded as gifts from the gods by roaming tribesmen.

The Darfur Campaign was the prototype of a form of operation which was frequently to be carried out in the Middle East by the Royal Air Force during the years between the two World Wars, and set the style for later operations. The first reconnaissance was made, on May 12th, by Lieutenant F. Bellamy, who dropped leaflets warning the local populace that attacks would be made by aircraft and instructing that the young, the old and all women should be moved to a safer place.

Great distances had to be covered in the air and the observer had to be sacrificed so that a spare petrol tank could be carried in the second cockpit. The high temperatures decimated the life of the engines and, to guard against an engine failure which, in that climate, could well prove fatal, mechanics rigged up a spare oil tank which could pump half a gallon of fresh oil into the Royal Aircraft Factory engine after every hour's flight. Thanks largely to this precaution, "C" Flight experienced no engine trouble, a tremendous achievement in those days.

On May 17th, Captain Bannatyne made the first air attack on Ali Dinar's army, at Melit, dropping 20 lb bombs with dramatic effect. After some brief opposition, during which Bannatyne's B.E.2c was hit in the propeller by a rifle bullet, the army fled, leaving the way clear for British forces. Bannatyne flew back and dropped a message telling them that the way was clear and, perhaps more important, that there were apparently water holes on the route. He spent a total of nine hours in the air that day. Melit was occupied during the next twenty-four hours.

Reconnaissance was not easy. A thin haze of sand was always blowing across the desert, even on days when sandstorms did not prevent flying. Even British troops were hard to locate. "One often did not spot our own column until right on top of it," says Air Marshal Sir John Slessor who, at that time, was a pilot with "C" Flight. "When looking down on the ground it suddenly became alive and you became aware of the slow-moving camels and men. Dervishes were easier to spot because they either wore next to nothing and appeared black, or dirty white Gibbah with large black patches. Our guns aften jammed and many good targets were missed."*

The next success for the R.F.C. came, on May 23rd, when Slessor located the remnants of the Dervish Army rallying around Ali Dinar's pennant. The pilot estimated that there were some 3,000 men milling around. Ignoring the rifle fire sent up at him, Slessor dived to the attack with bombs. One killed Ali Dinar's camel just as he was about to mount. Slessor, himself, was wounded in the thigh but returned successfully to his airfield.

This last attack completely broke the morale of the Dervish Army, which broke into small units and dispersed into the desert, where many men died. Survivors later said they were so afraid that if they returned to El Fasher, the capital city, they would be attacked from the air again, that they chose the horrors of the desert. The use of air power had been more than justified and the actual campaign was over in a few days. The aircraft were sent back to Egypt, while a small column of British troops searched out Ali Dinar. They caught up with him and a few of his followers on November 6th. After a brief battle, the ex-Sultan was found dead with a bullet in his head.

While "C" Flight of 17 Squadron had been trekking across the desert towards Darfur, the comparative calm of the Eastern Mediterranean sector of the Middle East was shattered in a rude fashion. During May, 1916, German aircraft made two bombing attacks on Port

* From *The Central Blue* by Marshal of the Royal Air Force, Sir John Slessor published by Cassell.

Said. This had not been entirely unexpected. As early as March, two British seaplanes operating from the aircraft carrier H.M.S. *Ben-ma-Chree* reported that enemy forces were building an airfield near Beersheba. Subsequent reports confirmed that the 300th Squadron of the German Air Force had arrived equipped with fourteen Rumpler C.1 two-seater aircraft, which were powered with 150 h.p. Mercedes engines. The Rumplers were faster than the R.F.C.'s B.E.2cs and it became obvious that better aircraft would have to be obtained from England if the Flying Corps were to fight on equal terms. The reinforcement of the Rumplers by a few Fokker single-seat fighters did not improve matters. But requests for improved aircraft met with no response, for the British aircraft industry was still lagging and any available new aircraft were urgently needed in Fance.

The German bombing attack was a signal for a series of bombing raids by both sides. In fact, the summer was so hot, and fighting on the ground so difficult, that the accent of the War in this region was moved to the air for a few months. These attacks may have been puny by modern standards, but the experience of the 1st Light Horse Brigade of the Anzac Mounted Division illustrates their effect. On June 1st, one German aircraft, flying at 8,000 feet, dropped eight bombs on the Division's camp. One officer and seven men were killed and twenty-one wounded. Thirty-six horses were killed, nine wounded and the rest stampeded. This was not the type of treatment to help the morale of men who were already suffering enough from inimical climatic conditions.

As a reprisal for this attack, the R.F.C. organized an attack on El Arish and its airfield on June 18th. Eleven B.E.2cs took part, two of them flying with observers, the rest being flown solo so that more bombs could be carried. The aircraft took off from Qantara and approached El Arish from the sea at 600 feet. There was stiff opposition from ground fire and one British aircraft immediately crashed in the sea; its pilot was rescued by motor boat. Captain R. J. Tipton was among those who reached the German airfield, where he released his bombs just before being brought down. He crashed outside the airfield and managed to set fire to his aircraft before Turkish troops took him prisoner.

Captain H. A. van Ryneveld had a bullet pass through the sump of his machine during the attack and was forced down on the sea-shore.

ight, Group Captain Gilbert Insall was rving in the 11th Squadron, R.F.C., as Second Lieutenant when he gained his .C. in 1915. *Below, left,* Lieutenant 'illiam Leefe-Robinson won one of ree V.C.s to be gained in England ıring the war by successfully attacking Zeppelin. *Below, right,* Lieutenant lbert Ball, described by Lord Trenıard as "the most daring, skilful and ıccessful pilot the R.F.C. has ever had"

Above, the D.H.2 was the first British aircraft to be designed primarily as a fighter. Immediately after it entered service it was given the name "Flying Incinerator" but eventually played an important part in the winning of air superiority for Britain. *Below*, one of the finest fighters of the war, the S.E.5a. Captain (now Air Chief Marshal Sir James) Robb is seen here setting the sights of his gun while serving with the 92nd Squadron in 1918

There he might have remained but for the sharp eyesight of Lieutenant D. K. Paris, the observer in Captain S. Grant-Dalton's aircraft. Paris saw van Ryneveld on the shore and waved his arm to indicate his plight to Grant-Dalton. The pilot immediately glided down towards van Ryneveld and brought off a neat landing nearby. The stranded airman ran across, scrambled into the observer's cockpit with Paris and, staggering slightly under this unaccustomed load, the B.E.2c carried all three men safely back.

The attack, despite the loss of three aircraft, was a success. One German aircraft was claimed destroyed on the ground, another was damaged, and two hangars were set on fire. One 20 lb bomb fell among a working party of Turkish troops and a 100 lb bomb fell in the centre of a camp. But perhaps the most worthwhile result was that German aircraft activity was kept to a minimum for at least a month, during which the R.F.C. were able to set up advance wireless stations to give warning of any further air attacks.

As could be expected, the desert took its toll of aircraft and crews, sometimes mysteriously. On June 15, two aircraft of 17 Squadron set out on reconnaissance, lost their bearings and eventually force-landed in the desert to spend the night. The engine of one aircraft refused to start the next day and so the other set out to find the base and get help. The pilot kept a careful note of the course he flew so that when he reached base, which he did successfully, he would know exactly where the other aircraft was. He returned with a mechanic but the B.E.2c had gone, and so had its crew. An intensive air search, which lasted for several days, failed to reveal a sign. The aircraft had vanished.

It was five days later when a patrol of the Imperial Camel Corps found the aircraft, in quite a different position, with both occupants dead. A diary kept by the observer, 1st Air Mechanic J. Garside, provided an answer to the mystery. He and the pilot had managed to start the engine, after all, and had set off to find their base. After twenty-five minutes the engine stopped again and they landed. They managed to coax it into life for just a few more minutes in which time they made another short hop, but then it stopped completely. Pilot and observer had no choice but to wait by the side of their aircraft and hope that help would come. Garside recorded that the pilot died three days after the initial forced landing. He, himself, had probably been dead less than twenty-four hours when found by the Camel Corps.

Action on the ground in this region remained negligible until towards the end of July, when R.F.C. aircraft reported heavy gatherings of Turkish troops at Birel Mazar, forty-two miles east of Romani. This was the first serious threat to the Suez Canal but, thanks to regular reports by British aircraft, the Army was prepared for the Turkish attack when it came on August 3rd. The German aircraft were backing up the Turkish ground forces effectively and, for the first time, pilots in the Middle East experienced air-to-air combat. That the R.F.C. succeeded in fulfilling most of its reconnaissance sorties against this opposition was not due to superiority in numbers, or aircraft performance. There were no more than seventeen British aircraft available during this battle, yet, with the loss of only one aircraft and one officer killed, the R.F.C. were able to keep the Army supplied with vital information.

The secret lay in the determination of the aircrew, like that shown by Lieutenant E. W. Edwards and his observer, Second Lieutenant J. Brown. Returning from a reconnaissance flight, their B.E.2c was attacked by a solitary German aircraft which soon showed its ability to outmanoeuvre and outshoot the elderly B.E. In this unequal battle, Edwards was hit by seven bullets, one of which broke his lower jaw on both sides, passing straight through his mouth, and another broke his shoulder. Despite these injuries, he managed to steady his aircraft, evade the German machine and carry out a forced landing at the Headquarters of Brigadier-General E. W. C. Chaytor, who commanded the ground forces.

Edward's first thought after landing was for his observer. He found that he had been shot through the chest, was unable to move and in great pain. Within minutes, the aircraft was surrounded by soldiers who began to prepare to move Brown. Hardly able to speak coherently because of the pain, Brown begged them not to touch him. He said that he must first communicate the news of his reconnaissance because he felt it was important information, but his chest was so painful that he was afraid he would faint if moved. So, still sitting in his cockpit, Brown dictated his report. Not until he had heard it read back did he allow himself to be moved. He fainted almost immediately and died two hours later.

The dedication of Brown, and many others like him who, however, were lucky in not having to make his sacrifice, was proved well worth while. Armed with a good knowledge of enemy movements, British forces subsequently defeated the Turks in the Romani area and a serious threat to the Suez Canal was removed.

CHAPTER TWELVE

Desert Airlift

REMOVAL of the threat to Suez did not mean an easier life for the R.F.C. men who had been sent out as part of the defence forces. No. 30 Squadron, with its outdated Maurice Farman Longhorns, its B.E.2as, which still used wing-warping for lateral control, and its B.E.2cs, found themselves flying east to support ground forces engaged in a somewhat unsuccessful battle against the Turks in Mesopotamia. Their new home was a 200 foot square landing ground, and the men of the Squadron found themselves housed with horse-lines on one side and a cholera camp on the other. The Squadron had only eight pilots and this meagre number was soon depleted by sickness brought on by the general unhealthy climate, the next-door neighbours and the somewhat foetid waters of the nearby Tigris River which, not infrequently, carried floating bodies.

By the beginning of March, 1916, the position of Major-General Townshend's Kut Garrison, at the confluence of the Tigris and Shumran rivers, was beginning to look serious; they were almost completely surrounded by Turkish troops. On March 7th, Lieutenant-General Aylmer launched a dramatic attack in an attempt to relieve the garrison. To achieve surprise involved a difficult move of 20,000 men and their equipment over a distance of fourteen miles during the hours of darkness. It was a well-conceived plan, but it failed.

There were delays in starting the night march, which had been planned to begin at 9 p.m., and there were more delays on the way. The force was still two miles short of its planned position at dawn but the Turks still had no inkling of the attack. Although first light was beginning to creep across the desert, there was little chance of the forces being seen by enemy reconnaissance aircraft because the long shadows cast by the sun would have made spotting from the air virtually impossible for several more hours.

In the event, it was Aylmer himself who revealed his plans to the enemy. His headquarters party was already in position and, as he was convinced that the Turks must have some knowledge of his move, he ordered the artillery to open fire. The Turks were immediately alerted. The time was 7 a.m. and the infantry were not yet ready to attack.

The attack was planned to capture the Dujaila Redoubt, a key point in the Turkish defences around Kut. The first reconnaissance aircraft from No. 30 Squadron were overhead soon after 8 a.m. but saw nothing of interest. A second aircraft, flown by Captain John R. McCrindle, had better luck. The pilot looked down and saw Turks, surprised by the artillery barrage, leaving their trenches and hurrying back across the river in an armada of coracles. He also saw a column of reinforcements coming forward, but these were still three miles away. He reached the airfield at 9.15, reported what he had seen and urged that the British attack should be pushed home immediately. McCrindle and other pilots, who returned with much the same story, were somewhat dismayed to find that their information and suggestions, apparently, had been ignored. They did not know, and this fact could not be discovered until some time later, that the majority of British ground forces were still not in position. The Turks had time to recover from their surprise and the attempt to relieve Kut failed. If 30 Squadron had been fighting in France, they would have had better aircraft and would have been more abreast of current military thinking on the use of airpower. The situation could well have been saved by carefully planned bombing attacks. But Mesopotamia was a backwater of the R.F.C. They had few bombs and little idea of when, or how, to use them. In this part of the world the R.F.C. was still merely the eyes of the Army and very little else. But the Squadron was soon to discover that their aircraft had another use.

Townshend, 13,840 troops and 3,700 town Arabs were completely cut off in Kut and no supplies could be got through. Aircraft from 30 Squadron had already made several flights over the garrison, dropping medical supplies and newspapers. On March 27th, in answer to a radio request from Townshend, they had even dropped a 70 lb millstone. But all this was a minor prelude to the task which lay in store for these sick and tired pilots and their equally frail machines.

The diet of the surrounded men, of necessity, was being supplemented by horse-meat provided by the unlucky inmates of the garrison stables, but, at the end of March, Townshend announced that this source of supply would soon be non-existent and he would be entirely dependent on material dropped from the air. His requirements, worked out to give every man a 6 oz ration each day, was 5,000 lb of flour, sugar, chocolate, salt, etc. to be dropped *each day*.

It was an impossibly tall order for the pilots, but they resolved to do their best. The aircraft were hastily modified to carry a long bar beneath the fuselage which would take two 25 lb flour bags, and a primitive release gear was fitted in the cockpit. Four 50 lb flour bags also were carried, two on top of each lower wing. These were tied with string, which the pilot cut when he was over the garrison. Then he pulled back on his control stick so that the aircraft nosed up and the bags slid off. The laden weight of the aircraft was such that it was impossible to carry an observer, or any armament except a service revolver—which would be of little use against the Fokkers used by the Turks. A more serious problem was the adverse effect on the take-off of the aircraft. The extra weight alone would have added to the length of take-off run needed, but the drag caused by the bulky sacks counted even more.

The regulation 200 foot square airfield was far too small and pilots suggested that it should be enlarged. But this suggestion met with little success. "There was quite a touch of the Indian Army about the establishment," one of the pilots recalls. "When we suggested increasing the size of the airfield we were shown the official regulations which said that airfields should measure 200 feet by 200 feet. And that was that." It is quite likely, however, that every available man on the Squadron, and this included many who, under normal circumstance, would be in the sick bay, was so busy loading, flying, modifying or repairing the aircraft, that there was no labour available to make major alterations to the airfield.

Luckily, the enemy aircraft showed little interest in the British machines and their strange loads, which was just as well, for the difficult flights with grossly overloaded aeroplanes gave the pilots more than enough to contend with. Even with the help of a small detachment of Royal Naval Air Service floatplanes, Townshend's needs of

5,000 lb a day could not be approached. Many pilots made four flights each day, but still the best which could be achieved was 3,350 lb of food and gold—the latter commodity being requested as Townshend hoped that he might be able to use it to buy wheat.

The target area was the disused airfield but the British aircraft had to fly high to avoid Turkish ground fire. The airmen became adept at aiming but, often, bags would burst open on impact, and one consignment of £30,000 worth of gold ended up in the Tigris.

Then, on April 24th, the Fokkers began attacking the supply aircraft. It became necessary to carry an observer and Lewis gun and the amount of supplies which could be carried was cut by about one third. The B.E.2s were no match for the Fokkers and, if attacked, had to turn away so that the rearwards-firing Lewis gun could be brought to bear. The return fire did act as a deterrent to the enemy fighters but there was little that the British aeroplanes could do except run away. One floatplane was shot down and Lieutenant D. A. L. Davidson in a B.E.2c, which he was flying without an observer, was wounded and his aircraft damaged. But he managed to return safely. During this strenuous airlift, Captain McCrindle offered to land on the Kut airfield at night and carry Townshend to safety. The offer was declined by the General, who was resolved to stay with his troops.

It was obvious that the garrison could not be supplied adequately from the air and that there was little hope of speedy relief from ground forces and, on April 26th, Townshend was ordered to negotiate a surrender with the Turks. This he did and, of the 12,000 men who were taken prisoner, 4,000 failed to live through their period of captivity.

In a two-week period, between April 15th and 29th, the aircraft had made 140 individual flights to Kut and had dropped 19,000 lb of supplies. It had been an almost superhuman effort and when, at last the pressure was off, the pilots, one by one, were admitted to hospital as the illnesses they had been fighting off finally took their toll. Soon, there was only one pilot left who could be classified as fit. The records do not mention the illnesses which floored these men but, according to the official war diarist of No. 30 Squadron, they were "seriously knocked up directly after the strain due to feeding Kut was over". There was no medical knowledge behind this opinion, but few who were there at the time doubt this diagnosis.

While 30 Squadron were thus licking their wounds in Mesopotamia, events were taking place elsewhere in the Middle East which eventually were to co-ordinate the various separate efforts of units dotted around Africa and the Mediterranean. This was the formation of the Middle East Brigade, R.F.C., which came into being in June, 1916, with Brigadier-General W. G. H. Salmond at its head. It was to be the headquarters unit of R.F.C. Squadrons in Egypt, Mesopotamia, East Africa and, in the future, Salonika. A useful offshoot of this new unit was the Twentieth Reserve Wing, whose training of pilots in Egypt where, during the winter months especially, flying tuition could be carried out almost without interruption from the weather, provided a source of manpower for the R.F.C. everywhere.

Slowly the tide of war in Mesopotamia turned and the British forces found themselves advancing. It was also time for a change in the fortunes of 30 Squadron. With a new Commanding Officer, Major J. E. Tennant, they were able to do good and rewarding work in reconnaissance and photography which helped the British advance. They also performed several bombing attacks and, as the Turkish retreat continued, the aircraft were used to find and attack any small pockets of resistance which might be left. It was hectic work and although, this time, the flyers were on the winning side, not always very pleasant, as one British pilot has recorded.

"Flying towards Azizaya," he wrote, "the spectacle was amazing and horrible; dead bodies and mules, abandoned guns, wagons and stores littered the road, many of the wagons had hoisted white flags, men and animals, starved and exhausted, lay prone on the ground. Few of these, if any, survived the attentions of the Arab tribesmen hanging around like wolves on their trail. Further on, I came up with the rear party on the march. Flying along, about ten feet off the road, I mowed down seven with one burst of machine gun fire: it was sickening, they hardly had the strength to run into the nullahs and fire back; those hit just crumpled up under their packs and lay still; others waved in token of surrender and supplication for rescue . . ."

But 30 Squadron did not always have to depend on such soul-searing sorties for their excitement. As the advancing British forces neared Baghdad, the Squadron found itself involved in a novel and, as it happened, somewhat adventurous piece of undercover work.

With the battle now going in their favour, G.H.Q. was anxious to take every opportunity of reaching a successful and speedy end to the campaign. Staff Officers noted a railway line, running north from Baghdad, which would enable the Turks to carry out a rapid evacuation. Reconnaissance reports had shown that this railway had one weak link, a bridge at Beled, some eighty miles north of the city. If this bridge could be destroyed, then the Turks would find evacuation extremely difficult. Rather than trust to the vagaries of bombing, it was decided to blow up the bridge by hand.

On the morning of March 7th, 1917, Lieutenants J. S. Windsor and R. K. Morris were busying themselves around their aircraft when Captain H. de Havilland, later to succeed Tennant as Squadron C.O., approached them.

"If you trot over to G.H.Q.," he said, "you'll find that they have a job for you." More he would not explain. At G.H.Q. the two pilots found that they were to take two B.E.2c aircraft and fly over to Beled, where they would land by the bridge. They were introduced to Captain Farley and Captain Cave-Brown, two officers from the Royal Engineers, who would fly with them and destroy the bridge.

The plans for this operation were simple in the extreme. The two pilots were to ferry the Engineer officers to the bridge, land, wait while the bridge was blown up with charges carried in the aircraft, take off with the soldiers and return to base. The only preparation needed was to load two B.E.2cs with gun-cotton and detonators, and to fit extra petrol tanks. This took only a few hours and everything was ready before lunch.

The more the pilots thought about the trip, however, the more complicated it seemed. There was no detailed map of the route which they were to take, only a very rough sketch map. Windsor was given custody of this and Morris had to depend on visual contact with Windsor's aircraft if he were not to get lost. There were, of course, the usual hazards of flying over the desert and the minor complication that the two soldiers had never before flown—a cause of some concern to the pilots.

Nevertheless, the take-off was made on time and the flight progressed without incident until the aircraft neared Baghdad. There, a Fokker Scout aircraft promised an early upset to the carefully laid plans, but Windsor and Morris, rightly reasoning that this was no time for heroic dog-fights, skirted the city and avoided the enemy aircraft. Windsor then glanced behind to make sure that he still had the mapless Morris with him and picked up the railway line north of Baghdad. From that point the navigation was simple.

The flight to the bridge was uneventful and, in just under two hours, the aircraft were circling the structure to make sure that the desert was suitable for a landing. This brief reconnaissance reassured them about the state of the desert, but also warned of an unexpected hazard, an Arab encampment a little way from the bridge. Whether these tribesmen were friendly or not the pilots had no way of telling—except by landing, and this they did.

Both aircraft made a good touchdown about two hundred yards from the bridge. From that moment, events followed each other quickly. The two engineers grabbed their gun-cotton and ran for the railway. At the same time, there was a spine-tingling yell from the Arab encampment and a flurry of disturbed sand as the tribesmen bore down on the aircraft, firing occasional shots.

The pilots looked across to the soldiers and hoped to see them running back to the aircraft, but Farley and Cave-Brown were intent on carrying out their task. When they arrived at the bridge they saw that their information about its structure had been wrong. They had come prepared to blow up a flimsy bridge: instead they found one of reinforced concrette. Their supply of gun-cotton and detonators could do little more than spit out chips of concrete.

The rapidly-nearing yells of the Arabs now entered into their deliberations. Realizing that little would be gained by standing there bemoaning their lack of powerful explosives, they ran back towards the aircraft, where the pilots were waiting with some anxiety, their engines still running. There followed an exciting race between the soldiers and Arabs from different directions. Cave-Brown was the winner and leaped into the cockpit of Windsor's aircraft, which lost no time in taking off.

For a few seconds, Morris was left to wonder dismally whether Farley would come second or third in the race. It was almost a photo-finish. The instant Farley had a foothold on the aeroplane, Morris opened the throttle. He did not bother to turn into wind for the take-off but charged straight forward. Even with these emergency measures, one Arab was able to catch hold of a wing-tip but the aircraft was moving too quickly for him to retain his grip.

The down-wind take-off meant a protracted run before the machine was airborne but, once up, Morris was determined to take his revenge on the blood-thirsty Arabs and turned and raked them with the machine gun which he had thoughtfully fitted to his aircraft to fire obliquely forwards, thus missing the propeller arc. He emptied one drum of ammunition into the Arabs with indeterminate results then, remembering that Windsor had the only map, set out hastily in pursuit of his colleague.

Luckily, Windsor was not yet out of sight and Morris soon caught up with him. The return journey was made without incident. After Morris had landed and checked his fuel tank, he found there was enough petrol left for, perhaps, five minutes more flying time. It had been a close shave.

The operation had been by no means a tactical success but it was one of the first instances of a new use of airpower, and one which was to be used many more times, both in that theatre and in France, with very useful effects. One thing was certain, however: the sortie had been a nerve-racking experience for the four men who took part. Morris recalls that there was a memorable party in 30 Squadron Mess that night.

The failure to destroy the bridge had no effect on the British advance and it was not long before Baghdad was in British hands and another phase in the Middle East war was over. But there was much more fighting left to be done in this general region, fighting in which the Royal Flying Corps was to play a leading—and extremely valiant—part.

CHAPTER THIRTEEN

The Flying Visionary

BACK in England, the War Office, with its overall responsibility for supplying the R.F.C., was much criticized for not providing the Middle East Brigade with the type of aircraft it required. These criticisms tended to be shrugged off by the War Office, for the demands from the Middle East were only a minor part of their supply problem: the R.F.C. in West Africa and, even more important, France, were also highly critical of their equipment. On the Western Front the shadow of the Fokker monoplane was causing no little alarm and better fighter aircraft were vital for Britain's needs. But there seemed little chance of firm action from the War Office.

In France, Sir David Henderson was understandably worried. He knew, however, that part of the trouble stemmed from the rival needs of the R.N.A.S., who had astute Winston Churchill as First Lord of the Admiralty to speak up for his Service's needs and to argue his way around the bumbledom of Whitehall. Henderson also had other immediate problems. Sykes, his chief staff officer in France, was an extremely able staff officer, an expert in polemics and a crafty politician. The fact that Sykes's ultimate aim was control of the R.F.C. was never more than thinly disguised, but this caused Henderson little loss of sleep. When, however, rumours began circulating that a lot of R.F.C. difficulties were due to the lack of a younger, healthier leader in France, and when Henderson traced this rumour to Sykes, it was obviously time for action.

It was not in Henderson's nature to be annoyed and this amiable, gentlemanly officer, invariably known to his pilots as "the oldest pilot in the world", merely decided that Sykes should be replaced. There was no rancour in this decision. Henderson, a patient, tenacious Scotsman, was merely doing what he thought best for the R.F.C.

With Sykes out of the way, he reapplied himself to the problem of equipment. Thinking about the many problems then filling the in-trays at the War Office, he decided that a man with both sound technical knowledge and up-to-date battle experience was needed in London. He would have to be a senior officer with sufficient presence to push his demands through the thickest of governmental indecision. In other words, Henderson decided that the man needed back in London was himself.

This was not an easy decision. The work in France was far more glamorous and more immediately rewarding. Nevertheless, Henderson ordered himself back to London in the interests of the Royal Flying Corps.

The problem of finding a successor in France was not so difficult as the decision to send himself back to England. With Sykes now in disgrace, as far as Henderson was concerned, he had little hesitation in visiting the First Wing Headquarters at Merville, where he told its Commander, Lieutenant-Colonel Hugh Trenchard, that he was to be recommended as the future General Officer Commanding The Royal Flying Corps in France. It was a decision as sound as any Henderson had made in the past, and one which was to have more far-reaching effects than anyone could have foreseen at the time. It was a decision which anyone who had taken the trouble to study Trenchard's past history would have immediately endorsed.

Hugh Trenchard, the son of a West Country solicitor, was no scholar. He had entered the Army through the back door of the Militia, after consistently failing his entrance exams. He finally scraped through, in the summer of 1893, to be gazetted Second Lieutenant in the Second Battalion of the Royal Scots Fusiliers. He served in India and in South Africa. There, during the Boer War, he was leading an attack against an isolated farmhouse in which some Boers were hiding, when he was hit by a bullet. It pierced his chest, went straight through the left lung and out at the back.

Trenchard should have died. The doctors, thinking him still unconscious, intimated that there was little hope. Trenchard heard them and, with a characteristic stubbornness, vowed that he would not die. He lived and confounded the doctors, but he was partially paralysed from the waist downwards and could only walk with the aid of two sticks. Invalided back to England and then sent to St. Moritz to convalesce, Trenchard refused to play the part of the invalid which he was. He took up the sport of bob-sleighing to prove that he was as fit as the rest. He used little skill or cunning when careering down the icy slopes but trusted to his own undoubted pluck and to his luck. He had many spills and, while practising on the Cresta Run, he took a sharp left-hand bend far too quickly. His toboggan skidded up the side of the banking and over the edge. Trenchard and his vehicle dramatically parted company and the convalescing invalid made hard contact with the ground two or three times before coming to rest in a snow drift. When anxious onlookers helped him to his feet, Trenchard gave a roar of excitement. Somehow, something had clicked back into place. He could feel his legs again—and use them.

Trenchard returned to England, to discover that he was a candidate for a permanent disability pension. The War Office was somewhat surprised, a little later, to learn that he had unofficially found himself a berth on a ship sailing to South Africa and was once again back in the fighting. After the Boer War, he found a place for his talents in Nigeria, where he led many expeditions to quell native uprisings. There, he proved himself an able administrator as well as a leader of men.

So far, the advent of the aeroplane and its potentialities had left Trenchard unmoved. Even the news that Blériot had crossed the Channel in one of his monoplanes was read with no more than passing interest. It was not until 1912, when Trenchard found a routine regimental posting in Ireland a dull contrast after his action in South Africa and Nigeria, that he was stirred by a letter from a friend, Captain E. B. Loraine, extolling the virtues of the new service. "Come and see men crawling like ants," he wrote. It was this phrase, rather than any vision of what aerial warfare could mean, that turned Trenchard's thoughts towards the R.F.C.

Theorizing had no place in Trenchard's life. At school he had shunned learning because books and theories bored him. Not until he started to lead the practical life of a soldier, did he discover that books could open the way to more practical deeds and experiences. So it was with flying. It was no vision of the future which drove Trenchard into aviation, just a combination of boredom and a graphic phrase in a letter. But later, when he was able to prove to himself that aircraft could be of immense use in warfare, he used his tremendous personality to further his beliefs.

Luckily for Trenchard, the politicians who had decided on the type of man who could apply for entry into the Flying Corps had not thought to stipulate that he should have two lungs. But they had stated that all entrants should be under forty years of age. Trenchard was thirty-nine. He arrived in London to train for his brevet on the day that the papers carried news of the death of his friend, Captain E. B. Loraine, the man whose letters had turned his thoughts towards flying. Loraine had been killed when his Nieuport monoplane had fallen out of control. The news only strengthened Trenchard's determination to conquer this new element.

The aircraft designers of those days had many problems of weight, which were aggravated by the small power available from the engines. No designer would have volunteered to build an aircraft easily capable of carrying Trenchard's large and heavy frame. His physical attributes inhibited aerial performance: his large body created considerable head resistance and his weight overloaded the aeroplanes. Probably it was for this reason that Trenchard never distinguished himself as a pilot.

But Trenchard was determined to fly, and for a man who decided to live when doctors had said that he should die, it was a comparatively easy task to will his way through the flying course which he took at Mr. T. O. M. Sopwith's school at Weybridge. Under the expert tuition of Copeland Perry, he gained his aviator's certificate in one hour and thirteen minutes of flying spread over thirteen days. Posted to the Central Flying School at Upavon, he was button-holed by Captain Godfrey Paine soon after arrival. Paine had some inkling of Trenchard's past record and wisely asked him to become Adjutant of the C.F.S.

Uncommunicative, monosyllabic when he did join in conversation, intolerant of gossip, evasive replies and lax discipline, Trenchard set himself the task of organizing the C.F.S. At first, this was just a task like any other, but then Trenchard took part in some combined Army–R.F.C. manoeuvres in East Anglia. He saw for himself how easily "enemy" formations were spotted from the air and, for the first time, realized what a revolution the aeroplane could cause in war. Then, and not until then, did his vision of the future begin to form—a future in which he was to play the leading role.

At Upavon he was hardly loved by the men under his charge, but he was certainly respected. His vision of the future left him in no doubt that the men required in this new force would have to be extremely able. If a man did not match up to his requirements, he did not complete the course at the C.F.S. The office work in organizing the C.F.S. took up much time but Trenchard lost no opportunity to fly, although his somewhat indifferent piloting alarmed his fellows, so that he should know as much as possible about the new element he was entering. By the end of 1912, he had decided the subjects in which would-be pilots at the school should be proficient.

He set tests in signalling, map-reading, the workings of the internal combustion engine, and aerial reconnaissance, sat the examination with the others and, in his official capacity as Adjutant, marked the papers himself. He was one of the thirty-two out of thirty-four who passed. To Trenchard this was the commonsense way of doing things under the prevailing circumstances.

If there was one black spot in Trenchard's life at this time, it was Sykes. The two men could never have worked closely together. Trenchard was suspicious of Sykes's smooth ability in argument—a sphere in which he could not compete because of an inability to express himself clearly. Sykes, in turn, was jealous of Trenchard's undoubted administrative and leadership qualities.

It was a great disappointment for Trenchard when, after the R.F.C. had mobilized in 1914, Henderson asked Sykes to join him in France and left Trenchard behind, with the old and unsatisfying sop that his work behind the scenes at the C.F.S. would be every bit as important as the more glamorous work at the Front. Recovering from his disappointment, Trenchard was no doubt pleased to see the problem which faced him. It was his job to recruit and train men to form new squadrons to be sent out to France. But the R.F.C. in France had taken all the serviceable aircraft from Upavon and most of the staff.

This was the type of impossible challenge in which Trenchard delighted. There were no half measures possible here. He bought up the Brooklands Flying School in its entirety—machines, buildings, men and even the nearby public-house. The move took the War Office by surprise and, for many months, minions were kept busy quibbling over the price to be paid for a piece of cooking equipment, some beer which had been in a cellar, or some bed-clothes. Together with Brancker, who was fighting for the Royal Flying Corps in the War

Office, Trenchard opened a recruiting office in London and offered rates of pay for riggers, mechanics and fitters which were as high as any paid to the top Army tradesmen.

After Sykes had carried out the first reorganization of the R.F.C. into Wings, in France, Trenchard at last returned to active service when he sailed across the Channel to take command of the First Wing in November, 1914. During this posting, Trenchard met Haig for the first time. Haig had a reputation for distrusting the R.F.C. but Trenchard managed to convince him that the R.F.C. had much to offer, and to show the C-in-C that the aeroplane would be playing an even more important part in the future.

When Trenchard was eventually gazetted as General Officer Commanding the Royal Flying Corps in France, on August 19th, 1915, it gave him the chance to realize some of his visions of the future, but there were many, many difficulties to be overcome first.

Not least was the fact that the Germans had air superiority through the able performance of the Fokker monoplanes. Trenchard knew that the only answer to this was more and better aircraft. These could not be obtained at a snap of his fingers.

Trenchard was one of the first air commanders to face the problems of running an air arm which did not have air superiority. There was one insidious trap in this situation which has been instrumental in losing several wars since Trenchard's time, and it is to his everlasting credit that he had the foresight to guide the Flying Corps around this pitfall.

In any war, if one side loses air superiority, its ground forces come under frequent attack from enemy aircraft. Naturally enough, they clamour for protection from their own aircraft. It might seem sensible that the air commander should give this protection in order to maintain the morale of the men in the front line. But all too often, and this was so with the R.F.C. towards the end of 1915, it means that aircraft have to be diverted from vital tasks such as reconnaissance or bombing to protect troops in the trenches. Even then, the cover they afford is often inadequate, the soldiers are treated to the spectacle of their own aircraft being soundly beaten and the all-important strategic work of the air arm lapses.

It needed someone of Trenchard's single-minded character to decide that the men in the trenches would just have to keep a stiff upper lip during the frequent attacks from the Germans. Not only did he decree that the reconnaissance work should continue, but on January 14th, 1916, issued the following order from R.F.C. Headquarters:

"Until the R.F.C. are in possession of a machine as good as the German Fokker it seems that a change in the tactics employed becomes necessary . . . It must be laid down as a hard and fast rule that a machine employed on reconnaissance must be escorted by at least three other fighting machines. These machines must be flown in close formation and a reconnaissance should not continue if any of the machines become detached. This should apply to both short and distant reconnaissances . . . Flying in close formation must be practised by all pilots."

Trenchard's policy, on the face of it, seemed a strange one. It was tantamount to a shrinkage of size of the already underpowered Flying Corps, because four aircraft had to go where one had sufficed earlier. But it did mean that the reconnaissance aircraft got through and, even more important, got back. It was hard luck on the "Tommies" in the trenches but Trenchard was gambling on their British phlegm to tide them over until the long-awaited reinforcements came from England.

The fact that things had not been going well with the war in the air was causing concern in England. Obviously, part of the trouble was the continual struggle which went on between the R.F.C. and the R.N.A.S. for aircraft—a struggle which the Navy, with its greater influence in high circles, was winning. To try and combat this, Prime Minister Asquith set up a Joint War Air Committee. The Committee was appointed on February 15th, 1916, under the chairmanship of Lord Derby, and its task was "to co-ordinate the question of supplies and design for material of the Naval and Military Air Services". It was not very effective and lasted just two months.

While this short-lived committee was struggling with the immense problems facing it, a new character appeared on the political front. His name was Noel Pemberton-Billing, a somewhat egocentric gentleman who had made his first acquaintance with aviation in an unusual manner. In conversation with aircraft designer Handley-Page during 1913, the question of how long it took to gain a flying brevet was mooted. Pemberton-Billing bet Handley-Page that it could be won in a day. A sum of £500 was involved in this wager. It is to Pemberton-Billing's credit that he won this bet. It involved many missed heart-beats for R. H. Barnwell, the instructor who pushed him through a concentrated flying course at the Vickers school.

"It was a terrifying ordeal," said an onlooker afterwards. "We who were watching held our breath at the hair-raising behaviour of his machine as it stalled at every right-hand turn and performed other amazing and unrehearsed feats. It was a wager pluckily won."

Pemberton-Billing later gained a commission in the R.N.A.S. as a pilot but he resigned during 1915 to stand as Parliamentary candidate in a by-election at Hertford East. He stood for the Liberal Party, won his seat and was sworn in on March 14th, 1916. In his maiden speech he explained, with characteristic lack of modesty, that he had resigned his commission so that there would be at least one person in the House competent to speak on air matters. That his presence was not likely to help the inequality which already existed between the R.N.A.S. and the R.F.C. in the matter of equipment was shown by the plea which followed this explanation—a plea for better aircraft in the R.N.A.S.!

But this was only an overture. On Wednesday, March 22nd, Pemberton-Billing was on his feet once again. This time, there was no mincing of words. It was a vehement attack which could have ruined a lesser man than Trenchard.

Pemberton-Billing referred to Lord Derby's Committee and the fact that the majority of those who sat on it had no knowledge of aviation. He said that the air services were generally in a muddle and that the only answer was amalgamation and the development of a joint force under one political chief. Then came his impassioned punch.

"We must create a new force, free from the inertia of the R.N.A.S. and from the blunders of the Royal Flying Corps as regards construction," he said. "I do not intend to deal with the colossal blunder of the Royal Flying Corps, but I might refer briefly to the hundreds, nay thousands of machines which they have ordered and which have been referred to by our pilots at the front as 'Fokker fodder' . . . I do not wish to touch a dramatic note, but if I do, I would suggest that quite a number of our gallant officers in the Royal Flying Corps had been rather murdered than killed."

Just what effect Pemberton-Billing thought his piece of splenetic acting would have is not known. Objection was raised to the word "murder", but Pemberton-Billing was unrepentant. "I repeat that statement," he retorted, "and if the Right Hon. member wishes to challenge that statement I will provide such evidence as will shock this House."

Pemberton-Billing sat down to cries of "Do it now!" But it was not until a week later that he produced his "evidence". This consisted merely of a long, long list of mishaps to aircraft all of which this outspoken M.P. attributed to faulty construction. There was no evidence to show that this was the case. Many of the accidents could have been caused by faulty maintenance or pilot error. Undoubtedly, aircraft construction was not all that it should be, but this was immediately attributable to the infancy of the art and not to any criminal negligence on the part of those who built, designed or ordered the aircraft. Any trouble with the air services—and trouble there was—could be directly attributed to the politicians whose ranks Pemberton-Billing had joined and whose general inability to understand the running of the Services he now showed that he shared.

This speech had two main effects. It came at a time when Trenchard's casualties in France were high, at a time when Britain was not enjoying air superiority. The word "murder" used at such a time only made Trenchard's burden heavier. But such was his already formed opinion of the politicians back in England that he could shrug it off. His frequent appearances at the squadron airfields had made him well known to his men and they were behind him. Pemberton-Billing's accusation had no effect on them. The Government, on the other hand, were sufficiently impressed to order an inquiry into air problems generally. An Air Tribunal was convened under Mr. Justive Bailache and soon began the long, tedious business of taking statements, sifting evidence and deliberating, before making a statement. It was obvious that there would be no immediate answer from the Air Tribunal.

Meanwhile, the Royal Flying Corps was having to struggle on with the equipment available. This was improving. The Vickers Gun Bus, with which Britain had first entered the serious business of air-to-air fighting, was proving no opponent for the Fokker monoplanes. The ability of the German aircraft to fire bullets from a machine gun straight through the propeller arc was a tremendous advantage.

Britain had not been particularly clever about synchronization gears for machine guns. A workable system for achieving fire through a propeller arc had been suggested to the R.F.C. *before the war* but no-one in authority had seen the need to take this up and it was forgotten. Later, towards the end of 1914, it was becoming obvious that fighter-type aircraft would be needed and the problem of firing forwards was seen—but no more work was carried out on the design and development of a synchronization gear. Not until the Fokker aircraft demonstrated how effective this apparatus could be did experiments begin.

The Vickers company then produced a so-called interrupter gear, early in 1916. Worked from a cam in the engine, these early gears pressed the trigger of the gun at intervals designed so that bullets would miss the propeller blades. At last, the British designers were freed of the necessity of designing two-seat "pusher" type fighter aircraft, and the day of the single-seat fighter ace was in sight.

But there was still another generation of two-seaters to appear. They were the F.E.2b and the D.H.2 and both owed their design to the gifted Geoffrey de Havilland. They had been designed around the ill-fated Green engine. Twelve F.E.2a aircraft had been ordered by the R.F.C. at the outbreak of war but, with the too-heavy Green engine, their performance was unsatisfactory. The airframe had to be modified to take a 120 h.p. Beardmore engine. This took time and the first modified aircraft, by now labelled F.E.2b, did not fly until March, 1915. The first to reach the R.F.C. in France flew over in May but, by November of that year, there were still only twelve aircraft of this type in service.

The D.H.2 was a single-seat "pusher" type aircraft powered by a 100 h.p. Gnome Monosoupape rotary engine, although some versions had the 110 h.p. Le Rhone. The D.H.2 first appeared in France with No. 24 Squadron in February, 1916.

These two aircraft, the F.E.2b and the D.H.2, had not been designed to combat the "Fokker menace" but were the normal development of British fighter aircraft at that time. But such was their performance that, in the hands of plucky and skilful men, they were to play a vital part in driving the Luftwaffe's pride from the sky.

CHAPTER FOURTEEN

The Fighters

EXCITEMENT was rife at R.F.C. headquarters, St. Omer, on February 7th, 1916. No. 24 Squadron, the first air unit to be formed primarily as a fighter squadron, was due to arrive from England. The uncertainty of the whole operation, however, served to heighten the tension. High winds were gusting across the French airfield and first the news was that the new squadron was arriving, and then that it was not. But the doubt at St. Omer was nothing compared to the indecision which reigned at Dover airfield on the other side of the Channel. There, the fourteen D.H.2s of No. 24 Squadron were lined up and ready to go. Their pilots had just flown down from Hounslow, where the squadron had been formed and the pilots were excited and ready for action.

"This was a real stop and go day," one of the pilots recalls. "We would get into our aircraft ready for take-off and then someone would come running across with a message saying that the weather had worsened. We would stand down, hear that the winds had dropped a little and the whole nerve-stretching operation would start over again. It happened several times."

The first result of the delays was a crowd of over-excited pilots: the second, the chance for the weather to worsen at Dover. By the time that a final "all clear" came from St. Omer, the winds at the British airfield were, in fact, too strong for the D.H.2s. Nevertheless, the squadron took off for France. Two pilots found their aircraft out of control before they were airborne and overturned on the field.

Thus, the arrival of this long-awaited squadron in France became a little inauspicious, but these minor tragedies were not allowed to detract from the excitement which was felt by the whole of the R.F.C. in France over the event. Great things were expected of the new unit, which was arriving at a time when the Fokker scourge was beginning to have an effect on the nerves of the British pilots as surely as it was taking toll of their aircraft. No. 24 Squadron with its D.H.2s was seen as the antidote to the Fokker and, moreover, its commanding officer was none other than Major Lanoe G. Hawker, V.C.

But the many hopes which focused on this squadron must have been shattered the following day when Lieutenant Archer, leader of "C" Flight, took his D.H.2 up on the first flight to be made from a French airfield. His aircraft was seen to enter a sudden spin. At this time, this uncomfortable manoeuvre was regarded as a certain killer for there was no set drill for recovery. Helpless onlookers watched Archer's machine spiral a jerky path earthwards and crash. The pilot was killed. After a short while, the shock caused by this event was dissipated by the openly voiced thought that, after all, one must expect accidents when flying. On February 10th, the Squadron moved to Bertangles aerodrome, which they shared with No. 11 Squadron, and the crash was almost forgotten until more D.H.2s spun and crashed. One caught fire on its way down and the grisly nickname of the "spinning incinerator" was immediately applied to the D.H.2. No-one now had any faith in its prowess against the Fokker.

Instead, hopes turned to the F.E.2b aircraft. The first of this type had arrived in France with No. 20 Squadron during January, 1916, but had been employed almost exclusively on reconnaissance work and had little opportunity to do battle with the Fokker monoplanes. Then, while No. 24 Squadron were still in serious trouble with their D.H.2s, No. 25, which was equipped with more F.E.2bs arrived and, after some weeks' familiarization with the local countryside and flying conditions, moved up to Auchel, a little mining village. They were given the task of covering the front line from Arras in the south to Armentieres in the north.

But it was left to No. 23 Squadron to be the first to pit the new aircraft against the Fokker. This unit arrived in France on March 16th, and, almost immediately, were pushed out to their operational airfield of Le Hameau, to the north-west of Arras. By March 23rd, an F.E.2b of this squadron had met a Fokker. It was one of a loose formation of F.E.2bs attacked by a solitary Fokker monoplane near

Queant. There was not much of a battle. The Fokker dived down from behind the British aircraft, fired and scored hits. The F.E.2b crashed almost immediately but, fortunately, the pilot was only slightly injured and the observer unhurt.

This loss only confirmed the fear which many pilots harboured concerning the F.E.2b—a serious drawback to its use as a fighter was restricted vision towards the rear. A successful look-out in this direction was only possible when the observer stood on his ammunition drums and peered backwards over the top wing. It was decided, therefore, that F.E.2bs should be flown only in formation with B.E.2c aircraft, which would be used to guard their tails. Hard-pressed reconnaissance pilots had been enduring the attention of Immelmann and his comrades for more months than they cared to remember, and this cumbersome fighting formation did not help them have much faith in the F.E.2b as a fighting machine.

Meanwhile, the pilots of 24 Squadron were still in trouble. On March 16th, one pilot on patrol in a D.H.2 in the Bucoy area had spotted an enemy machine and given chase in fine style. Then, without any warning, two cylinders flew from his engine, which seized up with a shudder which shook the entire aircraft. Fortunately, the pilot managed to glide back over the British lines and pulled off a successful landing near a balloon section.

It had been realized, by this time, that the Squadron's troubles stemmed mainly from the Monosoupape rotary engine fitted to the D.H.2. Basically, this was a fine example of aero-engineering, but it needed balancing within very accurate limits. The rough servicing received in the field often resulted in an out-of-balance condition which killed several pilots. One pilot who survived the dire results of an unbalanced engine was Captain R. Hughes-Chamberlain, leader of "C" Flight. His account of an accident which happened on June 17th is worthy of repetition, for it shows what pilots had to cope with in addition to attention from the enemy.

"I had just been sent off on a stand-by patrol," recalls Hughes-Chamberlain, "and had climbed to a height of some 4,000 feet by the time I was about nine miles from Bertangles. Then, without any warning, one cylinder left the engine. It knocked off one propeller blade at the root and sailed through the top mainspar of the aircraft. You always had your ears pinned back for engine trouble in that squadron and I managed to switch off the petrol and ignition almost immediately."

This smart action almost certainly saved Hughes-Chamberlain the further embarrassment of his engine catching fire in the air, but his troubles were by no means ended.

"The loss of the propeller blade was causing very serious vibration as the remaining blade made the engine windmill in the slipstream. The aircraft appeared to be shaking to pieces. The damage to the mainspar dislodged one of the centre struts which carried the control lines to the ailerons and elevator. I looked round to see the mainspar sagging and, at the same time, noticed the ammunition drums, which were fixed to the sides of the fuselage, flying away and bursting through the fabric of the wings.

"I had little time to consider the damage caused by the drums because at this moment the mainspar gave way and dropped down some six inches. My control stick was almost useless. You usually manoeuvred by moving the stick only a few inches in any one direction but I found that I had to swing the stick round about two feet to get any response from the aircraft. The vibration was making the Lewis gun—which was mounted in front of me—hop around madly and I had little forward vision.

"I realized that if I couldn't get the aeroplane to the ground soon, it would disintegrate in the air. In fact, it was disintegrating already. Luckily, I had not been very high and I managed to pull off a very good landing in a nearby field. I stood up in the cockpit and rested my head against the top wing for some time after I had landed, and then almost had a relapse when I realized that the tail booms, which carried the whole tail assembly, could be waved about quite easily with one hand. The aircraft was considered a complete write-off."

These early troubles, however, disappeared as servicing techniques improved and the D.H.2 soon proved itself a worthy fighter. Like all good fighting aircraft, it was sensitive to the controls, and this, coupled with the engine trouble, had led many pilots into unintentional spins and there was no doubt that the machine was regarded with awe at one time. That the name "spinning incinerator" eventually lapsed was due, mainly, to the effort of Lieutenant S. E. Cowan. Refusing to believe that the D.H.2 was naturally a dangerous machine, he proceeded to "wring his aircraft out", trying first one manoeuvre and then another. Soon, he was able to perform an impressive aerobatic show, which helped other pilots overcome the superstition with which they were liable to regard the aircraft.

No. 24's scoring opened on April 2nd, when Lieutenants D. M. Tidmarsh and S. J. Sibley returned from patrol with a report of a combat they had fought near Bapaume. There, they had met an enemy aircraft, which fell to Tidmarsh's gun. It was, moreover, a decisive combat for both pilots had seen the enemy machine crash.

Tidmarsh gained another victory on April 30th, when D.H.2s of 24 Squadron were escorting some reconnaissance F.E.2bs. Some half-dozen enemy scouts were spotted hovering in the distance but the D.H.2s were forced to stay with their charges. Then one German, a Fokker, ventured nearer. Tidmarsh turned to the attack but the enemy dived so steeply to avoid his guns that it crashed on a roof in Bapaume.

On May 4th, Cowan overtook an enemy two-seater close to the ground, near Clery, and fired a few rounds into it from almost point blank range. The German pilot was so harassed by this attack, that he flew into a wire fence and crashed into a field beyond. Cowan, anxious to make doubly sure of this victory, climbed to 200 feet and dived down firing the rest of his drum into the now stationary aircraft. This action almost proved his undoing.

Despite his excitement, he had remembered his correct drill and had switched off his engine at the start of his dive to prevent the fuel mixture becoming too rich. But, when he tried to switch on again with the thumb switch fitted to his control stick, he found the switch jammed. For a few seconds he devoted his attention to jiggling furiously with the switch and did not see the rapidly approaching ground until almost too late. He saw the danger just in time to flatten out and touch down with a bump in the same field as his victim. Luckily, the impact freed the switch and Cowan took off again without further incident.

Egged on by their indefatigable Commanding Officer, the pilots of 24 Squadron were soon regularly proving themselves more than a match for the Fokker monoplane. Hawker used as much ingenuity preparing his squadron for battle as he had in the earlier days when he was a "lone wolf" fighter. He rigged up what he termed a "rocking fuselage" at Bertangles. This was a device which allowed pilots to practise on the ground the art of firing from the somewhat unsteady gun platforms provided by the aircraft of the day. Pilots would sit in this and practise firing at a target placed against a nearby railway embankment, while colleagues applied synthetic aircraft movement to the fuselage. It proved valuable training but then, one day, the fuselage was rocked over-enthusiastically, a few bullets whistled over the railway line and one unlucky missile severed the telephone line which ran alongside the track. Hawker found himself faced with some fast talking to placate the indignant staff officer who came from R.F.C. headquarters to investigate this "act of sabotage".

The days of German air superiority were now undoubtedly numbered. Even the less manoeuvrable F.E.2b was beginning to prove itself in combat against the Fokker monoplane. This was decisively proved, on June 18th when two F.E.2bs of 25 Squadron took off from Auchel and met with three Fokkers at 9 p.m. The British aircraft dived to the attack immediately. One Fokker flew off at high speed, while the other two turned towards Lens with the British machine on their tails.

Suddenly, one of the two enemy aircraft reefed round in a steep, climbing turn to fire at the leading F.E.2b, which was flown by Second Lieutenant J. R. B. Savage. Savage was mortally wounded and his aircraft dived towards the ground. The second F.E.2b, flown by Second Lieutenant C. R. McCubbin, immediately turned on the attacking Fokker. The observer, Corporal J. H. Waller, opened fire. The Fokker broke off its attack against Savage, presumably to fire on McCubbin, but the German pilot never fully recovered from the dive and crashed headlong into the ground. McCubbin returned to Auchel with mixed emotion at the loss of his comrade and his own victory. Not until later did he learn of the identity of the German pilot. It was the legendary Immelmann himself.

It was characteristic of the fighting pilots of that time that British pilots should drop a message over a German airfield, extolling Immelmann's prowess and asking whether an aircraft from 25 Squadron could make a formal fly-past at the funeral. A return message from the Germans indicated that they were agreeable providing the aircraft carried no armament. This honour to an enemy was duly performed by Lieutenant "Fluffy" Dixon.

Despite its valuable work, the F.E.2b was never so effective in combat as the single-seat D.H.2. Two men in one aircraft trying to fight a battle with no satisfactory means of communication could find themselves in difficulties. A well-drilled team of pilot and observer could overcome many of the obvious problems but communication difficulties could loom large when the unexpected occurred—as two men from No. 25 Squadron found out.

This unit had rather more than the average number of sergeant pilots and one of these, Sergeant W. T. Walder, often found himself teamed up with a Captain Baynes as observer. Despite the disparity in rank, the two made a good team. While on patrol on one occasion, they saw an enemy aircraft flying above them which made no attempt to attack. At first, they were a little puzzled by its motives, but understood only too well when the enemy released some small bombs which fell towards the F.E.2b. Baynes was extremely annoyed and immediately signalled to Walder to climb and attack. Walder complied.

A brief but furious battle followed. There was no time for communication between the British pilot and observer, nor was there any need. Walder anticipated Baynes's intentions and flew the aircraft accordingly. The teamwork resulted in success; the enemy aircraft crashed to the ground—but not before quite a few shots had whistled past the F.E.2b. Walder was elated by this victory and, when Baynes turned round and shouted in clipped syllables, "Shot up arse!", the pilot returned a beaming smile and nodded his head joyously.

Then it was immediately apparent to Walder that the communications system must have broken down, for the reaction from the officer was the blackest of black looks. Baynes then took another deep breath and elucidated the situation by shouting back, "Not them. ME!" He had, in fact, received a bullet in the buttocks but this injury was not enough to stop his wrath at Walder's apparent lack of concern.

For most of that summer of 1916 the successes obtained by the D.H.2s and, to a lesser extent, the F.E.2bs, came from chance encounters between single aircraft or, at the most, pairs. The R.F.C. had to wait until July to prove its new fighter aircraft in an air battle of a considerable size. On the evening of that day, an offensive patrol of four D.H.2s of 24 Squadron took off from Bertangles and flew towards the front at 10,000 feet. The formation, which comprised Lieutenants

McKay, C. M. B. Chapman, and H. C. Evans, was led by Captain Hughes-Chamberlain.

At 8.20 p.m., precisely, the British pilots noticed eight enemy aircraft flying in formation southwards over Bapaume. Hughes-Chamberlain ignored the two-to-one ratio and led his patrol to the attack. As the four British aircraft dived, the enemy formation was joined by three Fokker monoplanes. Within less than a minute, the sky was covered with small groups of aircraft, each whirling around in their own private battles.

Hughes-Chamberlain pointed his aircraft at an L.V.G., which dived and turned towards the east. As he followed it down, the British pilot saw a Fokker beyond and shifted his aim to this, firing half a drum of ammunition. The Fokker immediately dived with Hughes-Chamberlain in pursuit. As the two aircraft flattened out near the ground, bullets began to whistle past the D.H.2 and Hughes-Chamberlain twisted his head, to see a Roland Scout diving towards him. He put his aircraft into a sudden climb and, in a desperate effort to out-manoeuvre the Roland, pulled his aircraft into a turn while still climbing. The home-made "Immelmann turn" worked. Hughes-Chamberlain found the Roland in his sights and emptied the remainder of his drum. The enemy aircraft dived earthwards but the British pilot was too busy changing drums to see what became of it.

Evans, meanwhile, had made a successful attack against another Roland, firing from a range of only 25 yards—until he found himself under attack from two Fokkers. In their exuberance the German pilots almost collided with each other and this near-accident enabled Evans to escape. An L.V.G. which he saw ahead gave him the chance to empty the rest of his drum, after which he found himself under attack from another L.V.G. He attempted to break the record for changing drums but was then horrified to find that his gun had jammed. He was saved from this predicament by Chapman, who dived on the L.V.G. and drove it away.

Chapman had, in fact, made his first attack against an L.V.G. when he, too, was attacked from behind. He escaped with a sudden turn which brought him into line with the enemy, and was just about to press home his attack, when he had seen Evans in trouble and had dived to the rescue.

Then he saw another D.H.2 spiralling earthwards pursued by a

Fokker. Once more, he played the part of rescuer. The spiralling aircraft belonged to McKay, whose engine had been running roughly since soon after leaving Bertangles. He had been unable to reach the same height as the others and had been flying at only 8,500 feet when the attack started. A Roland had dived down from the mêlée above and attacked him from ahead but McKay had held his course, opened fire and driven the enemy away. A Fokker then chased him and, with his ailing engine, McKay found the only evasive action he could take was a descending spiral. He was only 1,000 feet above the ground, and wondering desperately what his next move should be, when Chapman intervened. A well-aimed burst sent the Fokker straight into the ground where it burst into flames.

Hughes-Chamberlain had been completing his ammunition drum change during this excitement and, with this accomplished, looked up to see a Fokker diving towards him and firing about 400 yards away. Refusing to take evasive action, Hughes-Chamberlain lifted the nose of his aircraft slightly and returned the fire, keeping his finger on the firing handle until the Fokker had passed overhead. He saw it begin a dramatic tilt towards the ground but the sight of an L.V.G. within range took his attention.

The sky was rapidly clearing, but Evans found an L.V.G. and a Fokker and attacked both. All the fight seemed to be gone from the Germans, for these two allowed themselves to be driven off. Soon, the sky had cleared of all enemy aircraft except for one Fokker which tried to get behind Hughes-Chamberlain, who went into a spiral climb so that he would be in a better position to attack. The Fokker, however, took advantage of this manoeuvre to turn and climb away towards the east.

The dog-fight had lasted for twenty-five minutes and had been witnessed by British ack-ack gun crews on the ground and by the observer of a No. 9 Squadron aircraft which had been too far away to join in. Both these sources confirmed that three enemy aircraft had been brought down and that one of them crashed in flames. McKay had been unable to climb again after being forced down by the Fokker but had managed to nurse his limping D.H.2 back to Bertangles.

For four British aircraft to fight with eleven Germans and survive was excellent going by any standards. That three enemy should be shot down into the bargain was an unhoped-for bonus. The whole engagement had been seen by many British troops and the effect on their morale was as uplifting as the tale that the eight surviving Germans took back must have been depressing to the enemy.

This engagement marked the turn of the Royal Flying Corps' fortunes in France for some time to come. The number of attacks made on British reconnaissance aircraft decreased, less effort had to be made protecting them, and the single-seat fighters were allowed more time for purely offensive patrols against enemy machines. Although 24 Squadron had been the first complete fighter unit in France, many squadrons had one or two single-seat scouts on their strength, and these could now be used to much better advantage.

Up to this time, the anonymity which the War Office insisted should be given to all R.F.C. pilots had prevented any one man from being in the public eye for any length of time. With the greater freedom now possible for the scout pilots, the public image of the great fighter "ace" began to grow. Names like McCudden, Mannock and Bishop were soon to fill the newspapers and weekly reviews. Much was written of their deeds at that time and much is still written today. It is not the purpose of this book to retell the stories of these well-known men but, as we have already seen the emergence of Hawker as an "embryo" ace—because he was fighting at a time when conditions were not right for an ace—it is of interest to know something of the career of the man who became the first popular British air ace. He was a short, compactly-built young man with thick, black hair and dark, brilliant eyes, and his name was Albert Ball.

The son of Alderman Sir Albert Ball, one time Mayor of Nottingham, young Albert displayed an early passion for firearms and started to collect pistols when he was only nine years old. He would spend much of his leisure time on the tennis lawn, firing at a series of upright sticks and, by his early 'teens, was a remarkably good shot. Ball was also fanatically interested in engines and, when he was fourteen, acquired an old petrol engine which he trundled home on a wheelbarrow. It was little more than a wreck but, within a short time, Ball had it working again.

He was educated at Trent College which, at that time, was one of the new public schools, but his scholastic career was not brilliant. He left school with an inability to spell which was to stay with him for the rest of his life and fully deserved his headmaster's description—"an undistinguished pupil."

Ball had not long celebrated his twentieth birthday when the War started and he joined the Sherwood Foresters, later transferring to a cyclist unit stationed near Ealing. There, he saw many aircraft flying around, the machines captured his interest and he decided to become a pilot. He took flying lessons at his own expense, getting up before dawn, cycling to the flying school for lessons and returning in time for his 6 a.m. parade at Ealing.

Unfortunately, Ball was not a good pilot, but what he lacked in skill he made up for in enthusiasm. "I went up the other day and got out of sight of land," he wrote in one of his many letters to his family. "Then I turned straight down to earth with the tail pointing up. The ground seemed to rush up to meet me and my nose seemed to be bleeding but it was ripping."

Ball was seconded to the R.F.C. on January 29th, 1916, arrived in France less than a month later, and was posted to No. 13 Squadron. The commanding officer, Major Marsh, was not impressed with his new recruit and warned him that he might be sent back to England for further training. Before this threat could be put into effect, however, Ball managed to fly operationally. He was piloting one of six B.E.2cs, on a reconnaissance flight, when three Fokkers and a further gaggle of assorted German aircraft attacked them. One of the B.E.s fell behind and, despite hurried intervention from the others, was shot down. Ball's engine then began to run roughly and he was forced to land.

It was now that his skill with engines came to his aid. He spent the night with his aircraft and, by next morning, had succeeded in curing the engine trouble. He took off, ran into a snowstorm and was forced down again for a short while, eventually reaching No. 13's aerodrome at Le Hameau at 8 a.m. on the morning after his first forced landing. Major Marsh was impressed with Ball's tenacity and decided that he could stay in France.

Ball's first fight with an enemy aircraft came on March 28th. He was engaged in artillery spotting between Vimy and Givenchy, with Lieutenant S. A. Villiers as his observer. His uncannily accurate eyesight in the air had already been the cause of some comment on the Squadron and Ball was able to demonstrate it to some effect this day by spotting German aircraft at 5,000 feet and some miles away. He dived to the attack and Villiers was soon in a position from which he could open fire. Then the rattle of Villiers's gun was joined by another and Ball realized that yet another German had sneaked up behind but, as Villiers's bullets seemed to be having some effect on the first enemy machine, he remained in position until a drum and a half of ammunition had been drilled into it before turning to meet the second attack. The second German aircraft flew away before Ball could engage it.

Reconnaissance work was not to Ball's liking for he already regarded his primary mission in life to be shooting down enemy aircraft. Whenever he had time to spare, he would seek permission to make long "reconnaissance" flights, merely in the hope of finding a chance for combat. Nor was he happy with the B.E.2: this aircraft had not been designed as a fighter and the fact that it was a two-seater he regarded as a handicap. Although he and Villiers were the best of friends, Ball always felt responsibility for his passenger and was restrained from taking risks which, if he had been on his own, he would have felt justifiable. He therefore worried Marsh continually to be allowed to fly 13 Squadron's Bristol Bullet single-seat scout. Marsh was by no means confident that Ball's skill was sufficient, but sent him back to No. 1 Aircraft Depot at St. Omer to try his hand. Ball set off with a final admonishment from Marsh that, if he did not prove himself eminently capable of flying the Bullet, he would have to let another pilot have the honour. But the lively, sensitive scout seemed to have an affinity with the young pilot and there was little doubt that he could fly it better than the stately, foolproof B.E.

Ball's hopes, however, soon received a set-back. He had made only a few flights in 13 Squadron's Bullet when another pilot wrecked it. A replacement aircraft arrived, but when crossing the lines in it for the first time and test-firing his guns, Ball discovered that they were not synchronized correctly and had almost severed his propeller. His career as a fighter pilot did not start until May 7th, when he was posted to No. 11 Squadron under Major T. O'B. Hubbard.

This squadron was not exclusively a fighter unit but it did have more than the usual number of single-seat Bristols and Nieuports. Its pilots had also developed a usefully aggressive fighting spirit and it seemed to them that the young newcomer was unlikely scout pilot material. He was quiet and reserved, while most of his colleagues were hearty extroverts. They were vastly amused by Ball's habit of eating cake while flying—he rarely took off for any flight without making sure that he had an adequate supply. It was a great delight for Ball to race through the air, with his thick hair streaming in the wind, munching his mother's home-made cake. He was affectionately christened "John" by his new colleagues, who liked him in spite of his strange ways.

Within a week of joining No. 11 Squadron, however, Ball gave the other pilots cause for some consideration. On May 15th, he was flying in a Bristol Scout at 12,000 feet, when his keen eyes spotted an Albatros at about 5,000 feet above the German lines. He pushed his aircraft downwards, achieved complete surprise and pumped 120 bullets into the enemy machine which, in Ball's own words, "turned over and was completely done in."

He repeated this success on May 22nd. This time, he was flying a Nieuport. Near Givenchy, he saw an Albatros some five miles away and gave chase. He opened fire from 100 yards but the German dived away steeply to shelter among the guns at Douai. Ball refused to do combat under such conditions and continued his patrol.

At his southern turning point, near Moyenville, he saw another Albatros at 6,000 feet. Ball dived down from 10,000 feet and, this time, held his fire until he was within thirty yards of the enemy. Some twenty shots had left his gun when the Albatros nosed down in a continually steepening dive. Ball tried to keep it in sight but was unable to do so. Confirmation of his victory came later from witnesses on the ground.

Climbing back to his 10,000 feet patrol level, Ball turned on to a northerly course and saw an L.V.G. accompanied by two Fokkers. Two other Fokkers then joined the formation, while Ball kept watch, waiting his chance to attack. The Fokkers branched off for Douai, while the L.V.G. turned for the trenches at Oppy. This was the opportunity and Ball dived, opening fire at fifty yards. He emptied one drum into the enemy machine, broke off the attack to change drums and went in again. This time, the enemy gunner put up a spirited opposition and Ball found himself on the receiving end of a gun. His aircraft was hit eight times and once, after he completed a firing pass, a following German bullet narrowly missed his back and smashed in a strut near his face. The return fire did not deter Ball, who continued to attack, but he was forced to break off when the L.V.G. flew down almost to ground level and remained there. With his fuel running low, Ball had to return to his airfield. His Nieuport was badly hit by anti-aircraft gunfire while crossing the trenches but, although his tail was damaged, he returned safely.

It was the start of a fighting career which was brief in duration but spectacular in results. Ball was the first British pilot to receive wide publicity at the time of his deeds and his performances not only lifted the morale of the soldiers in the British trenches but gave heart to civilians at home.

When his career ended, Ball was a flight commander with No. 56 Squadron. Late in the evening of May 7th, 1917, he was seen in combat with a German single-seater near Lens. What happened in the fight is not known. Ball's aircraft was seen diving into a cloud and it seems that he never recovered. The S.E.5 which he was flying crashed and Albert Ball was killed. He is credited with forty-four confirmed victories.

CHAPTER FIFTEEN

The Greatest Battle

ON FRIDAY, June 23rd, 1916, a thunderstorm suddenly rent the air over the British lines along the Somme. Many R.F.C. observation balloons which were flying were destroyed when they were hit by lightning. Most of the observers escaped by parachute. Not so lucky were the two observers of a balloon of Number 5 Section in the Third Army area. Second Lieutenants J. W. Jardine and G. D. S. M. Pape suddenly found themselves surging higher as their balloon was wrenched from its winch, and soon they were soaring over the trenches. Their first thought was to prevent their maps and papers from falling into enemy hands and they began to tear up all their documents. It was a difficult task to carry out when confined to a small basket which was swaying madly to the whims of a strong and extremely variable wind and, by the time they had finished, they had reached 13,000 feet, where they were gyrating in a swirling snowstorm pricked by frequent flashes of lightning.

When the storm had first struck, the parachutes of both officers had been accidentally broken. Jardine had cut his free but Pape had remained attached to his, resisting its insistent tugging. The balloon crossed the German lines near Monchy but, almost immediately, began to blow back again and to drop towards the earth. Pape suddenly found that his parachute was above him and, before he had time to cut it loose, was lifted forcibly from the basket. The ropes of the parachute became entangled with the ropes of the balloon, which was sinking fast. Pape looked down and saw that the envelope was rapidly losing shape and that flames were licking around the valve. Realizing that his parachute was helping to check the descent of the balloon, he secured himself to it.

This strange ensemble slowly sank to earth near a British gun emplacement by Arras. Both officers were severely shaken by their fearful ride at the mercy of the elements and Pape's left arm was badly frost-bitten but, apart from this, they were none the worse for their experience.

The sudden, violent storm was, perhaps, a fitting prelude to that which was to follow for, on the next day, began one of the longest and most bitter conflicts ever fought, the Battles of the Somme. In five months of terrible fighting, the German forces were to be pushed back by a small, but vital, amount. The overall value of the successes achieved in the Somme are still open to discussion but, as far as the R.F.C. were concerned, it was an invaluable, although harrowing, experience. It was a battle in which Britain's meagre air forces were to play a major part. The many lessons which had been learned during the trial-and-error years were to be put into operation and many new difficulties were to be discovered. For the first time, airpower was to play a key part in a land battle, but this could not be achieved without superhuman efforts by the men of the Royal Flying Corps, nor without firm, almost clairvoyant direction from the man at the top, Trenchard. Hundreds of thousands of British lives were to be lost in the coming battle, many of them the lives of pilots or observers, but these men did not die in vain. They gave the final proof of the value of air power and, perhaps more important, the Battles of the Somme fired for all time the mould in which the spirit of the R.F.C. and the Royal Air Force was already cast.

The River Somme forms one of the great natural military barriers of northern France. In the early summer of 1916, British Forces had taken over from the French a great part of the line on their own right, and now the British line extended almost to the north bank of the Somme between Amiens and Peronne. It was here, along a front running about twelve miles north of the river and a similar distance to the south, that the grisly battles were fought. Over a period of seven months, the Germans, entrenched in huge underground labyrinths hewn out of the solid chalk undersoil, were slowly pushed back a distance of seven miles. For the British it was a time of innovations. During these battles they used the creeping artillery barrage for the first time and, in September, tanks were unleashed against the enemy. But perhaps the most important innovation of all was the intelligent use of airpower.

When the battles opened, Trenchard had 27 squadrons in France which owned, between them, 410 serviceable aircraft. With this small force the R.F.C. C-in-C set himself the task of establishing air superiority for the British. This meant a series of frequent attacks on German airfields, which called for aircraft carrying bombs and others to act as escort. He also had to supply aircraft for artillery spotting and, a new task, the support of infantry units at the front. All this had to be achieved without lessening the number of aircraft used for the primary task of pure reconnaissance.

Trenchard's first efforts to establish air superiority were directed against German observation balloons and, during the week preceding the start of the battle proper, he organized attacks against all enemy balloons in front of the four British armies. Two new weapons were brought into use for these sorties, a phosphorus bomb designed by Lieutenant R. B. Bourdillon and the Le Prieur rocket which had been designed by a French naval officer. The latter was an electrically-fired missile carried on the inter-plane struts and, on June 25th, four balloons were brought down by them and one by a phosphorus bomb.

Attacking balloons was no easy mission. The Le Prieur rockets had a curved trajectory and it was vital to get to within 400 yards of the target if it was to be hit. Successful rocket delivery also required a pilot to dive with his engine at full throttle—never a very popular manoeuvre in the aircraft of those days. As late as September, the task of shooting down balloons was regarded as something of a special mission. On September 16th, a Rolls-Royce car drew up at No. 60 Squadron's airfield at Vert Galand. Trenchard stepped out and, after the pilots had been assembled, told them that three enemy balloons had been hoisted and that these had to be shot down because they were overlooking the tank park—the tanks had only just been brought into the battle.

Three pilots were chosen from those who stepped forward. "Remember," Trenchard said to them, "it is far more important to get these balloons than to fail and come back." The balloons were shot down and all three pilots returned to base but each aircraft had been badly shot up.

Lieutenant Roderic Hill was another pilot who made an attack with Le Prieur rockets, a few days later. His target was a balloon over the Bapaume–Arras railway. He approached at a height of 7,000 feet and put his Nieuport fighter into an almost vertical dive. He was so busy concentrating on his aim that he was almost oblivious of the ground fire coming up at him. He held his dive until within the 400 yards limit and then fired his rockets.

The balloon blew up in flames almost in his face and, as he pulled hard on the control stick to come out of his head-long dive, he found himself ensnared by phosphorus anti-aircraft shells which were bursting all around him and enveloping him in black smoke. Not until he was down to one thousand feet and speeding homewards amid a hail of ground-fire, could he really see where he was going.

But perhaps the most important new use of aircraft during the Somme offensive, was as direct support for the infantry. The duty was known as "Contact Patrols" and, more than any other type of sortie, brought the pilots and observers right into the thick of the fighting on the ground. Just how the airmen could help the infantry was ably demonstrated on July 14th. Captain A. M. Miller of No. 3 Squadron was detailed to fly his Morane monoplane to the area of High Wood where the 7th Division and the Secunderabad Cavalry were starting an advance. With his observer, Second Lieutenant C. W. Short, he watched the progress of the combined advance. The two men could also see German infantry hidden among standing crops to the front and east of High Wood. They immediately realized that the high ground in front of the Germans would hide them from the British forces which were, in fact, advancing into a trap. Communications between air and ground were, as always, a problem and Miller reckoned that there must be a quicker way of warning the British forces than dropping a message. He dived down to three hundred feet and flew straight over the German forces who, as he had reasoned, began to fire up at him, immediately giving their position away to the British troops.

Miller and Short continued to fly up and down the German lines, raking the ground with their Lewis gun but taking tremendous punishment themselves, until they saw that the infantry had achieved their objective and were in a good position to attack the concealed troops. Then, because their Morane was so badly holed that it was becoming difficult to fly, they decided they would have to return to their airfield. But, before they did so, Short made a detailed sketch of the German positions and dropped this in a message bag to the cavalry.

This use of aircraft in what was virtually a ground attack role was greatly assisted by a new bullet, known as the Buckingham Tracer, which burned when it hit its target. Its greatest asset, however, was the smoke trail it left from the gun to the ground, which greatly assisted aiming. Buckingham Tracer bullets were effectively used, again in the High Wood area, by Captain H. E. F. Wyncoll, who was the observer in a 22 Squadron F.E.2b on July 15th. Parties of enemy infantry were seen in Flers, just to the north of High Wood, and the pilot, Captain J. G. Swart, flew low while Wyncoll fired. They saw many of the enemy fall as they were hit. A little later, as they flew south, they came across another party of Germans with some wagons and a gun limber. Once again they attacked, this time killing one horse and causing others to bolt.

The one serious drawback to this close co-operation between air-crew and soldiers was the difficulty which the airmen had in identifying the particular British unit which they had been detailed to assist. Rain had transformed the thin top-soil of the battlefield into a sea of sticky mud which stuck to transports and personnel alike. From the air, the picture was of open, shell-scarred areas dotted by odd woods and copses, with many homogeneous groups of mud-bespattered, squirming humanity. The infantry did use mirrors strapped to their backs to attract the attention of aircraft, but the use of flares lit on the ground was found to be the most successful method, though many infantry units were reluctant to light these in large numbers in case they should attract enemy fire. Nor were the flares always lit at the best time for the airmen to see them. As a result, many aircraft were fitted with Klaxon horns. These could be clearly heard on the ground over short distances and told the infantry when they should light their flares. Pilots making these contact patrols were surprised at their comparative immunity from ground fire when flying extremely low. Not one aircraft engaged on this duty was shot down by ground fire, although they often returned with their fabric almost in tatters from the bullets which had passed through the wings. But one very real risk for these airmen was British artillery shells. Pilots and observers could often see these whistling through the air, overtaking the aircraft. One British aeroplane was hit by a British shell and blew up in the air.

That this ground work and the constant reconnaissance and air photography could be carried out over the front lines was due entirely to Trenchard's bid to establish air superiority. If German aircraft had been around in large numbers, then the close support work would have been almost impossible. The air opposition, which undoubtedly was there all the time, had been drawn off by the process of mounting almost continual bombing attacks on targets well behind the lines, thus forcing the German Air Service on to the defensive.

Many of these attacks did not achieve a great deal in the way of damage but Second Lieutenant A. L. Gordon-Kidd, flying a B.E.2c of No. 7 Squadron, on July 1st, spotted a train approaching a deep cutting, on the line between Aubigny-au-Bac and Cambrai, a spot which the pilots had been told at their briefing would be one of the most difficult places to clear of wreckage. Gordon-Kidd selected his moment carefully and, as the train entered the cutting, flew down and dropped two 112 lb bombs which his aircraft was carrying. He made his attack from 900 feet and scored a direct hit on the middle coaches of the train, which began to catch fire and then exploded. Other pilots saw the flames and added their bombs to the holocaust.

Another attack on St. Quentin, the same day, caught two German battalions at the station just as they were loading their arms and transports on to trains. There were also two hundred ammunition wagons in the sidings. The first British aircraft appeared at 2 p.m.; one bomb hit an ammunition shed and others hit the train, destroying it and all the equipment piled on the platforms. Panic-stricken German soldiers fled from the scene, leaving behind them 180 dead and wounded. In the panic there was no time to move the ammunition wagons and sixty of these also caught fire. Seven British aircraft made the attack and four did not return. The cost of success had been high.

On the following day, more attacks were made, this time with unspectacular results but with the loss of three more bombing aircraft. Among the escorting aeroplanes were the Moranes of No. 60 Squadron, led by the C.O., Major F. F. Waldron. This escort was essential, for the heavily-loaded, slow-manoeuvring B.E.s were quite unable to protect themselves, but the asset of having few enemy aircraft hampering work at the front was paid for by the tremendous opposition met behind the lines. In heavy air-to-air fighting over Cambrai, Waldron was shot down and killed.

Despite these losses, Trenchard kept up his offensive against distant targets, although he called off the low-level attacks against moving trains. By July 18th, the first phase of the battle was over. A little over two weeks of intensive fighting under terrible conditions had won the Allies some six thousand yards. Trenchard, taking stock of the situation, was pleased to see that his offensive policy had borne fruit. Not one British aircraft had been molested from the air while working over the front lines. But it was becoming obvious that this would not last forever. Intelligence carried reports that the German first Army, which had been temporarily dispersed, was being reorganized under General Fritz von Below and that air reinforcements for this army were being brought into the battle area.

The attacks behind the lines continued, despite the growth of opposition. It should be remembered that these attacks had to be carried out by men who were also needed for artillery co-operation and reconnaissance. Pilots were often working for as much as ten hours a day on a variety of duties, of which the bombing sorties were, without a doubt, the most tiring. The story of just one pilot on one raid illustrates what this type of warfare was like. This was no dramatic attack which made headlines, but a typical sortie.

Second Lieutenant R. H. C. Usher, later to find fame as a rugby footballer, was one of seven pilots of 27 Squadron who were briefed to bomb Marcoing on the evening of July 30th. They took off from Fienvilliers aerodrome with an escort of Sopwith two-seaters from 70 Squadron, which shared the airfield with them. As they crossed the lines a thick mist came up and the pilots lost contact with one another. Usher looked around him, saw that he still had a Sopwith with him, and so continued with his flight.

The outward trip to Marcoing was uneventful and Usher released the two 112 lb bombs which his Martinsyde was carrying into the centre of the village. As he pulled his aircraft up and banked for the return flight, he almost rammed a German L.V.G. Recovering in time to pump the best part of a drum of Lewis gun ammunition into the enemy before he flashed past, Usher saw his quarry dive, hotly pursued by the Sopwith, which stuck to the enemy, firing continually until within 1,000 feet of the ground where it was swallowed in the mist.

Usher, in the meantime, was busily changing drums, and had just completed this operation when he saw a Roland Scout diving at him from ahead. Again he fired but, this time, the answering fire came from behind him. He slewed round in his seat, to see three more Rolands diving at him from the rear and, as he did so, was hit in the leg. Despite this injury, he was able to bring his gun to bear again and the German scouts made off. Usher's relief at this achievement was short-lived, as his engine spluttered and then died completely. The cause was obvious; there was a large hole in the petrol tank and, within a few seconds, the pilot's left leg was soaked in fuel.

As he glided down to what seemed a certain crash-landing in enemy territory, Usher managed to jam his left knee into the hole in the tank and decided that, if he used the hand pump, he might be able to build up sufficient pressure inside to force a little fuel through to the engine. At first, he could feel little resistance to his frenzied pumping effort but, after a short while, the engine gave a couple of coughs and started again. By this time, he was down to about 200 feet, and still fifteen miles behind enemy lines.

Determined by now to keep going until he had recrossed the lines, Usher started an exhausting return flight. The engine would start to miss whenever he eased up on the pumping, and often threatened to quit despite his most frenzied efforts. For more than fifteen minutes, Usher willed himself to continue. He was weak through loss of blood from his wounded leg, he rarely managed to coax the aircraft above 50 feet on its faltering engine and, at this height, could see little of the ground below him and was lost. To add to his confusion, enemy forces on the ground frequently made their presence known by a shower of small-arms fire.

The fuel pumping had become a desperate, almost automatic motion by the time that Usher spotted a French biplane which was also flying low. He hoped that it was returning to its airfield and followed behind. Eventually, in a semi-conscious state, he brought his aircraft down at Moreuil aerodrome. The Martinsyde was wrecked in the heavy landing but Usher, completely exhausted, suffered no more injuries.

Despite the reinforcement which the German Air Service had received in the Somme area, not one British bombing attack was completely stopped by the opposition. Many pilots reported on their return from bombing or escort operations that resistance was often half-hearted. Trenchard's policy was, in fact, continuing to have a serious effect, not only on the morale of the German soldiers at the front who saw only British aircraft and none of their own intercepting them, but on the troops behind the lines, and on the pilots whose job it should have been to put a stop to the British attacks.

But it must not be thought that the British aircraft were completely unopposed. Casualties continued to mount and, as all British pilots were well aware of the general shortage of aircraft, many brave and desperate efforts were made to get back in damaged machines. On August 24th, Second Lientenants A. M. Vaucour and A. J. Bott were caught by the burning wad of an anti-aircraft shell near Cambrai. The fuselage of their Sopwith two-seater caught fire but Bott immediately tore away the burning canvas and beat out other flames with his hands.

Their troubles by no means were ended, for they immediately met two enemy aircraft and, in the ensuing fight, a petrol feed pipe was broken and the engine stopped. Vaucour managed to glide over the trenches and land near Carnoy. He stayed with his aircraft while Bott went to get help. Air Mechanic Herbert Warminger was sent out to make the repairs, which took him the rest of the day and most of the night. Next morning, he took off with Vaucour, but the Sopwith was immediately attacked by three enemy aircraft and was then hit by anti-aircraft fire. Again the engine stopped, and again Vaucour carried out a successful crash-landing, this time well inside British lines. Warminger, unfortunately, died the same evening of wounds received in the fight.

Even if they could not get their aircraft back, the pilots lost no time in returning to their airfield, on foot if necessary, because men, too, were in short supply. Roderic Hill of 60 Squadron had his engine shot during a fight on October 26th, but managed to glide back and crash-land just behind the British front line trenches. The ground was a mass of shell holes, the aircraft turned over and Hill received a sharp crack on the head. Apparently unperturbed, he crawled from beneath his aircraft, cadged some whisky from gunners in a nearby dug-out, and then walked two miles further back to where he knew he might pick up some form of transport. That two-mile walk took all of two hours, as Hill frequently found himself up to his knees in mud and water.

The third phase of the Somme battle had started on September 15th, a day marked not only by the first use of tanks in warfare, but by the biggest air effort yet made by the Royal Flying Corps during the war. More hours were logged in the air on that day than on any other. Trenchard's policy was still having gratifying results, but German air reinforcements were increasing and the doubts which Trenchard had at the start of the second phase were magnified. On September 17th, the R.F.C. suffered particularly heavy casualties, most of them at the hands of a new German fighter squadron under the command of Oswald Boelcke. Trenchard realized that the Germans were likely to try his own technique of attacking but resolved that he would not ease his own attacks, even if it meant ignoring requests for air protection from units at the front or behind it. With this resolution in mind, he wrote a memorandum to the War Office which he called "Future Policy in the Air". This document, dated September 22nd, 1916, stressed the fact that the aeroplane was essentially an offensive weapon and not a defensive one. "The sound policy which should guide all warfare in the air," he wrote, "would seem to be this: to exploit the morale effect of the aeroplane on the enemy, but not to let him exploit it on ourselves. Now this can only be done by attacking and by continuing to attack."

It was a sound policy and Trenchard adhered to it. Like most of his decisions and edicts on aerial warfare, it was prophetic. In only one aspect of the air war was Trenchard wrong. It was, perhaps, a minor detail, but it could have helped save many lives, lives which the British nation could ill afford. The parachute was already a well-known and proved device for saving life in the air but Trenchard, true to his spartan upbringing, would not have it in the Royal Flying Corps. He believed that a pilot facing heavy odds would take to his parachute rather than press on with the fight. There is little doubt that in this decision he was doing the R.F.C. a grave injustice. The aggressive spirit of this force had always been high. Few, if any, pilots would have taken to their parachute rather than fight.

So the pilots and observers fought without any means of leaving their aircraft in an emergency. Only the balloon observers, who were reckoned to be defenceless and entirely at the mercy of the enemy, were issued with these life-saving devices. Many hundreds of pilots and observers, trapped in aircraft completely out of control and, perhaps, on fire, had the unpleasant choice of staying with their machines until final obliteration on the ground, or jumping clear to an equally certain, but perhaps cleaner, death.

This obvious need for parachutes was never more keenly felt than in the third phase of the Somme Battle. The Somme had already seen the development of "contact" work and the continued exploitation of bombing techniques. Now, with the arrival of more, as yet not dispirited, German fighter units, the technique of fighting air-to-air battles moved forward with a tremendous surge. It was the beginning of the great dog-fights which were to continue until the end of the war.

No longer were the Germans despondent. Boelcke and his pilots soon proved that they were, indeed, skilful. On September 27th, a flight of six Martinsydes from 27 Squadron was attacked by five Fokker biplanes led by Boelcke. The German leader shot down the aircraft flown by Second Lieutenant H. A. Taylor immediately and then turned his attention to the machine piloted by Second Lieutenant S. Dendrino. His aircraft outclassed, Dendrino tried valiantly to shake the German fighter off. The Martinsyde was riddled with bullets, but Dendrino persevered until he was hit himself. The British pilot was probably killed at this instant. He was certainly unconscious, but his aircraft continued to fly round in circles, much to Boelcke's amazement. Finally, the German pilot flew alongside and saw Dendrino slumped in his cockpit. After noting the number of this Martinsyde, Boelcke took on another, which eventually escaped and returned to Fienvilliers with bullets in the petrol tank, in the seat, radiator, engine, and wings, and with its control wires damaged.

Trenchard, noting that his forebodings were proving well-founded, asked for reinforcements as soon as possible. It was obvious, however, that these would take some time, and so the R.F.C. continued to fight against the increasing odds. October 28th was a notable date for the British pilots. On that day, two D.H.2 pilots from 24 Squadron, Lieutenant A. G. Knight and Second Lieutenant A. E. McKay, met six German fighters led by Boelcke near Pozieres. As the fight began, six more German fighters flew up. Two dived simultaneously on to Knight's tail and collided, but both flew away again, apparently under control. Hopelessly outnumbered, the De Havillands could do little more than use all their skill in beating off the continued German attacks.

The fight lasted for fifteen minutes, until the whirling and diving aircraft had drifted over Bapaume, where the Germans lost heart and broke off the attack, allowing the two British aircraft to return to their base. Not until some time later was it learned that one of the two German aircraft which had collided was piloted by Boelcke. Badly damaged in the collision, it had later broken up in the air. Boelcke, who in two months of fighting had shot down some twenty British aircraft, was killed.

As October gave way to November, the number and size of these aerial battles continued to grow and, on November 8th, culminated in the biggest air battle which had been seen to that date on the Western Front. Twelve aircraft from Nos. 12 and 13 Squadrons were briefed to attack an ammunition dump at Vraucourt. With them, as escort, went fourteen scout aircraft from 11, 60 and 29 Squadrons. Some enemy aircraft tried to break up the British formation as soon as it had crossed the lines, but the target was reached and the bombs dropped on their objective. By this time, however, the number of attacking German aircraft had grown to about thirty and a huge fight developed over the village of Vraucourt.

The first British casualty had been Lieutenant A. D. Bell-Irving from 60 Squadron whose aircraft had been hit as it crossed the lines. Wounded in the leg, his petrol tank punctured and his Very lights set on fire, Bell-Irving had no other course open but to crash-land by the trenches, where his aircraft was wrecked.

Over Vraucourt, the fight split up into many different sections. The escorting aircraft fought hard to protect the slower bombers, but two escorts from 12 Squadron were shot down and the pilot of another was wounded but got back. Two de Havillands from 29 Squadron failed to return and were last seen being forced downwards in a running battle. An F.E.2b of 11 Squadron, with its observer dead and pilot wounded, crashed in no-man's-land from where the pilot managed to drag his way to the British trenches. At least three of the enemy aircraft were shot down.

The last shots of the Somme battles were fired on November 18th. That day a thaw set in, turning the snow-covered battleground into a sea of mud once more. It had been the greatest continuous battle which the world had seen at that time. Whether it had been worth the bloodshed to the Allied forces as a whole is debatable but, for the R.F.C., it was an overwhelming victory in the air—a battle which had been fought almost entirely over enemy territory in face of increasing odds. Three hundred and eight pilots and 191 observers had either paid with their lives, were wounded or were missing, but Trenchard's policy of attack whatever may happen, had been vindicated.

There is one postscript to the battle which should be recorded. Among the pilots chosen by Boelcke for his new fighting squadron was a young man called Manfred von Richthofen whose name, at that time, was practically unknown. He first came into the limelight on November 23rd, a few days after the battle had ended. Richthofen's aircraft was spotted by three English machines which were flying above it and one peeled off to give chase. Approaching from astern, the English pilot opened fire but, almost immediately, Richthofen pulled round in a tight turn and, for long minutes, the two aircraft circled tightly round in a tail chase, so that it was impossible to tell who was after whom. The object of the contest was to be the first to get above and behind the other aeroplane. The first to succeed was von Richthofen, but his ascendancy was short-lived, for the British aircraft turned and dived unexpectedly and, once again, the two machines were circling madly in the air. Then the British aircraft caught von Richthofen unexpectedly, but the German escaped. So far, apart from the few shots fired at the opening of the conflict, neither pilot had been able to bring his guns to bear. The dog-fight evolved into a series of circlings the monotony of which was broken by the odd break and dive.

All the time, the aircraft had been getting lower and lower and, because of the prevailing wind, which was always to the R.F.C.'s disadvantage, were being blown further behind the German lines. The two protagonists were down to a few hundred feet when the British pilot momentarily had von Richthofen in his sights. He opened fire but again the German escaped. The British pilot saw the German aircraft above him and realized his danger. He had also noticed that, by this time, they were over Bapaume. If he was to have sufficient fuel to get back, the British pilot knew he would have to start straight away. He was aware of the danger of flying away from the enemy, but had little choice.

Practically on the ground, the British aircraft turned and flew eastwards on full throttle, but the embryo ace had fast reflexes. Wings tilting crazily from side to side, he followed the British machine and

Above, the Sopwith Camel was another first-class fighter, but not for insensitive pilots. The torque of its rotary engine gave added manoeuvrability to skilful pilots but would lead the inexperienced into a spin. *Below,* ground crews on the Western Front during the 1917–18 winter had a difficult time getting the Camels of No. 8 Squadron under way

Lord Brabazon of Tara was respo[illegible]
for the R.F.C. Photographic Sectio[illegible]
the development of aerial photog[illegible]
during the First World War

Jan Christiaan Smuts was given the task of cutting through the political struggles and red tape stunting Britain's air defences. The result was a unified air arm and the formation of the R.A.F.

opened fire. Then his gun jammed and the German cursed. But the damage had already been done. The British machine flew into the ground some 150 yards inside the German lines. When the pilot was dragged from his cockpit, it was discovered that he had been shot through the head. It was also discovered that he was none other than Major Lanoe Hawker, V.C.

"Thus did he die as he had lived, a very gallant gentleman," was von Richthofen's somewhat unctuous epitaph when he heard the news.

CHAPTER SIXTEEN

Death of the Zeppelin

FLIGHT SUB-LIEUTENANT J. C. Northrop of the Royal Naval Air Service bounced across the turf of Covelithe airfield, in a hopeful frame of mind, on the night of July 30th, 1916. He was one of many pilots being sent up to try and intercept Zeppelins which were over Britain. No pilot had yet succeeded in destroying a Zeppelin in the air, although the Home Defence squadrons—by this time more than thirty of them—had been trying for over a year. But Northrop fancied his chances, for his Lewis gun was armed with the new explosive bullets. If only he could make contact with one of these airships, then he stood a more than even chance of shooting it down.

But, as the dreary patrol passed with no sight of an airship, his excitement waned. Dutifully he maintained his steady course, up and down the east coast, watching the dawn breaking over towards Holland. Then, at 5.15 a.m., he saw a shape in the sky, some thirty miles out to sea. He pulled his B.E.2c round in a soggy climbing turn, as he tried to make speed and height to investigate the flying object. Soon, there was no doubt. Ahead was a Zeppelin, returning from a nightly saunter over England.

Determinedly Northrop kept his throttle wide open and slowly overhauled the airship. It seemed an age before he was near enough to fire and, when he was, he literally had to turn his head to look from one end of his target to the other. He could not miss. Taking his time, he emptied two drums of ammunition towards the cylindrical object before him. Sooner or later, he knew, one of his explosive bullets must hit the metal skeleton inside the Zeppelin and then it would explode. It was infuriating to see his bullets passing straight through the flimsy structure.

The cold, high-altitude air seemed to slice straight through his thick fur gloves as, with numb hands, he loaded his third drum of ammunition. Then, as he was about to open fire yet again, the drum flew off the gun and hit him in the face. For a split second he wondered what it was, suddenly realized that he was losing control of his aircraft and struggled to recover an even keel. But, when he looked around for his quarry, it had disappeared. A Zeppelin which Northrop felt should never have returned to its base had escaped.

It was a story which was becoming almost commonplace during that summer. Time and again, the R.F.C. or R.N.A.S. would engage a Zeppelin, but the monsters seemed immune to any form of attack. Three days later another R.N.A.S. pilot, Flight Lieutenant C. T. Freeman, who was flying a Bristol Scout from the seaplane carrier H.M.S. *Vindex*, encountered another Zeppelin over the North Sea. Freeman was armed with Ranken Darts, which called for the pilot to climb above the airship before he could release his weapons—an almost impossible task. Yet Freeman succeeded. Flying steadily above the Zeppelin, he aimed his darts carefully and watched them whistle down into the airship. They passed into the fabric as cleanly as a bullet into butter—and had just as little effect. The Zeppelin stayed serenely on course. Then Freeman's engine spluttered and died. He had no option other than to sit impotently in his cockpit nursing his aircraft down to a forced landing in the North Sea, where he stayed for a few hours before being picked up and taken to Holland.

Despite these and many other valiant efforts by the pilots of the Royal Flying Corps and the Royal Naval Air Service, the steady drone of Zeppelins high in the night sky had almost become part of life for those living in eastern England during that summer of 1916. There was no great public despondency over this. The bitterness of the previous year had been overcome, for the Zeppelins, although their bombs caused many minor family tragedies, achieved very little in the way of systematic destruction. The British were almost inclined to accept these raids as their part of the war effort and shrugged them off with the thought that, after all, their boys were going through much worse in the trenches. But there was still the individious, almost unconscious thought that the airmen could be achieving much more.

It was hard for the public to appreciate that the Home Defence squadrons were achieving some success. They were reaching Zeppelin heights regularly and often made contact with the airships, whose commanders rarely made determined efforts to reach their targets in the face of any opposition. The Home Defence squadrons were, in fact, acting as a useful deterrent.

Then, as the month of August passed, the Zeppelin activity dwindled away. There was the real hope that perhaps the R.F.C. and the R.N.A.S. had been successful, but it was known to HQ Home Defence that Germany was busily building up an even greater fleet of better airships. Indeed, the Battle of the Somme in France was warning Germany that the war was no longer going entirely in her favour. A big, surprise onslaught on British cities would, it was thought, turn the flow of events into Germany's favour. The month of August was just the lull before the storm that was to break over England.

The storm broke on the night of September 2nd. That evening, sixteen airships left their sheds in Germany. By night time, all but two had reached the British coast. Morale among the German crews flew high as they anticipated a very unpleasant surprise for the English, asleep below. But the surprise was to boomerang.

A little after 2 a.m. the Zeppelin L.16 was over St. Albans, the L.32 was near Tring and the L.21 over Flitwick near Hitchin. To the south the L.14 was at Thaxted in Essex and, away to the north, the S.L.8 was near St. Ives. These five aircraft were quietly going about their business, secure in the thought that attack was unlikely when, simultaneously, their lookouts saw a vivid glow in the distant sky. The glow was at their own height and the Germans quickly realized that it was far too great a fireball to be an aeroplane. There was no doubt in their mind what had happened.

The effect was magical. The five airships, almost as one, turned back towards the east, shedding their bombs haphazardly as they scuttled back to the securer skies of Germany.

The dramatic conflagration was also seen by many British pilots within a radius of some fifty miles. The two with the closest view were Second Lieutenant J. I. Mackay from a flight of 39 Squadron based at North Weald, Essex, and Second Lieutenant B. H. Hunt from Hainault Farm. Both had seen a Zeppelin caught in searchlights to the north and were climbing to the attack when, suddenly, their quarry disintegrated into a great ball of fire.

But none of them had seen the aircraft responsible for this victory.

Lieutenant W. Leefe-Robinson had taken off from Sutton's Farm, Hornchurch in his B.E.2c, a little after 11 p.m., to patrol on a line between Hornchurch and Joyce Green. For two hours he droned drearily back and forth but saw nothing. Then, at 1.10 a.m., he spotted a Zeppelin held in searchlights to the south-east of Woolwich. He was at 12,900 feet and immediately gave chase, trying to head the airship off in an eastwards direction. He was about 800 feet higher than the Zeppelin and gaining steadily. His chances seemed good—until the airship disappeared into a cloud and he had to break off.

Dejectedly he returned to his patrol area. It seemed too much to hope that he would be given two chances in one night and when, at 1.50, he saw a glow over to the east, he assumed it was a fire on the ground. Determined not to let even a forlorn hope pass, he headed in its direction and, after fifteen minutes, saw that the glow was, in fact, a Zeppelin held in searchlights. Swearing that he would not allow this one to escape, he lowered the B.E.2c's nose to sacrifice height for speed and set off in pursuit.

As he drew near, he saw heavy anti-aircraft fire bursting around the Zeppelin. Ruefully he reflected that this anti-aircraft gunfire stood much more chance of hitting him than the Zeppelin because the majority of shells were bursting a good 800 feet behind the airship, and all were too high or too low. Dismissing the risk of being hit by the shells, he positioned himself below his quarry, pulled back on his control stick and took his first good, close look at the great, ghostly fish-shape above him. Wasting no time on admiration for the genius which could produce such a craft, he fired his first drum of ammunition upwards from some 800 feet below the airship. He was using explosive ammunition mixed with tracers and was grieved to see his bullets entering the Zeppelin without any apparent effect.

By now, he was completely unconscious of the shells which were bursting around him. He took his B.E.2c out slightly to one side and hosed another drum of bullets along the cylindrical envelope—again without seeming effect.

"I then got behind it," he reported later. "By this time I was very close—500 feet or less below—and concentrated one drum on one part, the underneath rear. I was then at a height of 11,500 feet."

Hardly had the last bullets from this drum torn into the Zeppelin, when Leefe-Robinson saw the rear portion become incandescent.

There were no flames at this time and the searchlights had gone out. For a few seconds the airship seemed to glow red-hot from some interior source.

Then, the flames suddenly burst through, and the whole holocaust began to topple down on to the British pilot below. With the flames scorching his face, he pulled his aircraft out of the way of the falling, blazing airship and suddenly realized his achievement. In a burst of high spirits, mingled with the relief of tension, he fired off a series of red Very lights and dropped a parachute flare.

But this individual display of fireworks went unnoticed. All eyes, both in the air and on the ground, were on the falling, blazing Zeppelin. It was the S.L.11, an old wooden-framed ship. Slowly it fell downwards, to crash at Cuffley where it burned for two hours on the ground. The fall was seen from the ground over a radius of fifty miles and the effect on the morale of the thousands who watched the terrible descent was as magical—if in a different direction—as it had been on the other Zeppelin crews.

No one at that time knew who had shot the airship down, but he was already a public hero in the eyes of most of those living in London, Essex, Hertfordshire and Cambridgeshire. Leefe-Robinson landed back at Sutton's Farm at 2.45, well pleased with his night's work but with little idea of the dramatic effect it had had on the German raid and British public morale. He was not long left in doubt. Public adulation knew no end and the award of the Victoria Cross which followed had the nation's whole-hearted approval. Not only had the Zeppelin menace been successfully met, but the victory had been witnessed by thousands over a wide area.

While Britain rejoiced on what the public confidently thought to be the end of the Zeppelin scourge, Germany was examining the events of that September night in some detail. The Zeppelin crews discussed the awesome sight. It required very little imagination to look up past the ropes and wires to their own hulls and see that dreadful incandescence spring up as if some huge gas mantle had been lit. A few gave voice to the question of whether they would be burned alive before they were dashed to pieces on the ground, as there seemed but a remote chance that the fall of a Zeppelin would blow the flames away from the gondolas. Some even vowed that they would jump and make sure of a clean death.

Then, as the days passed, so the discussions took on a less personal meaning. Perhaps it could happen to them, but surely the British success had been luck. This train of thought was officially encouraged, for Germany was anxious to try once again for her revenge. The date chosen was September 23rd. This time, eleven naval airships left their moorings bound for England. They included three of the new "Thirties" series—the latest and best of the Zeppelins, the L.31, L.32 and L.33. Mercifully, the crews did not know what was in store for them.

That the lesson of September 2nd still lingered was proved when the bulk of the raiders set course, not for London, but for an area north of the Wash. Only the three new airships made for the capital, and even then, the L.31 and L.32 used the much safer southern approach, coming in over Kent. The L.32 came in over the Crouch estuary.

The crew of the L.31, commanded by the veteran Kapitanleutnant Mathy, had every reason to continue regarding the loss of the S.L.11 as ill-fortune. To the seasoned crew members it seemed like old times as they passed over Tunbridge Wells, dropped a few bombs in the Kenley area, had a little trouble from searchlights but successfully blanketed them by dropping flares. Unchallenged, they made their way across London, dropping bombs all the way, between Mitcham, Streatham and Brixton. Over the Thames, and then more bombs in the Lea Bridge Road area, and away from England via Great Yarmouth. The airship had been almost unmolested. It was a model raid. The L.33, under the command of Kapitanleutnant Boeker, the only commander who had dared to take the east coast route, had made landfall at 10.45 p.m. at Foulness and approached London by way of Billericay and Wanstead. Over West Ham she was held in searchlights and soon found herself in the centre of much gunfire which, despite its general inaccuracy, was not encouraging. Dropping his bombs hurriedly, Boeker then set off on a north-easterly course and, by 12.30, was over Chelmsford.

Among the pilots flying that night was Second Lieutenant A. de B. Brandon, who was patrolling between Hainault and Sutton's Farm. Just before 12.30, he caught a glimmer of an object in the sky to the north and turned his aircraft in that direction. His action was rewarded by the sight of the L.33 and he lost no time in attacking.

Brandon was under no illusion that this would be an easy victory but, even so, after pumping in drum after drum of ammunition, he began to lose heart a little. By the time that Brandon thought that the airship might be losing height a little, he was out of ammunition and had to break off his attack, disappointed that his target had not caught fire.

It was then that he saw a remarkable sight. Not far away was another Zeppelin caught in searchlights. As he had no ammunition, there seemed little point in making towards it but, even as he watched, a sudden stream of liquid fire was injected into the airship from an invisible source close to it. Fascinated, he watched.

The Zeppelin was the L.32, commanded by Kapitanleutnant Petersen, which crossed the Kent coast with the L.31, bombed Dungeness and, after loitering a little, came up to Dartford by way of Tunbridge Wells. As it crossed the river it had been caught by searchlights which it had tried to bomb. While thus engaged it had been seen by Second Lieutenant F. Sowrey.

It was a long chase. The R.F.C. pilot had first seen the airship, away to his east, while patrolling between Joyce Green and Sutton's Farm at 12.45. Even with his throttle wide open it was 1.10 before he was near enough to attack. Steadily he tried to match his speed with that of the airship as he came up beneath it. The searchlights holding it gave it an almost transparent appearance against the black of the sky. With his aircraft nose pulled as far up as it could go without the aeroplane stalling, Sowrey was conscious of the Zeppelin's propellers, now turning, now stationary, as Petersen manoeuvred to try and escape from the embarrassing beams. Then Sowrey opened fire and it was his tracers streaking into the hull which had caught Brandon's attention.

Doggedly he laced the Zeppelin from stern to bows and back again with a stream of bullets. Two drums were emptied in this way. Sowrey reloaded and applied himself to his task once more. He was rewarded with a sudden, meaningful tongue of flame which leapt out amidships, followed immediately by another at the bows. Within seconds, the whole craft was dipping and turning like a huge, slow-motion catherine wheel. Pulling his aircraft out of the path of the falling ship, Sowrey circled as he watched its graceful but terrible final descent. It hit the ground between Great Burstead and Billericay in Essex and burned for an hour after crashing. Not one of its crew survived.

All this was seen by Brandon, but his disappointment at what he thought was his own failure was soon dispelled after he had landed. The L.33 had, in fact, been losing gas rapidly from the perforations which Brandon had so industriously drilled through her gas bags. Boeker had crossed the coast by West Mersea at 1.15 and was hoping that he might make the German coast. His crew were still throwing every movable object that they could find overboard when the commander realized that he did not stand an even remote chance of reaching safety. Rather than crash into the sea, he turned back for England and landed in a field near Peldon. The Zeppelin caught fire, but there was so little gas left that only light damage was sustained. The entire crew survived to be taken prisoner, while the framework of the airship gave Britain one of her most valuable war prizes to that date. L.33 later proved the basis for the British R.33 Class of airship.

The Germans had learned the lesson that Leefe-Robinson's success was not luck, and it had cost them two of their latest airships. There was now every reason to believe that, as far as heavily-defended London was concerned, the Zeppelin scare could be relegated to the history books. Indeed, the German Navy, which operated the majority of the Zeppelins, had received a blow to its morale from which it never fully recovered. More Zeppelin raids were mounted, but London was left alone—except by one commander—Mathy. When, on October 1st, eleven Zeppelins left their sheds, ten set course for the Midlands and north-east England but Mathy, trusting in his own undoubted skill and in his luck, took a different course and, once again, headed the L.31 towards London.

But this time the reception was too hot, even for Mathy. He came in by way of Lowestoft but, by the time that he had reached Ware, was slowed down by the accuracy of the searchlights and ferocity of the anti-aircraft guns. He came as far south as Cheshunt, where he released his bombs and set off westwards, twisting and turning with the skill of a master to throw out the aim of the ground defences.

Among the R.F.C. pilots up that night was Second Lieutenant W. J. Tempest who was patrolling between Joyce Green and Hainault. Before he landed, he was to taste the success of Zeppelin chasing—and to learn several of its hazards.

He saw the L.31 from fifteen miles away, held at the peak of a great white mountain of searchlights. His chase took him through what he described as "an inferno of bursting shells"—British shells which were meant for the airship. Ignoring this hazard, he fired an experimental burst of fire as he approached the Zeppelin head on and another as he passed below it. Then he hauled his aircraft round in as tight a turn as he dared to make at an altitude of 14,500 feet and made his main attack from the rear.

The L.31 began to glow like an enormous Chinese lantern. For a few seconds there were no flames and then, in an instant, there was nothing of the airship but flames. Tempest was rapidly overtaking the Zeppelin as the fire brought her to a halt. He was below her when he suddenly realized that the whole flaming mass was toppling down on top of him. For a few age-long seconds he struggled to manoeuvre out of the way. So close was the L.31 as it passed him that he could hear the flames roaring like a great furnace, even above the noise of his own engine.

The moment of danger passed and Tempest relieved the tension by shooting off Very lights, before yet another of the risks of Zeppelin chasing overtook him. The controls and his cockpit seemed to become magically remote and the pilot realized that he was distinctly light-headed. Fighting sickness, dizziness and sheer exhaustion, Tempest began looking round hazily for the flares on the ground which marked the extremes of his patrol area. It was not until he had been descending for some time that his head cleared. He was a victim of the high-altitudes at which the night battle had been fought and his strenuous efforts, both in attacking the Zeppelin and avoiding its fall, had proved too much for his oxygen-starved body. Feeling very much more in charge of his aircraft, he picked up his flares and came down for his landing—only to meet yet another hazard, ground fog. This insidious gossamer sheet which covered the ground was invisible from the air but all too apparent once a pilot descended into it. Tempest's landing could not be classified a good one by any standards. He wrecked his aircraft and sustained a cut on his head. But it was an insignificant price to pay for one of Germany's latest airships and the lives of her greatest Zeppelin commander and his crew. It was also the last Zeppelin raid on London.

For a while, the Midlands and the north-east of England still suffered attacks, but the successes around London led to the formation of more home defence squadrons and it was not long before even this part of England became unpleasant for the Zeppelins. More fell to the pilots of the R.F.C. and the R.N.A.S. By the end of 1916, some sort of score sheet could be drawn up. Since the beginning of the war Zeppelins had dropped 162 tons of bombs on England, which had killed 500 people. At first, these raids had some effect on British morale and perhaps production was affected slightly. More important was the fact that squadrons which could have been usefully engaged in France were kept busy clearing the skies of airships. The total expenditure of manpower on British home defence was some 17,000 officers and men. Against this, the Germans had lost six airships over Great Britain and others had been lost in accidents and some damaged through the attentions of defending aircraft or anti-aircraft guns.

The Zeppelin had started as an invincible juggernaut of the skies but, after 1916, its appearances over England were extremely rare.

Perhaps there is only one other Zeppelin raid which deserves mention. The awfulness of death in a burning Zeppelin could only be surmised for obvious reasons but, on the night of June 17, 1917, the terrible facts became known. On that night four Zeppelins set out for a timid attack, two turning back before the British coast was reached. One of the others, the L.48, commanded by Kapitanleutnant Eichler, was carrying Korvettenkapitan Schutze, Commodore of the North Sea Air Ship Division. It did not get very far. Over Harwich it fell to the guns of Second Lieutenant L. P. Watkins of No. 37 Squadron.

In the front gondola of the Zeppelin, Eichler was beginning to realize what little chance he stood against winged aircraft, as he desperately tried to outmanoeuvre the British fighter. The first intimation he had that he was not successful came as a brilliant glare lit the gondola from behind. The aft portion of the hull was alight and the nose took a sickening lurch upwards.

The ship settled in a sixty-degree nose-up attitude and began falling, still burning from the rear. Eichler remained calm throughout. Convinced that they were still over the sea, he began calmly to remove first his leather jacket, and then his overalls. Minutes passed and still the airship was falling, still the front gondola was intact. The flames were closer—and so were the hideous screams of those in the gondolas which were slowly being eaten by the flames of the burning hull. Schutze, the Flag Officer, remained immobile throughout, grimly clutching the sides of the chart table. There was no panic. The sounds were the rush of air, bass-note roar of flames and the chilling paeon of those screaming their last breath. The terrible question for those in the front car was how long it would be before they would be joining the dreadful chorus.

The fall took five whole minutes. Still outwardly calm, Eichler jumped overboard as the ground loomed up. Four others followed him. All were killed. The front gondola was still intact when it hit the ground hard. Schutze was burned alive. Another man in the front car, Leutnant Mieth, survived by a miracle, although he was hideously injured. The story of the five-minute fall of the L.48 which he was to relate would have been sufficient to demoralize the entire German airship service—if they had not been already disheartened. The Zeppelin, as a weapon of war, was finished—but Germany was not to forgo her revenge on Britain so easily. She had other plans.

CHAPTER SEVENTEEN

Daring in the Desert

THE MANY R.F.C. successes at home and in France were being echoed in the Middle East sphere of operations. In the Egyptian desert the work of 14 and 17 Squadrons was eased by the arrival of No. 1 Australian Squadron in September, 1916. The many Australians in the unit, which was later to be renamed No. 67 (Australian) Squadron, were soon proving their fighting worth in no uncertain manner. Perhaps the greatest of the many heroic deeds performed by these Australians took place on March 20th, 1917. Four aircraft of 67 Squadron were detailed to carry out a bombing raid on a section of enemy railway just across the Wadi Hesse. This bombing force comprised two Martinsyde single-seaters and two B.E.2cs which, on this occasion, were being flown without their observers. There was the usual shortage of bombs, so each aircraft carried six 4.5 inch howitzer shells which were specially fused to give a time delay of 40 seconds after release from the bomb racks. The Martinsydes were flown by Lieutenants McNamara and Ellis, and the B.E.2cs by Captain Rutherford and Lieutenant Drummond.

The flight out to the target was made without incident and Ellis opened the attack as soon as a train appeared. McNamara followed Ellis down, dropping three shells on the train and one on the railway lines. He released yet another shell, aimed at the railway, but this action resulted in a violent explosion almost as soon as he pulled the release toggle. The fifth shell had, in fact, exploded prematurely and McNamara was severely wounded in the right buttock. The mainplane and other parts of the aircraft were ripped open but luckily the engine was not damaged.

McNamara wisely decided that his best course was to return to base before his wound caused him to faint but, as he turned to fly back to the airfield, he saw one of the B.E.s on the ground. The pilot was standing beside it and igniting a distress smoke signal. McNamara also saw that a body of Turkish cavalry was approaching. Ignoring his own difficulties, McNamara immediately landed nearby and shouted to the pilot to join him. The stranded airman, who was Rutherford, ran across to the Martinsyde, climbed on to the engine cowl because there was no room for him in the single-seat cockpit, and hung on to the rigging wiring of the centre section for support as McNamara opened the throttle and turned into wind for the take-off.

McNamara's wounded buttock had almost paralysed his right leg. The ground was soggy and uneven, and he found it almost impossible to operate the rudder bar to keep the aircraft moving in a straight line. The Martinsyde had just gained flying speed and the pilot was about to take off, when the aircraft swung violently to one side. The undercarriage was torn off and the machine came to an abrupt halt with its nose buried in the ground.

As the two airmen scrambled out of the wreckage, the Turkish cavalry dismounted and opened fire. Ignoring this opposition, McNamara put a pistol bullet through his petrol tank and fired a Very light into the resulting trickle of petrol. This effectively set fire to the Martinsyde and, confident that it would not now fall into enemy hands, McNamara turned his attention to the other problems which faced him and Rutherford. He noticed that the stranded B.E.'s machine gun was still intact and, with Rutherford, made his way across to the aircraft with the idea of opening fire on the Turks to drive them away. To Rutherford it seemed an optimistic plan, but help came from an unexpected quarter. The two British airmen had just reached the B.E., when the remaining shell on McNamara's burning aircraft exploded, blowing the machine to pieces. The Turks were deterred by this and stopped their advance.

This unexpected interlude gave McNamara and Rutherford the opportunity to examine the B.E. In his forced landing Rutherford had ripped a tyre from one of the wheels, broken the centre-section wires, cracked a longeron in the fuselage and dropped several Lewis gun ammunition drums under the rudder bar. The only "first-aid" possible in the circumstances was to clear the drums from the rudder bar. This McNamara did and, still seated in the cockpit, he called to Rutherford to swing the propeller. At first there seemed no life in the engine but, after several swings, it fired and Rutherford sprang into the observer's cockpit while McNamara turned the aircraft into wind.

By this time, the Turks had realized what was happening and were galloping down towards the B.E. The sogginess of the ground almost proved McNamara's undoing for a second time. Three times the B.E. bogged down and could be freed only by violent revving of the engine. The Turks were almost near enough to throw stones at the aeroplane before it finally staggered into the air.

The bombing operation had been made from an airfield known as Kilo 143, which was some 70 miles distant from the scene of the crash-landing. It was not until he was safely in the air and setting course for Kilo 143 that McNamara realized how much blood he had lost from his wound and how faint he felt. Several times he almost lost consciousness and had to revive himself by pushing his head to one side into the cool air of the slipstream. In this manner he covered the 70 miles back to the airfield safely and made a good landing. At last, he and Rutherford were safe.

There was little doubt in the minds of the men of 67 Squadron that McNamara's action of going to Rutherford's rescue, despite his own serious wound, and his subsequent organization of the escape from the Turks was worthy of recognition. They were not to be disappointed. On June 8th, 1917, the *London Gazette* carried the following announcement:

His Majesty the King has been graciously pleased to approve of the award of the Victoria Cross to . . . Lieutenant Frank Hubert McNamara, No. 67 (Australian) Squadron, Royal Flying Corps.

A conspicuous deed had been rewarded in an equally conspicuous manner and McNamara who, during the Second World War rose to the rank of Air Vice-Marshal, became the first Australian airman to receive this highest award, and the only one to receive it during the First World War.

Further east, in Mesopotamia, the advance which had followed the capture of Baghdad continued and No. 30 Squadron found the tempo of their work increasing. They were aided by No. 68 Squadron which had been sent straight from their training in Northumberland to this inhospitable area and, as a consequence, suffered so much ill health that, for many months, they were unable to contribute much to the war effort.

By late 1917, the R.F.C. were beginning to enjoy air supremacy but did not always find their reconnaissance or bombing tasks could be performed without difficulty. On October 31st, for instance, 1 Corps were about to attack on the Tigris front, and six Martinsydes, led by Lieutenant F. Nuttall, were sent to bomb Kifri aerodrome on the Diyala front as a diversionary measure. As they came in to the attack, an enemy aircraft took off and engaged one of the B.E.2cs of the British force. The pilot, Lieutenant A. P. Adams, his aircraft heavily laden with bombs, was unable to take sufficient evasive action and received tremendous punishment. With his engine useless, he had no option but to land in an area close by some Turkish troops. Nuttall saw Adams's predicament and, ignoring the danger of the troops, flew down to rescue the other pilot. As he touched down, Adams was busy destroying his aircraft. By the time he had finished this task and had half run, half stumbled across to Nuttall, the line of retreat was cut off by Turkish troops. A few brief bursts from a machine gun soon dispersed this hazard and, with Adams clinging to one wing and the fuselage, Nuttall took off again and reached his base safely.

Two other aircraft were lost in this attack. One, flown by Lieutenant J. B. Welman, was forced down on Kifri itself, with its pilot wounded. Welman was taken prisoner. Another Martinsyde, flown by Lieutenant C. Cox, was hit by anti-aircraft fire and had to be crash-landed eighteen miles inside enemy territory. The pilot reached British lines on foot, constantly eluding Turkish patrols, in the creditable time of six and three-quarter hours.

A little later, No. 72 Squadron helped to swell the R.F.C. effort in this area. The work in Mesopotamia reached its climax on the night of March 31st, 1918. Sudden gales lashed through the whole of the Euphrates area, hangars and tents were blown down and camps flooded. Kite balloons and aircraft were blown away. Three aircraft were wrecked and seven others damaged. It could well have been a severe blow to the R.F.C., but Nature had left her somewhat violent intervention too late as far as Turkey was concerned. The war in Mesopotamia was over. Turkey had capitulated. It was, appropriately enough, the end of an era for the Royal Flying Corps for, on April 1st, the R.F.C. became the Royal Air Force.

* * *

Above, the Bristol Fighter proved invaluable in the closing stages of the war, but not until hard-earned experience had taught crews not to rely solely on the rear armament. *Below*, Lord Trenchard and, on his left, Prince Henry watch a display at the Hendon aerial pageant in July, 1920

Fifty years on: officers and men of No 1 Squadron R.A.F. (Fighter Command) with their S.E.5a aircraft on the Western Front in July, 1918, and, *below*, with Hunter jets at R.A.F. El-Adem during the R.F.C.'s Golden Jubilee celebrations in May, 1962

There remained one other area in the Middle East where the R.F.C. was to distinguish itself, and this was in Macedonia. Macedonia was split between Serbia, Romania, Bulgaria and Greece when the War started. Serbia and Bulgaria were by no means happy with this arrangement and so it was easy for Germany to push Bulgaria into the war, thereby facilitating the supply of ammunition to Turkey. British troops first landed at Salonika on October 5th, 1915, at the request of the Greek Government and, on October 14th, Britain declared war on Bulgaria.

Both France and Germany already had aircraft units in the area and when it was decided to swell their numbers with British machines the War Office declared that these should come from the Middle East Brigade. The first British air unit, No. 17 Squadron under Major E. N. Fuller, did not arrive until July, 1916, when it made its base at Mikra Bay. It was later joined by No. 47 Squadron, under Major C. C. Wigram.

There was little call for bombing support for the fighting in this region and, ostensibly, all that the R.F.C. had to do was reconnaissance work. Nevertheless, the air war in Macedonia soon took on a colourful character, heightened, no doubt, by the romantic nature of the surrounding countryside and of the peoples engaged in the Balkan war. The R.F.C. had often been used, both in the Middle East and in France, to drop secret agents behind the lines, and this task was also performed in Macedonia. On December 10th, Lieutenant W. S. Scott of 17 Squadron was detailed to fly a Greek observer to the Drama area and there find a suitable landing ground for the dropping of secret agents. This he did and, on the return flight, was set upon by a German aircraft which he promptly shot down. One week later, Scott took off again, this time carrying a secret agent, found the landing ground in the Drama Valley and, despite a thick layer of mist, landed safely, unloaded his passenger, watched him disappear in the suitably mysterious swirls of mist and took off for base again without incident. Scott repeated this ferry trip on several other occasions.

But it was in air-to-air combats that the Macedonian campaign was so rich. Two pilots quickly rose to prominence, one of them English and the other German. The English pilot was Captain G. W. Murlis-Green who, on December 13th, 1916, opened his score by shooting down an enemy two-seater near Fort Rupel. On January 4th, he shot down another over the British lines and yet another victory, this time shared with Lieutenant F. G. Saunders, was achieved over the British airfield at Lahana. Murlis-Green normally flew a B.E.12 aircraft. This was a modified B.E.2c machine hurriedly converted into a single-seat fighter by the Royal Aircraft Factory during the time that the R.F.C. in France was crying out for aircraft to beat the "Fokker scourge". The B.E.12 shared the B.E.2c's inherent stability, and thus was practically useless as a fighter. It was discarded in France after very little use.

The German ace of this campaign was Lieutenant von Eschwege. The German aircraft were undoubtedly far superior to the British machines and von Eschwege's list of victories grew rapidly. On February 18th, 1917, Murlis-Green decided to tackle von Eschwege in the hopes of shooting him down. Accompanied by Lieutenant J. C. F. Owen flying another B.E.12, he flew over Drama airfield where the enemy fighter aircraft were stationed and, entering the spirit of the challenge, von Eschwege took off alone to meet the British pilot. Murlis-Green dived for the initial attack but his guns jammed and he was forced to break off the combat to try and rectify the fault.

Owen continued the fight but anti-aircraft fire came up from the ground, the B.E.12 was hit and Owen forced to land. Von Eschwege immediately flew down and landed nearby so that he could complete what he regarded as his victory by personally taking the British pilot into custody. As the German ace approached on foot, Owen was busy setting his aircraft alight. He held von Eschwege at pistol point until he had completed this task to his satisfaction and then, when the arrival of Bulgarian soldiers made further resistance fruitless, capitulated. He was later tried by a Bulgarian court-martial for having the effrontery to destroy his aircraft. His action was strenuously defended by von Echwege, who still maintained that Owen had fallen to his guns and not to anti-aircraft fire from the ground.

Thus, von Eschwege was still able to give his unwelcome attention to British aircraft and his toll of 17 and 47 Squadron machines mounted steadily. But his career was to come to an untimely end.

German pilots were fond of attacking British observation balloons. There were few fighter aircraft available to give these adequate protection, so the balloons were extremely easy targets and there was little risk in attacking them. Balloon attacks reached an all time high during October, 1917, and the men of No. 17 Balloon Section determined to attempt to do something themselves to stop or, at least, lessen these attacks. A balloon which had reached the end of its useful life was inflated and the observation basket filled with 500 lb of explosives. These were packed with detonators from which wires ran down the main cable to contacts on the ground.

This formidable trap was first sent aloft when a German aircraft was reported to be approaching on November 21st. The unmanned balloon, which must have appeared to the German as a special test rig, was an irresistible target. The German fighter circled round for a few moments and then dived in a leisurely manner to the attack. Down on the ground one of the men from the balloon section waited patiently by the switch. He judged his moment carefully and then completed the electrical circuit. The result was both spectacular and gratifying. The basket and balloon erupted violently into an orange fireball and the German fighter was enveloped in the resulting smoke. Within a few seconds, parts of aeroplane were seen tumbling earthwards. The German machine had obviously broken up with the force of the blast.

The fuselage section, with the body of the pilot still strapped in his cockpit, fell nearby and men from the Balloon Section rushed over to see the fruits of their ruse. When they pulled the body from the fuselage and examined the papers found in the pocket, they found that they had trapped no less a pilot than the almost legendary von Eschwege. At this time, he was credited with the destruction of twenty British or French aircraft and the Balloon Section was, justifiably, proud of its achievement. In the fighter squadrons, however, there was much discontent. The British pilots regarded the explosive balloon as an unsportsmanlike trick. To them it was unthinkable that a man they regarded as an honourable and brave opponent should die by any other means than open combat.

During the early months of 1917, the R.F.C. in Macedonia found themselves facing yet another problem in the shape of large formations of German heavy bombers. They were first noticed on the morning of February 26th, flying down the Vardar in a large "V" formation to bomb a French airfield at Gorgop. In the afternoon, the bombers visited 47 Squadron's airfield at Yanesh. As soon as their approach was reported, the pilots rushed to their aircraft and took off in the hopes of making an interception, but the British machines had little chance of reaching the Germans in the short time available. There were twenty-eight casualties caused by this attack; seven were killed on the airfield alone.

The next day, the Germans attacked the British Summerhill Camp. All available aircraft of No. 17 Squadron—seven of them—were sent to intercept, and this time the British machines succeeded in breaking up the enemy formation. They also forced one of the Halberstadt fighter escorts to land. But bombs still fell and 115 British soldiers were killed and 261 injured.

Bombing attacks which achieved such results obviously had to be stopped, but the R.F.C. resources in Macedonia were already taxed to the utmost with calls for reconnaissance, observation and artillery direction. In addition, their aircraft were not suitable fighter machines. Intelligence soon established that the German Bombing unit was No. 1 Kampfgeschwader, which had just arrived at Hudova Airfield from Bucharest after a successful bombing campaign in Romania. The aircraft were A.E.G.s powered by two 260 h.p. Mercedes engines, Rumplers with two 150 h.p. Benz engines and Friedrichshafeners with two 260 h.p. Mercedes. In addition, there was one Gotha bomber and a number of single-seat Halberstadt escorts. It was, in all, a most compact, complete and self-contained bombing unit which used a railway train to house offices and stores to air general mobility.

It was obvious that the R.F.C., with their puny B.E.12 aircraft powered by one 150 h.p. engine, could do little against the might of these bombers. They tried to give the Germans a taste of their own medicine by making bombing attacks on Hudova. In two attacks they achieved little. The only aircraft vaguely suitable for bombing were B.E.2cs and Armstrong Whitworth F.K.8s, and the weapons which they could carry were hardly sufficient to be more than pin-prick nuisances to the Germans, although much damage was done during the second attack when hits were scored on an ammunition dump at Cestovo. Even so, many of the British aircraft were damaged and one, flown by Second Lieutenant D. H. Glasson, was shot down, the pilot dying shortly afterwards from a stomach wound.

In later bombing attacks made by the Germans, the British pilots found that, if they could take off in time, they stood a fair chance of disrupting the enemy plans. On March 18th, the enemy formation twice crossed the British lines but the British aircraft, led by Murlis-Green in a B.E.12, were up in good time and were able to attack the enemy force before they had time to release their bombs. They were, therefore, heavier and less manoeuvrable. Murlis-Green flew up below and behind the rearmost of a group of six bombers, got to within thirty yards of the enemy machine, and fired two drums from his Lewis gun. Most of his bullets found their target, the engines of the bomber began to splutter and it was forced down in no-man's-land where British artillery immediately began to shell it.

A little later, Murlis-Green found a group of five bombers and repeated his tactics with the same success. This time, he emptied three drums and had the satisfaction of watching petrol stream from the fuselage of the crippled machine. One of the German crew members, who was obviously attempting to bring a gun to bear on the fighter, was hit and slumped across the side of the bomber. He was still hanging out when the bomber dropped from the sky.

But it was still obvious that the paltry British air forces could have little more than a nuisance value as far as the Germans were concerned. The Royal Naval Air Service was called in to help and four Sopwith 1½ Strutters and one Sopwith Triplane were sent from the R.N.A.S. Eastern Mediterranean Squadron. These aircraft, together with the B.E.12s from 17 Squadron and two D.H.2s and one B.E.12 from 47 Squadron, were formed into a special fighter unit whose specific task was to deal with the German bombing group.

This specialist unit soon brought results and the German bombing unit began to limit its attentions to targets nearer the front line. On April 8th, they once more ventured as far as Yanesh. The British fighter unit managed to break the formation and one bomber was forced down, its crew of three being taken prisoner. In the aerial fighting that day Lieutenant F. G. Saunders was shot down and wounded.

Whenever aircraft could be spared, retaliatory raids were carried out on Hudova aerodrome or on various ammunition dumps used by the Germans. On April 25th, the two bombing formations, one from the R.F.C. and the other from the German Air Force, met in the air. There was a brief bitter skirmish as the paths of the two groups of aircraft crossed and one British machine, flown by Lieutenant G. A. Radcliffe, was shot down in flames. Honours were even, a few minutes later, when a large Friedrichshafen fell from the sky in a slow, almost majestic spin. The spectacle was heightened by the fact that this aircraft, too, was in flames.

Attack and counter-attack followed at regular intervals, despite the weariness of the overworked R.F.C. and R.N.A.S. pilots. The last attack made on Hudova aerodrome took place on May 10th. On that day, the British pilots saw that there were no bombers on the field and that the large special train which housed the German bombing squadron's support units had pulled out of the railway siding. The British efforts had been successful and the German bombers were no more seen on the Macedonian theatre.

Despite the fact that there were no British aircraft in the region which were eminently suitable for bombing, this type of sortie continued to come the way of the R.F.C. from time to time. It was asking much of the pilots and observers to make these attacks under the conditions which prevailed but the British flyers invariably pressed home their attacks bravely in the face of opposition which, at times was overwhelming. A bombing raid made on August 20th provides a notable example.

Three aircraft—two B.E.12s flown by Lieutenants A. Maxwell and Scales, and an Armstrong Whitworth F.K.8 flown by Lieutenant Thomas with Lieutenant H. A. Jones as his observer, were detailed to make an attack at Prilep. Their slow aircraft were allotted a fighter escort of Nieuports from French squadrons in the region. The take-off was made in the early hours of the morning, and the splendid beauty of the Greek countryside—a view heightened by the splendid sight of the early morning sun just tipping Mount Olympus in the distance—gave no hint of the troubles in store for the small British formation.

Enemy fighters made their presence known as soon as the formation crossed the front line, but the Nieuports peeled off and dealt with these while the three bombers continued their flight to Prilep. There more Nieuports joined them as they were dropping their bombs. The attack was almost completed, when the whole formation was attacked by another group of enemy machines. One Nieuport was shot down immediately. Jones and Thomas in the F.K.8, the rearmost of the three bombers, saw this and Jones managed to bring his guns to bear on the German and shoot him down.

Pleased with this victory, Jones was busily engaged changing his ammunition drums when he felt a sudden searing pain in his stomach. At the same time he became conscious of the whine of bullets. One had hit him but his Sam Browne had taken most of the shock of the bullet. Struggling to overcome the muzziness he felt from the shock and pain, Jones straightened up in his cockpit and tried to sight his guns on the five enemy aircraft which were not attacking. Unaware that Thomas, his pilot, had been shot in the back and had lost consciousness, Jones yelled at him to swerve a little to port so that he could bring his guns to bear on one of the enemy aircraft, which was masked by the F.K.8's rudder. When he got no response, he turned round, to see Thomas almost on his back in the cockpit and apparently dead. The F.K.8 continued to fly on an even keel, so Jones merely returned to his gun and continued to fight back. There seemed little else he could do.

In this way he emptied another drum into the Germans. As he was about to reload, an explosive bullet smashed into his left hand. Ignoring this injury, Jones concentrated on changing drums, using his right hand only, succeeded, and resumed firing. His first burst with the new drum entered the engine of one of the German fighters, which immediately went down. A few moments later, he got another, which also went down out of control. Then another explosive bullet hit his gun. The Lewis gun seemed to explode in his face and pieces of metal embedded themselves in his chin. His whole jaw felt numb and he saw large patches of blood forming on his tunic. Jones wanted to feel his jaw but was afraid that if he did, it would sag and he would be unable to close his mouth.

The gun was now useless, and in a dazed state, Jones looked at Thomas. At that moment, he saw him rise from his almost prone position and slump forward on to the stick, causing the aircraft to dive towards the ground. Whether or not it was a voluntary movement Jones never knew. The enemy aircraft were left behind in the dive and Jones was almost too dazed to realize the danger of the situation. He was sure Thomas was dead but could not grasp the implication that the aircraft was now pilotless.

German horse-lines began to loom up below and, automatically, Jones reached for his Lewis gun to fire at them. He realized the fruitlessness of this at the same time that he sensed the aircraft, its engine spluttering hideously, was coming out of the dive. Somehow,

Thomas seemed to have rallied and appeared to be attempting a crash-landing in enemy territory. Then the engine picked up and the F.K.8 continued to fly. Barely conscious and with the whole of his left side paralysed by the bullet in his back, Thomas nevertheless managed to fly a zig-zag course to avoid enemy fire now coming up at them from the ground. As they crossed the line, Jones gave what he later described as a "blood-soaked cheer" and Thomas managed to raise a smile. He refused to land as soon as he had crossed the lines but flew on another twelve miles to his own airfield where he brought off a good landing.

Despite immediate hospital treatment, Thomas died, after lingering for four and a half months. Jones survived to become, a few years after the end of the War, the author of the six-volume official history of the Royal Flying Corps, Royal Naval Air Service and Royal Air Force during the First World War, an invaluable work of painstaking scholarship which is, perhaps, marred only by the sparseness of the account it gives of the heroic exploits of that August day in 1917.

With their out-of-date aircraft, the R.F.C. were forced to continue the air struggle in Macedonia at unequal odds until the start of 1918 when new equipment began, at last, to arrive from England. Among the new aircraft were a few S.E.5as, remarkably good fighter aircraft produced by the Royal Aircraft Factory. In the hands of experienced flyers like F. G. Saunders, by this time a Captain, these turned the tide of events with dramatic rapidity. On January 31st, Saunders and Lieutenant G. E. Gibbs were flying over a ceremonial parade of troops near Orlyad when an enemy two-seater approached. The two S.E.5as immediately turned to the attack and the enemy machine was sent crashing into the Bulgarian lines.

During the afternoon of the same day, Saunders received a report that an enemy aircraft was working over the lines. He took off immediately, caught up with the enemy machine and, after a brief tail chase, shot it down in flames, the German pilot and observer hurling themselves from the burning wreck at about 8,000 feet.

With the S.E.5as came air superiority for the R.F.C. The slower and older aircraft, which had been such liabilities only a few months before, now could carry out bombing, reconnaissance or observation work with little resistance from enemy machines, which were fully occupied with avoiding the attentions of the British fighters. It was a lesson which was to be learned, time and time again, by the R.F.C. during the course of the war: superior aircraft meant not only the ability to shoot down enemy aircraft; it meant that the air units could carry out their prime purpose, which was to aid the Army, in a satisfactory manner. It meant the winning of wars.

CHAPTER EIGHTEEN

Men and Machines

WHEREVER the R.F.C. flew, whatever their task, the call was not only for more and better machines, but for more men. There was no shortage of volunteers for the flying service but training problems were many and varied. The sudden exodus of the bulk of the R.F.C. to France in August, 1914, had left the Central Flying School practically bare of aircraft and instructors, yet more trained pilots were wanted than had ever been produced before. The old practice of making an officer earn his "wings" at his own expense was obviously outmoded and the War Office resigned itself to teaching pupils from scratch. Trenchard's bold purchase of the Brooklands Flying School on behalf of the War Office—a shock from which officials at that establishment took a long time to recover—enabled quick replacements to be found for pilots being killed in France. Another emergency measure was the conversion of the aerodrome at Netheravon into a C.F.S. annexe where *ab initio* training could be carried out and pupils passed on to the C.F.S. itself for more advanced instruction.

The new units at Brooklands and Netheravon became known as reserve squadrons. By the end of 1914, there was a total of three reserve squadrons but the numbers of pilots they were producing was still inadequate for the needs of the R.F.C. and, in January, 1915, each R.F.C. squadron which was based at home was ordered to give a complete course of instruction to volunteers. This provided another valuable source of pilots and, by the end of that year, the number of reserve squadrons had grown to eighteen and there were eight operational squadrons engaged in flying training in addition to the Central Flying School.

These moves were instrumental in turning out pilots in quite satisfactory numbers but, unfortunately, they were not normally efficient airmen. Little thought had been given to the problems of instruction. It was reasoned that any proficient pilot should be able to pass on his knowledge to a novice: no provision was made for the fact that a good pilot was not necessarily a good instructor. Training methods differed little from those used in 1912 and there were still no dual-control aircraft. A pupil's first flights were made as a passenger watching the movements of the pilot and subsequent flights with the instructor in the passenger seat warily watching the antics of his charge and slapping him in various parts of his anatomy to indicate control movements to be carried out. Obviously, there were few instructors who would let their pupils make difficult manoeuvres when they, themselves, were unable to get at the controls in an emergency, and so pupils rarely progressed beyond the fundamentals of the art of flying during their training. Once a pupil had passed this scrimpy *ab initio* training, he was given no further instruction purely in the art of flying but, instead, initiated into the problems of artillery spotting and reconnaissance.

The majority of new pilots, therefore, were insufficiently trained when they were sent to France, and this fact accounted for many deaths. When the Fokker monoplane was beginning to take its toll on the Western Front, it was said that the first fortnight of a new pilot at the front was the most vital. It was a fact that many new pilots perished through their own inexperience during this period. If, on the other hand, they survived, they had received far more practical training than was ever given them in England and their chances of survival were many times greater.

Even some of the great pilots of the first World War suffered through hasty training methods. Among the great aces was Major James McCudden, V.C., who was credited with shooting down fifty-seven enemy aircraft before his death in 1918. In 1916, McCudden was a sergeant pilot not long out of training. He was posted to a squadron which flew D.H.2 aircraft and, because he had seen other pilots perform the feat, was anxious to loop the loop—a basic manoeuvre which had never been taught him during his training. One day, he attempted it. He pulled back on his control stick several times, trying to get the aircraft over but failed. Then, with one last effort, he managed to get the nose up beyond the vertical. The aircraft tumbled untidily over the top and began to dive. McCudden had achieved his ambition, had looped the loop, but his engine was running roughly and the whole airframe vibrating in a most dangerous fashion.

McCudden had forgotten that he was carrying ammunition drums, and these had tumbled out of the aircraft when it was inverted. The slipstream had blown them back into the pusher-type propeller where they had been scattered in all directions, damaging not only the propeller but the fuselage longerons and the tailplane. Fortunately, the D.H.2 held together just long enough for McCudden to get down safely and to profit from his lesson.

Another hour spent on his flying training could have initiated him safely into the mysteries of the loop and a brief warning should have put him on his guard about carrying loose objects in the cockpit when carrying out flying manoeuvres. His accident could well have been fatal. How many other budding aces were not as lucky as McCudden will never be known.

When McCudden finally met his death it was through another accident which could well be blamed on scrappy flying training. During July, 1918, he was appointed Commanding Officer of No. 60 Squadron. Taking off from Aux-le-Château airfield to take up this new command, McCudden felt and heard the engine of his S.E.5a fail just as he left the confines of the aerodrome. His training should have stressed the importance of not trying to turn back to the airfield, with a dead engine, at low altitude. The thing to do was to pick a spot for a crash-landing straight ahead. It seems that this had not been impressed upon McCudden because he tried to turn back, lost flying speed, stalled and crashed to his death.

The R.F.C. were never really aware of the omissions in their flying training and the many accidents which were directly attributable to pilot error, and could have been prevented, were put down simply to the dangers of flying. But there was one man who was appalled at this state of affairs. He was Robert Raymond Smith-Barry, mentioned earlier as one of the R.F.C. originals, an eccentric character who delighted in terrifying his colleagues with abrupt aerial manoeuvres. He was wilful and a trial to his senior officers but his antics were endured because he undoubtedly had a most active and agile mind.

When the War came, Smith-Barry appeared to take life a little more seriously. He went to France with No. 5 Squadron but, on August 18th, 1914, while flying an R.E.8 aircraft, commonly known as "The Bloater", he crashed. His observer, Corporal Gerrard, was killed and Smith-Barry was taken to hospital with two broken legs and a smashed knee-cap. During the retreat from Mons, Smith-Barry was immobilized in hospital at Peronne. Fearing that he would be taken prisoner if he remained there, he told a nurse to call him a cab and, lying on a stretcher in an old horse-drawn four-wheeler, he was taken to St. Quentin and from there escaped to Rouen in the guard's van of a train. He eventually reached England, where his broken legs at last received the attention they deserved, but they never set satisfactorily and for the rest of his life he had a distinct limp and could only walk with the aid of a stick.

His colleagues in No. 5 Squadron never expected him to fly again, but by March, 1915, Smith-Barry had talked someone into giving him another flying training course at Northolt. He found great difficulty in operating the rudder bar with his crippled legs and those who watched his first efforts at flying after his accident were quite sure that, sooner or later, he would crash yet again. But he soon overcame his difficulties so well that, after a short period in England, he was sent back to France with No. 60 Squadron, just in time to take part in the bitter fighting of the Somme. He was appalled at the R.F.C.'s losses and realized that many of these were attributable to poor training. When he became Commanding Officer of the Squadron a little later, he refused to send some of his pilots over the lines. "They've only seven flying hours to their credit, sir," he said to Dowding, who was his wing commander. "It's bloody murder."

When any staff officer visited the Squadron, he could always expect a lecture from Smith-Barry on the half-trained pilots who were sent to France as "Fokker Fodder". Then, during the last few months of 1916, he set down his thoughts on flying training in a series of letters to Trenchard. He stressed the fact that many instructors were reluctant to allow pupils to take full control of an aircraft because of the dangers involved. He insisted that this attitude should be scrapped because no pupil could be satisfactorily taught in this manner. "The writer cannot see," ran one passage, "why, in wartime, instructors should consider it their duty to carry out their work with a minimum of risk to themselves and the minimum of risk to their pupils and their machines . . . The service rendered to the country is comparable to that rendered by going over the lines and is therefore worth the risk."

But Smith-Barry's ideas did not end there. He stressed the importance of aircraft with dual controls and of instructors who had been taught their art at a special school. He was emphatic that pupils should not just be taught how to fly straight and level and make gentle turns but should be encouraged to place their aircraft in any position and be taught how to recover. This, he believed, was of the utmost importance for scout pilots who would find the experience invaluable when they fought with enemy aircraft.

At the time of these letters appointment as an instructor at a flying school was regarded as a rest period. Smith-Barry regarded this as completely wrong. "The present day pupil is often discouraged on entering the Flying Corps by being regarded as an odious hun," he stated in his third letter written on December 10th, 1916. "He is taught to fly by people who are altogether without enthusiasm and whose indifference is, as always, contagious . . . It is suggested that the mental attitude towards flying of an instructor is reflected in all the pilots he turns out."

Trenchard was among the officers who had received personal lectures from Smith-Barry on this subject, yet he took the trouble to read the letters carefully, decided that they made sense and, in a typically brusque manner, told Smith-Barry to go back to England, choose his own budding instructors and put his ideas into operation, as an experiment. Thus, Smith-Barry arrived to take over the duties of commanding officer at No. 1 Reserve Squadron at Gosport. Although his primary purpose in life was to instruct instructors, the first course at Gosport had to turn out trained pilots from complete novices. The instructors, however, were all ordered to use Smith-Barry's methods and the result was that the course was completed in nine weeks instead of the usual fifteen.

Smith-Barry observed progress carefully throughout the nine weeks. The lessons he learned were summarized in a pamphlet called: *Notes on Teaching Flying for Instructors.*

"The chief thing is dual," he stressed yet again. "We use it to teach every possible manoeuvre from taking off across wind to spinning . . . The object of the course has not been to prevent flyers from getting into difficulties or dangers but to show them how to get out of them satisfactorily and, having done so, to make them go and repeat the process alone. If the pupil considers this dangerous, then let him go and find some other employment as whatever risks I ask him to run here he will have to run a hundred times as much when he gets to France."

There were a few dual-control aircraft at Smith-Barry's disposal for this first course and he lost no time in agitating for more. These he fitted up with speaking tubes—later to be immortalized as the famous "Gosport tube"—so that instructors could communicate directly with their pupils without either stopping the engine or slapping him on the shoulder.

The success and fame of Smith-Barry's school at Gosport grew. Before the war ended a big demonstration was held for visiting dignitaries, who watched with wonder pupils with only fourteen days' training to their credit, looping and spinning. Later, thirteen embryo pilots took off for a demonstration formation flight and only one pilot spoilt the overall effect, landing too far up the airfield and coming to rest with his tail sticking ignominiously in the air.

The Avro 504 aircraft, which made its appearance in 1917, greatly helped Smith-Barry's work. This was a fully aerobatic machine and Smith-Barry exploited it as a trainer. In October of that year the notes which he had compiled from his experiences in tuition were printed and issued throughout the Royal Flying Corps under the title *General Methods of Teaching Scout Pilots*. Thus, his influence was carried throughout the R.F.C. and the calibre of the new pilots being sent to the front was improved almost beyond recognition. The skill and dash of pilots trained under the Gosport system became a by-word. Smith-Barry never believed that aerobatics should only be practised at a safe altitude. "In combat there is no such thing as a safe height," he would say. So "stunting" became the hall-mark of the Gosport pilot, and cross-wind take offs, side-slipping landings or landings made with a final swish of the tail just as the engine was cut in front of the hangars and the aircraft rolled to rest in its parking place—all these feats invariably showed that a pilot had come under the Smith-Barry influence.

The new approach to training had the immediate effect of cutting the wastage rate of new pilots when they were sent to operational units. Britain's final ascendancy in the air can be attributed to many factors but one of them was undoubtedly the methods evolved by Smith-Barry whose basic system is still in use today. Instructors for the Royal Air Force and many other air arms are currently turned out at the Central Flying School at Little Rissington, Gloucestershire. The Charter of this institution contains the following words: "The tradition of organized flying instruction which was born at Gosport in the days of the First World War has grown with the passage of time and is now a major factor influencing R.A.F. efficiency in peace and war."

But the better pilots produced by Smith-Barry would have been of little use to Britain if there had not been a corresponding improvement in aircraft. The machines with which the R.F.C. had entered the war, and most of those that followed during the early years, had been the result of trial and error designs. Only the young Edward Busk had combined the assets of pilot and scientist and the valuable work he was doing stopped with his death in 1914. The handsome, dashing Frank Gooden also played an important part but his non-scientific reports did not always please the scientists who were soon drawn to the challenge presented by the Royal Aircraft Factory.

Among some of the bright young "boffins" who arrived during 1915 were William Farren, who was to be knighted in 1952, and Frederick Lindemann, who later became Viscount Cherwell and Winston Churchill's scientific adviser during the Second World War. There was constant friction between the scientists and pilots because they did not speak the same language. Lindemann and Farren tried to overcome this difficulty by asking permission to learn to fly. Mervyn O'Gorman, the Superintendent of the R.A.F., refused, as he regarded the task of flying as belonging to the professional aviators. He further stated that it would be pointless his seeking permission for the scientists to fly as the War Office would never countenance such a measure.

When, in 1916, Noel Pemberton-Billing launched his broadside against the Government's policy in aircraft construction and used the word "murder", a committee was set up and a scapegoat had to be found. The scapegoat was O'Gorman. Pemberton-Billing's outburst was, in the main, unfounded, for there was no criminal neglect at the R.A.F., but the criticisms had caught the imagination of the public and the press and O'Gorman left Farnborough.

His departure was the signal for Lindemann and Farren to renew their application to be taught to fly which, contrary to O'Gorman's prediction, was granted at once. The scientists—the third was Keith Lucas—thus presented themselves at Upavon for their tuition in September, 1916. Farren and Lucas looked most business-like in smart khaki but Lindemann, who liked to specialize in small eccentricities, turned up wearing a neat, dark suit, a bowler hat and carrying an umbrella. This did not upset the staff at the Central Flying School who merely decided that, because Farren and Lucas were suitably dressed, they should attend the regular morning parades. These two scientists, much to their disgust, had to drill like soldiers, while Lindemann was excused because he did not have a suitable uniform. This amazing scientist stuck to his own clothes throughout the course and even flew in a dark suit and tall white collar.

Back at Farnborough as trained pilots, these three soon proved the value of scientists who could fly. They could hardly be called test pilots because they were not skilful pilots, merely adequate ones, but they bridged the gap between the first "artistic" test pilots and the skilful, scientifically-trained men who carry out the exacting task of testing aircraft today.

Perhaps it was Lindemann who most dramatically showed the value of the scientist-pilot. He has often been called the first man to demonstrate spin recovery in an aircraft. This is a gross overstatement of the facts which must not be allowed to overshadow his true achievement. One of the first pilots to recover from a spin successfully, and to realize how this was achieved, was Wilfred Parke. On August 25th, 1912, he was returning to Larkhill from a lengthy flight when he tried to spiral down to a landing in front of the hangars. Despite his skill, the Avro cabin-biplane he was flying entered a spin. His natural reaction was to try and pull the aircraft out of its dive before attempting to stop the circular motion—an instinct which was to kill many pilots. When he failed, Parke had the sudden inspiration to try and stop the spinning—the jerky, circular motion of the tail which at that moment was whirling around above him. He applied rudder in the opposite direction to the spin, which immediately stopped. This left him in a straight-forward dive from which recovery was simple.

Parke's experience was widely published and discussed but the mechanics of the spin were still little understood and the manoeuvre was regarded by almost every pilot as a "dive of death". Lindemann made one of his first tasks as a pilot that of providing a fully scientific explanation of the spin. His observations of other pilots spinning and conversations with Frank Gooden had given him some insight into the problems, but he needed a set of accurate performance figures on which to work. He had two valuable assets which enabled him to get these figures, a phenomenal memory for figures and a head whose thinking was not befuddled by the sick-making centrifugal force of the spin.

Lindemann made an historic series of flights from Farnborough in the late summer of 1917. He would fly to a pre-determined height and there put his aircraft into a deliberate spin. During the spin he would watch, and remember, the readings of the bubble level indicator and the airspeed indicator and note the angle of the airflow over the wings, which was measured by tapes on the interplane struts. He also made a mental note of the heights at the beginning and end of the spin and the number of turns. All this he would keep in his head until he had regained level flight, when he would jot down the figures in a notebook.

The results of his experiments were eventually published by the Advisory Committee for Aeronautics under the title *The Experimental and Mathematical Investigation of Spinning*. This proved that he had achieved a complete scientific understanding of the nature of a spin and it took much of the mystery from the manoeuvre. Pilots could then be taught why they got into a spin, which made their mental attitude towards recovery much less overawed. Perhaps even more important was his success in working out exactly the forces which affected an aircraft when it was in a spin, for this provided important criteria to which designers could work.

The scientific methods which Lindemann and his colleagues used, both before and after they had qualified as pilots, were inevitably reflected in the quality of the aircraft supplied to the R.F.C. The most notable to come directly from the Royal Aircraft Factory was the S.E.5, a single-seat scout biplane. The first tests on this aircraft were performed by Frank Gooden but at the end of January, 1917, the prototype broke up in the air and Gooden lost his life. This was the price of not fully understanding the stresses affecting an aircraft in flight, for the S.E.5, basically, was an excellent design and, after it had been strengthened, it provided a valuable mount for fighter pilots.

The work of the scientists at Farnborough was also to affect the private companies in a British aviation industry which was beginning to thrive. Among the many designs which were started roughly half-way through the war were the Sopwith Camel and the Bristol Fighter, the De Haviland D.H.4 and D.H.9, which were used as bombers, and the incomparable Avro 504. None of these aircraft would have been successful if it had not been for the individual genius of their separate designers, but the unsung work of Lindemann and his colleagues cannot be dismissed. The scientific facts which they were rapidly uncovering not only enabled the general performance of aircraft to be improved, but allowed designers and constructors to build airframes which were just strong enough to withstand all likely stresses which would occur in flight and to avoid the opposite extreme—aircraft which were unnecessarily heavy. The number of lives saved when British pilots threw their aircraft into drastic manoeuvres during air battles, confident in the knowledge that their aircraft would not break up, can never be calculated.

CHAPTER NINETEEN

Death Comes Again to London

WEDNESDAY, JUNE 13th, 1917, dawned a fine morning in London, if a little hazy. After the costly victory of the Somme, the war had not been going too well for Britain; the Nivelle campaign, an expensive offensive which had brought no compensating victories, had collapsed, there was increasing U-boat activity on the seas and Russia had defected from the Allied cause. Yet, to the man in the street, life seemed little different. The Zeppelin menace had been overcome and, although there had been a few sorties by winged bombers, their punch seemed comparatively puny compared with the onslaught of the Zeppelins in their hey-day. The British at home were by no means down-hearted.

It was a little after 10.45 a.m. that those living on the eastern outskirts of London first heard the distant drone of aero-engines. It was a strange and, although distant at first, an immensely powerful throbbing in the air. Groups of people ran into the streets and gardens to look towards the east, where they soon spotted fourteen small dots silhouetted against the sky—fourteen aircraft, large ones, flying in diamond formation.

No one knew whether these were British or German machines, yet, as the steady, almost stately formation passed slowly overhead on an undeviating course for London, many people were filled with an inner feeling of foreboding.

These people were justified in their fears for, before the noon hour had been reached, 162 dead bodies were to be left in the streets of London, and almost four times as many wounded. In one fell swoop, the feeling of well-being in Britain was shattered. The Zeppelins, even in their most terrible raids, had never achieved destruction such as this.

Perhaps the public could be excused their stunned surprise at the sudden power shown by the German Air Force, but there was little excuse for the politicians. They had sufficient knowledge to have deducted that this type of attack could be expected. The German Air Force had had plans for large-scale bombing attacks on England for some time. Following the fall of the Belgian ports, some of the most experienced German pilots were formed into a unit known as "The Ostend Carrier Pigeon Squadron". Their task was to bomb London but, at that time, the range was beyond their aircraft, which had little more than nuisance value in spasmodic attacks against British coastal targets.

It was not until November, 1916, that the first successful raid took place. In the early morning of the 28th of that month an L.V.G. two-seater aircraft took off from Mariakerke airfield. In the German Air Force the pilot was not necessarily the commander of an aeroplane, and although the L.V.G. was piloted by Deck-Offizier Paul Brandt, the man who took all the decisions was Leutnant Walther Ilges. Ilges must have felt his responsibilities keenly that morning, for he was charged with dropping bombs on the British Admiralty in London.

The weather was on Ilges's side. A slight mist and patches of fog covered the British soil as he flew west towards London. The mist cleared in time for him to position himself over the capital for his attack but, fortunately for their Lordships at the Admiralty, the Leutnant's geography was not good. This fact, allied with the necessity of making the attack from a considerable height, caused his bombs to fall along a line between Harrods and Victoria Station. They fell on a baker's shop, private houses and the Victoria Palace Music Hall.

Luckily, the six bombs did little damage and only ten people were injured, but the surprise of the attack had been a shock for Londoners. No-one had paid any attention to the lone aircraft which could be heard high above. The whistle of the small missiles had hardly been audible above the London street noises and the attack had been literally a "bolt from the blue."

Although Ilges could now see the ground clearly, he was still virtually invisible from below. But he did not realize it and this was to prove his eventual undoing. Several aircraft were sent up on fruitless searches while Ilges, unaware that he was perfectly safe, was plotting a long, laborious course back, to miss known British airfields. His return flight took him south over Tunbridge Wells and across the Channel to Abbeville, where he turned left to fly along the coast. But the long flight had proved too much for his engine and it was missing badly as he passed the mouth of the Somme. He was forced to land at Boulogne and was captured—a success for which the R.F.C. could take no credit at all.

The Germans, sobered by Ilges's failure to return, cancelled any further plans they had for attacking London in daylight. They did not venture over the British capital again until May 6th, 1917. Once again, the attack was made by a solitary aircraft, but this time it was at night. The German aircraft returned safely because the R.F.C. had little chance of intercepting it in darkness, but the effect of the raid had little more than nuisance value, as did the periodic attacks on targets nearer the British coast.

During all this time the German aircraft industry had not been idle. Several companies were busy building giant aircraft with the main idea of bombing London successfully. The first to have an aeroplane ready for service was the Gothaer Waggonfabrik which, during 1915, flew a large biplane, with a wing span of 66 feet 6 inches, and powered by two 150 h.p. Benz engines, known as the G–I. In 1916 this was superseded by the G–II which had 220 h.p. engines and a top-wing span of 77 feet 10 inches. It carried three machine guns and had provision for 1,000 lb of bombs. Top speed was 90 m.p.h. at ground level.

Three crew members were carried in a roomy cockpit which allowed unhampered movement from the front section housing the pilot and aircraft commander to the rear cockpit, aft of the wings, where the gunner sat. The rear Parabellum machine gun could be fired in a wide arc either side of the rudder and, a novel feature, also downwards through a channel cut in the underside of the rear fuselage. The problems of gun oil congealing in the cold of high altitude were overcome by connecting the thin metal casings of the rear gun and one, sometimes two, forward guns, to a dynamo driven by the starboard engine. The electrical current produced heated the casings.

German scientists also provided the Gotha with an effective though cumbersome bomb-sight. Built on a telescopic principle, the sight itself was connected electrically with a dial placed in front of the pilot.

When the aircraft commander took aim through the telescope his movement of the sight was transferred to the dial. The pilot would correct accordingly and, with much practice, a good pilot would soon learn to fly the precise course required by his commander without need of awkward shouted instructions or waving of arms.

Despite some of its modern features, the G–II was by no means a superlative aeroplane. It was frail, even by the standards of that time. The sections of the wooden main spars, for instance, were not screwed or nailed together, merely glued. The ailerons were too small and an extremely wide movement of the controls was necessary to produce a small, sluggish movement of the aircraft. The aircraft was intolerant of any small lapse in pilot concentration and the accident rate was high. The flimsy structure could not withstand the strain of rumbling over normal aerodromes and specially levelled fields had to be used for Gotha operations.

But the Gotha II did enable bombs to be carried to London and, during February, 1917, No. 3 Bombengeschwader began forming at St. Denis Westrem and Gontrode aerodromes near Ghent. The best pilots in the German Air Force were selected and began training under Kapitan Brandenburg. The German war machine was recovering from the setbacks of the Somme and morale in "Bogohl 3", as the unit became known, was high. Every man was convinced that he was working for the final, successful revenge against England.

Excitement on the Squadron reached its peak during the morning of May 25th, 1917, when it was learned that, that very afternoon, the raid which they all knew was imminent was at last to take place. At four o'clock that afternoon, the combined roar of forty-six Benz engines throbbed through the air around the Belgian airfields as twenty-three bombers prepared to take off for London. Overhead the sky was clear but a cloud-bank covered the western horizon.

One by one the large aircraft lumbered across the aerodrome and clawed their way into the air. One crashed almost immediately at Thielt. The remaining twenty-two took up formation and set course for England. Over the North Sea the formation separated into three distinct groups. The clouds were thickening slightly, which would not make their attack easy, but the German aviators were secure in the knowledge that their arrival would be completely unannounced. Even if a spy had stumbled across their last-minute plans for take-off, it was impossible for him to relay this news to London before their own arrival.

In fact, the first inkling that Britain had of any attack came at 4.45 p.m., when the crew of the Tongue lightship saw ten enemy aircraft. Fifteen minutes later, the first formation of Gothas had made landfall between the River Crouch and Blackwater estuaries. But the cloud had increased and it would have been impossible for the Gothas to bomb accurately from the height—about 12,000 feet—which they had to maintain for their own safety. The formation leaders called off the attack against London and spread out to make individual attacks against many targets in Essex and in Kent, where the visibility was better.

The Gothas were over British territory for one hour fifty minutes. During this time a total of some 160 50-kilogramme bombs fell, killing ninety-four people—twenty-six of them children. The result was many individual tragedies but, to a nation which had weathered the Zeppelin storm, this aeroplane raid was negligible. During the time that the Gothas were over Britain, thirty-three R.F.C. aircraft were sent up to attack. None of them was successful. Lieutenant G. W. Gathergood, a ferry pilot stationed at Lympne, took off in a D.H.5 aircraft and met one Gotha at a height of 14,500 feet. He successfully manoeuvred into firing position but his guns jammed. By the time he had freed the stoppage, the enemy aircraft was beyond effective range.

The only other R.F.C. pilot to get near the Gothas was a Lieutenant Baker who was ferrying a new Bristol fighter from the factory to France. His aircraft had not yet been fitted with armament and, when he accidentally encountered a Gotha near Ashford, he was forced by the German's fire to land at Lympne.

Royal Naval Air Service aircraft sent up from English bases had little more success. One, flown by Flight Lieutenant Leslie, managed to intercept a Gotha between Dover and Gravelines and attacked. He saw his bullets enter the fuselage and engines, which began to smoke. Other Gothas came to the rescue and Leslie was forced to break off the attack, got into an accidental spin and had lost the bombers by the time that he recovered. R.N.A.S. aircraft stationed at Dunkirk were airborne and waiting for the return of the raiders. They intercepted them as they neared the French coast and one Gotha was brought down. Another crashed mysteriously over Belgium, its pilot apparently suffering from vertigo, no doubt induced by a long period spent at comparatively high altitude.

That the German High Command thought these losses acceptable was proved less than two weeks later when, on June 5th, the same Gotha unit made another attack. Again London was spared and the bombs fell mostly in the Thames Estuary area. Again the R.F.C. and R.N.A.S. pilots were sent up in defence of Great Britain : again they had no success. But the anti-aircraft guns did.

Gotha number 660, piloted by Vizefeldwebel Erich Kluck and commanded by Leutnant H. Franke, came down to 9,000 feet to bomb Shoeburyness. Maintaining this height, it turned south across the Estuary and headed for Sheerness. Kluck realized his mistake, too late, as he suddenly came under the combined fire of guns on both sides of the river. Shrapnel from one close burst thudded into the starboard engine which immediately ground to a standstill. The asymmetry thus caused was too much for the feeble controls to correct and Kluck, after struggling with his controls for a few futile seconds, switched off the port engine so that, at least, he would be able to glide down to the water below. He was too late.

While he had been attempting one-engined flight, the good port engine had pulled the port wing up and round, and the nose dropped. By the time that Kluck had shut down this engine also, the Gotha was in a large, ungainly nose-down spin. While the gunner and aircraft commander hung on grimly to prevent themselves from being thrown out, Kluck strove to right the aircraft. He was unsuccessful. The Thames Estuary continued to revolve sickeningly below and grow visibly nearer.

Kluck, Franke and Unteroffizier Georg Schumacher, the gunner, had to endure this motion and the thought of certain death for 4½ minutes. Then the aircraft smashed into the water, still nose down. Miraculously, Franke and Schumacher survived, although the former lived for only a short time. Kluck was killed instantly.

The rest of the formation returned safely to Belgium. The Germans regarded the operation as a success but, by Zeppelin standards, the raid was puny. Thirteen people had been killed and damage was negligible. Perhaps the unremarkable results of these two aeroplane raids could excuse the feeling that all was well in Britain, but the fact that in neither raid had the defending aircraft been anything more than privileged spectators should have warned the Government that, when this German Squadron made a determined effort to reach the capital, casualties and damage would be high. But no one seemed worried. It was left to the Germans themselves to bring this point home, on June 13th.

Eighteen Gotha bombers took off from St. Denis Westrem and Gontrode during the morning and set course for the Crouch Estuary on the Essex coast. While some miles out to sea, one aircraft detached itself and steered for Margate. Over Foulness Island three more peeled off and made attacks in the Thames Estuary area, while the remaining fourteen throbbed inexorably on towards London. At a height of 14,000 feet they had little to fear from anti-aircraft guns and, as fighter aircraft could expect no help from the ground, it was largely a matter of luck whether they met airborne opposition or not.

Passing over Wickford and Brentwood, they approached the outskirts of the city from the north-west. No bombs had been dropped by this main formation and, to the staff at G.H.Q., Home Forces, it was obvious that the main onslaught, this time, was being reserved for the capital. Not until the formation was over East Ham did the first bomb whistle earthwards. It exploded in the air and did no damage. Another followed and fell in Park Avenue, East Ham, but did not explode. Six others fell in the same area but did no damage. Then one solitary bomb fell on the Royal Albert Docks, killing eight men and causing considerable damage. This was but a prelude to the devastation which was to follow.

The raiders were approaching the City and, at 11.40, were over Liverpool Street Station. Two minutes later, no fewer than seventy-two bombs had fallen and each had hit inside a circle of one mile radius round the station. Three people were trapped in a railway coach which caught fire, and were burned to death. Thirteen others were killed elsewhere on the station.

In Fenchurch Street, a 50 kilogramme bomb burst when it hit the top of a ten-storey building, killing ten people. At Upper North Street School, Poplar, where the children had been taken to the ground floor for safety, fifteen of sixty-four children were killed by a direct hit from another 50 kilogramme bomb. After this attack the enemy formation split up and made further individual attacks, spread uniformly inside a district bordered by Barking, Bermondsey, Aldgate and Hoxton. As the air cleared of the throbbing sound of German engines, so it was filled with the noise of British aircraft searching—for the most part unsuccessfully—for the intruders. But the hard-pressed public were not educated in aircraft recognition and could not tell friend from foe. How could Britain's armed forces leave those at home in such a vulnerable position, even in broad daylight, they asked.

On this occasion, one pilot of the R.N.A.S. was able to bring his guns to bear on an enemy machine but had to break off when the Lewis jammed. The R.F.C. were more successful and several pilots made contact with the enemy. A Bristol Fighter, belonging to No. 35 Training Squadron and flown by Captain C. W. E. Cole-Hamilton from Northolt, met three enemy machines flying eastwards over Ilford. He flew into position for his gunner, Captain Keevil, to attack but return fire from the raiders killed Keevil. Other aircraft which made visual contact with the enemy reported either that the bombers outflew or outclimbed them, or that their own fire had little effect. No German aircraft was shot down.

When the grisly business of working out British casualties had been completed, the total was 594 killed and injured in the one raid—almost as many as the casualties of all the Zeppelin raids of 1915 added together. The press echoed the public's indignation in asking where were the aircraft supposed to be defending Britain. The War Office, of course, knew the answer. Britain had an excellent anti-Zeppelin defence in the stable aircraft which had been used so successfully against these lighter-than-air craft. But now, it needed speedy, manoeuvrable single-seat fighters, and these were all serving in France. It made the obvious move and brought back two squadrons—Nos. 56 and 66. These squadrons did not prove very effective in a raid on Harwich on July 4th and were sent back to France where they were sorely needed.

The Gothas returned to London on July 7th, and this time more R.F.C. aircraft made contact but the raiders seemed strangely impervious to machine gun fire. The wide span of the bombers was not appreciated by the British airmen, who misjudged their range when attacking.

Captain J. B. McCudden, a man who was soon to be one of Britain's leading aces on the Western Front, met a formation of bombers returning from London over Southend. His story illustrates the punishment which the bombers were able to absorb in spite of their flimsy structure.

"I attacked the rear machine of the formation," McCudden said. "I fired a single drum at a range of fifty yards without apparent effect. I changed drums and dived again at right angles to the enemy aircraft and fired another single drum at close range, again with apparently no effect. I changed drums and then dived at the enemy at right angles, passed over it and did a quick turn in from the other side and fired a drum at close range. I observed my tracer entering the wings of the enemy machine but it went straight on and took no notice."

By this time McCudden had used all his ammunition and had been with the bomber for twenty-five minutes. Then, seeing some Sopwith Scouts and Camels following the enemy formation, he deliberately positioned himself as a sitting target in the rear to draw the enemy fire while the other fighters attacked, but the enemy carried on, apparently unscathed.

Captain J. Palethorpe and Airman A. G. James, flying a D.H.4 from Martlesham Heath, encountered a large formation near Rochford. Palethorpe made a beam attack on the leading aircraft on the starboard side, firing with his own guns while James was standing up shooting over the top of the wing. Both saw their shots going home, then one of Palethorpe's guns jammed. He tried to clear it but could not. Refusing to break off the combat, he positioned his D.H.4 on the other side of the enemy formation so that James could fire, which he did, although under fire from three of the enemy machines. Still the Gothas seemed unmarked.

Palethorpe then felt a tingling in his left hip and looked down to see his boots filling with blood from the wound. Worried that he might lose consciousness through loss of blood, he finally broke off the combat and dived for the ground, landing at Rochford. There had been little visible damage to the enemy aircraft, but Palethorpe's own machine was badly shot up.

But success did come to Second Lieutenants F. A. D. Grace and G. Murray, pilot and observer respectively of an Armstrong Whitworth fighter of No. 50 Home Defence Squadron. On patrol between the

Rivers Crouch and Blackwater, they spotted some Gotha bombers on their homeward journey. They attacked several of them without success and found themselves under heavy fire from the enemy. Grace then saw one straggler bomber some way below and made for this. It was not flying as fast as the others and seemed to have engine trouble. The Armstrong Whitworth had little trouble in overtaking this aircraft and Grace manoeuvred into position, to the right of the enemy and a little above, as Murray opened fire. Black smoke streamed from the centre section and the Gotha dived into the sea, the starboard wing crumpling as it hit. Grace circled as he watched two of the crew climb out to the port wing of the rapidly-sinking aeroplane, and fired Very lights to try and attract attention to the spot. Shortage of fuel caused him to leave and the bomber sank soon afterwards. Two other bombers were brought down by aircraft of the Royal Naval Air Service as they flew back over the North Sea.

Slowly the British successes in interception were mounting but the pilots still had many difficulties. They could never be sure when the enemy were coming and, when the warning came, took a considerable time to reach the height used by the bombers. Then it was largely a matter of luck as to whether they had chosen the right spot to meet the Gothas. Although those on the ground had little difficulty in piecing together an overall picture of how the attack was developing, it was quite another matter to relay this information to those in the air. Not surprisingly, the fighters had most of their successes when the bombers were on their way home. The Gothas did not carry enough fuel to make wide deviations from the course back to Belgium and the British machines could lie in wait. Over a period, this caused losses which gave the Germans some embarrassment and, as a long-term policy, it was one way to deter the bombers—but the hard-pressed Londoner who still had to endure the attacks could not find this policy very satisfying.

The British fighters were further hampered by over-enthusiastic anti-aircraft gunners. During a raid on July 22nd, many pilots complained of being shot at by British guns. Lieutenant D. F. Holden was shot at over Southend and protested in his report. "The coloured rings are perfectly distinct on the machine," he grumbled. At least six other cases of individual British aircraft or formations being fired on by British guns were reported on this occasion.

Despite these difficulties, it seemed that the fighters were being successful as deterrents. Weeks passed and, although there were raids around the east coast and Thames Estuary, the bombers did not return to London. Fortunately, G.H.Q. Home Defence did not regard this as a victory for, during this lull, the Germans were practising for further onslaughts against the British capital. If reaching it in daylight was proving too costly, then they would attack by night. They had set themselves a difficult task. The stodgy manoeuvrability of the Gotha by day was irksome: at night it became dangerous. Night flying had been a hazardous business from the start and had not improved very much during the war. There were still no adequate instruments and many aeroplanes tumbled mysteriously out of the sky as their pilots became hopelessly disorientated. Yet the Germans persevered.

During this period the British Home Defences were being reorganized in order to deal better with daylight raids. Major-General E. B. Ashmore, an artillery officer who had served with the R.F.C. in France, was given charge of all ground defences in south-east England over an area stretching from Portsmouth to Harwich. The defending aeroplanes were placed under Brigadier-General T. C. R Higgins and, as the number of Home Defence squadrons grew, so the Home Defence Wing became the VI Brigade.

This reorganization was just getting under way and was well able to cope with the daylight raids, when the Germans began their night offensive. Once again, the defenders found themselves useless and when, on the night of September 3rd, an attack on the Naval barracks at Chatham killed 130 men and one woman, the public again began to look askance at Britain's air defence.

Again the R.F.C. and other ground forces changed their techniques to combat the night raiders. The manoeuvrable, spirited aircraft used in daytime were thought to be far too dangerous to fly at night, but Major G. Murlis-Green, recently returned from his successes in Macedonia, sought special permission to try his day fighter out at night. Lieutenant C. C. Banks of No. 44 Squadron joined him and, on the night of September 3rd, these two took off to try and intercept the enemy. Their departure was watched with foreboding by their colleagues who fully expected them to crash. They did not crash but returned safely. They had seen no enemy aircraft but had demonstrated that, with vigilance, day fighters could be used at night. It did not take long for the remaining day fighter pilots to follow suit and the number of aircraft which could be put up on defensive patrols at night was greatly increased.

Shooting the enemy down, however, was another matter. There was still the problem of being in the right place at the right time and the additional difficulty of poor visibility. Raids were normally carried out only when there was a full moon. Even so, a fighter had to be extremely close to a bomber before it could be seen and any sudden movement on the part of the quarry could mean its escape.

For months the only success went to the anti-aircraft guns. A binaural listening system had been used for gun-ranging in France for some time and this was now brought in to help the anti-aircraft gunners. Listening posts were set up throughout south-east England. The distinctive throb of the Gotha engines were easy to pick out and the listening posts, manned for the most part by blind people, were able to provide reasonably accurate figures for range and distance to help searchlight and gun crews.

A complex operations room was set up at the Horse Guards Parade headquarters of the London Air Defence Area, and the staff there soon became adept at assessing the overall development of a raid. Even minor improvements resulted in more successes for the anti-aircraft guns. Orders to synchronize all watches, for instance, ensured instantaneous firing from several different sites.

The Germans kept pace with developments in London. During September even bigger aircraft were introduced to the bombing programme, the so-called "R" planes. The "Riesenflugzeug", or giant aircraft, covered several makes or types, all of which had more powerful engines than the Gothas and were more strongly constructed. Most of them, too, were more heavily armed and carried a much greater load of bombs. At first, the giants filtered into English skies in the middle of formations of Gothas but, as more became available and whole squadrons of "R" planes bore down on London, the fine calculations of the listening post crews, who had just become used to the Gotha engine beat, were thrown out.

Meanwhile, the R.F.C. were still struggling to play a more important part in the battle over England. It was the Zeppelin story over again. For a long time the majority of reports turned in by tired pilots who had spent most of the night patrolling, read: "No hostile aircraft seen." Then, a few bombers were seen and attacked, but without results. This run of failures was broken, appropriately enough, by Murlis-Green.

On the night of December 18th, he was on patrol over London when he became aware of a shadowy outline in the sky near Goodmayes in Essex. He gave chase and could soon see that his quarry was a Gotha. He crept nearer and nearer, and then opened fire. Immediately he had to stop because the flash of his guns blinded him. As his vision cleared, he fired again, and kept up his attack in a series of short bursts interspersed with periods of partial blindness. He was sure that his bullets were entering the enemy bomber but then, after one spell of blindness, he failed to find the Gotha again. During his attack Murlis-Green had seen the aircraft drop a bomb and was also fairly certain that one engine had stopped. He could hardly claim this aircraft as "destroyed".

But the Gotha was, in fact, in serious trouble. The pilot had lost one engine but was just able to cope with the difficult task of keeping control. He set a shaky course for the French coast and then became aware that his aircraft was losing height steadily. Over the Channel, the second engine stopped and the pilot turned the aircraft round to try and crash-land on English soil. He fell short and came down in the sea off Folkestone. The aircraft remained afloat and the crew were saved, but when it was being towed ashore, the bomber exploded.

Other successes followed that of Murlis-Green, but they were not enough to keep back the waves of bombers sent over by the German Air Force. It was something the British public had to learn to endure. They learned this painful lesson eventually but, from the mass complaints and outcries which rose from the country, especially London, during the early days of the bomber raids, came one very beneficial thing—the formation of the Royal Air Force.

CHAPTER TWENTY

Reprisals!

"RIGHT NOW—tomorrow at the latest—we must send five hundred aeroplanes to Berlin!" The raucous voice of the public speaker grated its way clear of the background traffic noise around Tower Hill, London, a traditional site for the airing of grievances. The date was Thursday, June 15th, just two days after London had been stunned by the first great German aeroplane raid. Normally, Tower Hill was a debating ground where one would hear the minority view but on this day it was different. A murmur of approval rose from the lunch-time crowd of onlookers.

"We must pay back the enemy in the same way that he has treated our country," the speaker continued. "We must kill his women and children if necessary. We must make five raids for every one he carries out over our country." The murmurs grew into cheers and clapping, for this was the feeling of London. The people wanted reprisals.

Nor was it left to the odd street-corner orator to demand this. In the House of Commons no less a person than Joynson-Hicks was demanding reprisals. "Every time the Germans raid London," he stormed at an unhappy Lloyd George, "then British airmen must blot out a German town."

Nobody stopped to think that perhaps the Royal Flying Corps was incapable of this. The general feeling was that the Government was being far too sportsmanlike in its conduct of the war. If the Germans bombed and killed women and children, then Britain should do likewise. British scruples should be scrapped and the Germans should learn to take what they were giving.

London was alive with rumours. A well-timed spurious report, originated by a German news agency, said that the British Government were preparing to move away from London to some safer meeting place. Another rumour, and it was impossible to trace its source, said that a Royal Flying Corps pilot who had taken off to try and intercept the raiders had been court-martialled because he had been given no orders to defend the United Kingdom. Both rumours were patently false but they had the advantage of circulating among a community ready to believe anything detrimental about both the R.F.C. and the Government.

In the House of Lords, Lord Derby, trying to pacify the country, said that Britain would be playing straight into the enemy's hands if squadrons of fighters were brought back from France to defend England. "As for reprisals," he continued, "many, many more bombs have been dropped behind enemy lines in France than have fallen on England—and what's more, they have all been on military targets."

But this was not what the public wanted to hear. They were no longer interested in the R.F.C. attacking military targets; they wanted to strike directly at the German civilians. Nor did the public want to hear the brutally frank speech delivered by Lord Montagu of Beaulieu who warned that more raids would follow and casualties could well reach thousands. He also stated that the Germans had a right to attack London which was a chief centre for the production of munitions. Finally, he urged the Government to tell the people frankly that they could not be adequately protected and would have to bear their casualties just as those who were fighting in France were doing.

All this was undeniable commonsense, but the nation was in no mood for it.

The Government was also severely criticized for its failure to provide warning of air attacks. This was not a matter of unpreparedness but was firm Government policy. The War Cabinet feared that news of a forthcoming raid would not cause Londoners to seek refuge but would bring them out on the streets in their thousands to watch the attack. There were few more dangerous places than the streets, not only because of falling German bombs, but because of the shrapnel from British anti-aircraft shells and also shells which failed to explode until they hit the ground. These often outnumbered German bombs.

By the weekend following the raid, the Lord Mayor of London had told a noisy open air meeting that he, personally, would arrange for some warning to be given, even if the Government would not help. A few days later, he announced that he would arrange for the great bell of St. Paul's Cathedral to be rung if an air raid was expected, but this scheme was sabotaged from an unexpected source : the Dean of St. Paul's refused permission because, he said, the bell would be ineffective.

The Vicar of St. Peter's church in Dalston had no such worries and made it known that he would ring his church bell if he could be given advance notice of approaching raiders. From Folkestone came the news that a "compressed air hooter" had been installed as an air raid warning.

As London suffered more raids the clamour for warning increased, but the Government remained adamant. It was left to the people of London to find their own answer and this they did. The advantages of the underground railway were realized, as was the fact that raids normally occurred when there was a good moon. A nightly trickle of the timid or sensible few to the underground stations soon became a regular procession of thousands, if conditions seemed remotely right for an air raid. Handcarts piled high with bedding, food, valuables and even pet birds accompanied Londoners to the haven offered by the Metropolitan Line. At times as many as 300,000 Londoners spent the night underground.

The result was a definite saving in lives but, because there was no official warning, people often spent the night there when there was no raid. Difficult sleeping conditions, coupled with forced conviviality, often carried on until the small hours, meant that many were late at work the next morning and production was threatened. The Government saw the danger at last and reluctantly agreed to provide an official warning of approaching enemy aircraft. Londoners soon began to accept adversity and their naturally resilient spirit overcame their fear of this new method of warfare. The provision of air raid warnings seemed to prove to them that, after all, the Government did care about their fate and public morale climbed back to a healthy level, despite the regular sounding of maroons which betokened a raid and the subsequent trek to the underground. Public criticism of the R.F.C. diminished.

But if the public was happy with the Flying Corps, the Government certainly were not. Soon after the first large aeroplane raid, Lloyd George found himself facing an indignant House of Commons in secret session. The political running of the R.F.C. was spared no criticism. The sorry history of the first, short-lived air board was dragged up and the work of Lord Cowdray's Second Air Board dismissed with short, angry phrases. Cowdray had, in fact, been quite industrious in his main task of building aeroplanes, and had even reached the point at which he could forecast sufficient extra aircraft to build up a separate air formation, which would be completely independent of the Army and which could be used for bombing German cities. But neither Members of Parliament nor the public were in the mood for Cowdray's leisurely deliberations. They wanted quick, deliberate action. This was obvious to Lloyd George but, as he looked at the politicians around him, he could see no-one with the strength of character or brilliance necessary for an almost impossible task. He was forced to look outside the Government, and his choice fell on a man who was not only foreign but who had recently been a declared and active enemy of Great Britain—Jan Christiaan Smuts of South Africa.

Smuts had come to London in April, 1917, as South African representative at an Imperial War Conference called by Lloyd George. His arrival had been marked with a broadside of publicity. "Here is the rebel who fought against Britain during the Boer War but who has also been the first successful Allied general in the World War, having driven the Germans from East Africa. Now he is coming to Britain in her hour of need." So ran the propaganda on Smuts's behalf.

Smuts had soon given proof of a cool, fast-working and nimble brain and Lloyd George seized upon him as the one man he could trust to get on with a specific task at a time when inter-Service rivalry and personal bickering was threatening to turn the War Cabinet into an arena where feuds could be settled between Ministers. He invited Smuts to sit in the War Cabinet, quite unmoved by critics who said that it was wrong for a man who was not a Member of Parliament, nor even a British subject, to help govern the country or critics, like Mrs. Asquith and the Liberal Party, who sought to keep old quarrels open and harped back to the Boer War.

Unmoved by this controversy, Smuts accepted the invitation and was ensconced in a luxurious suite of rooms at the Savoy Hotel, with a brief enabling him to act as chief trouble-shooter to the Government. He worked hard and late and slept but little, yet when Colonel House, confidential adviser to President Wilson of the United States, visited London he said of Smuts: "He is alert, energetic and forceful—one of the few men here who do not seem tired."

Thus, it was Smuts who was entrusted with the task of examining, not only the immediate problems of home defence against aerial attack, but the whole future of the Royal Flying Corps. He wasted no time and his first report was ready on August 17th. Perhaps it was his suggestions for a better air defence which impressed Members most, but it was his comments on the future of the R.F.C. which made the greater history. He reviewed the future of air power in these prophetic words:

"There is absolutely no limit to the scale of its future independent war use. And the day may not be far off when aerial operations with their devastation of enemy lands and destruction of industries and populous centres on a vast scale may become one of the principal operations of war, to which the older forms of military and naval operations may become secondary and subservient."

Smuts concluded his report with the statement that there was an urgent need for an Air Ministry to be formed to run both the R.N.A.S. and the R.F.C.

The logic of Smuts's arguments carried the War Cabinet and his report was accepted. It seemed that an independent air force, for so long the dream of many politicians and airmen, was to be accepted. But, over in France, Haig was far from happy with Smuts's conclusions. Even Trenchard, a firm believer in the value of independence for the air arm, thought that the plan was an untimely pipe dream. The R.F.C. was operating well with the Army and it seemed foolish to divorce the two at such a critical stage of the war. Trenchard was afraid that Smuts had been misled by Cowdray's forecast of plenty of aircraft. Extra fighter and bomber squadrons were urgently needed in France for which Trenchard had been waiting since 1916.

Lloyd George, depressed and overworked, left London for a holiday. During his absence, the War Cabinet was assailed with doubts. The wisdom of changing the constitution of the R.F.C. in mid-war was critically questioned but, despite this, Smuts's proposals passed successfully through Parliament.

As Trenchard had feared, Smuts had not been aware of the critical shortage of aircraft and did not learn of this until he met Trenchard after the measures to form an independent air force had been taken. When Smuts learned of this shortage he was worried, but it was too late to stop the moves which he had started. Perhaps this was, for Britain, a fortunate mistake. If there had been no independent air force in Britain by the end of the First World War, it is doubtful whether there would have been sufficient incentive to form one during the inter-war years. Britain could well have entered World War Two with an air arm which was either twenty years out of date in its conception, or which was still newly forming and suffering the inevitable teething troubles.

As the year 1917 waned to the bursting of bombs in London and the continual shell-fire in France, Smuts worked on to put his accepted proposals into action, seemingly oblivious of the controversy which continued to storm about the changes. Details of discipline, Pay Warrant and King's Regulations for the independent air arm were discussed, and the words, "Royal Air Force" were used for the first time. The Air Force Bill was introduced to Parliament and received Royal Assent on November 29th. On January 2nd, 1918, an Order in Council was issued stating that the Air Council would be brought into being the next day. At last, there was a unified air command—but there was anything but unity at the embryonic Air Ministry.

Cowdray had confidently expected to be appointed Air Minister, and the fact that he received no inkling to the contrary from Lloyd George seemed to confirm this. He learned the truth from an unexpected source. One morning, the Northcliffe newspapers carried an open letter from Lord Northcliffe to Lloyd George which revealed that the Prime Minister had, without saying a word to Cowdray, asked Northcliffe to be Air Minister. Northcliffe's letter was a refusal to accept a post under the present Government. Lloyd George then offered the post to Northcliffe's brother, Lord Rothermere, who accepted. Rothermere then sent for Trenchard to be Chief of Air Staff but, when he came to London to accept the post, Trenchard was angry and dismayed to discover that he was to be part of a plot by the Harmsworth brothers, Rothermere and Northcliffe, to remove

Sir Douglas Haig from France. There followed a night of furious argument between the Harmsworths and Trenchard in which the latter upheld the work of Haig. He finally agreed to accept the position of Chief of Air Staff because he thought that, somehow, he might be able to thwart Rothermere's plans. This was the act of a man who sincerely thought that he was doing the best for both England and Haig, but it was also the act of a man who was politically immature.

More shocks were in store for Trenchard. When he took up his position at the Hotel Cecil, which housed the Air Ministry, he soon discovered that Rothermere had very few qualifications for the task of Air Minister. He was a bungler because he would refuse to listen to professional advice. Trenchard's life became a series of bitter arguments, except for blissful interludes when the two men were not on speaking terms. This state of affairs did not seem to upset Rothermere but it was obvious to Trenchard that the work of the Air Ministry would never proceed efficiently if the two men at the top could not agree. He took a long, cool look at his predicament and knew that there was only one course open to him.

The Royal Air Force was due to come into being on April 1st. Two weeks before this date, the R.A.F. lost its first Chief of Air Staff when Trenchard resigned. Reluctantly he agreed to defer his departure and the public announcement of his resignation until two weeks after the formation of the Air Force.

Trenchard was replaced by Sykes who was, by this time, Sir Frederick Sykes. It was hardly a fortunate choice. Vice-President of the Air Council was Sir David Henderson, the man whom Sykes had previously tried to remove from France by spreading rumours. Understandably, Henderson followed Trenchard in resigning from the Air Ministry because he found it impossible to work with Sykes.

All these moves had been carried out with great secrecy so that news of the internal strife at the Air Ministry should not undermine the morale of the men at the front. This had helped to strengthen Rothermere's position but when Bonar Law, the Deputy Prime Minister, began to look into the events which had triggered two resignations, he made a long telephone call to Rothermere. What passed between the two men has not been revealed but the result was that Rothermere joined the exodus from the Air Ministry. With him went Sir Norman Brook, a member of the Air Council.

The Royal Air Force was just twenty-five days old. It seemed that those who had been against the change in mid-war were to be proved correct. It seemed obvious that those at the Air Ministry were far too busy untangling their own internal differences to be bothered with the many pressing problems of the men flying and fighting in France.

CHAPTER TWENTY-ONE

The Fight to the End

THE ROYAL AIR FORCE was born at a time when Britain was probably as near final and overwhelming disaster as she had ever been before. An all-out German offensive had been expected on the Somme since mid-February. The expectation did not diminish as days, and then weeks, passed without the expected attack materializing. The attack did not come until 4 a.m. on the morning of March 21st. Thick fog shrouded the lines of the Fifth Army, commanded by General Sir Hubert Gough, when the expected battle became a reality along a 44-mile stretch of front between Croiselles and La Frere. The British soldiers had been fatigued by the suspense of waiting and the German attack succeeded. By Sunday, March 24th, a three-mile gap had been cleaved between the right and left flanks of the Fifth Army, and still the onslaught continued.

The weather was atrocious and flying was impossible, but the situation was such that the impossible had to be achieved. The following order went out from the R.F.C. Headquarters on the night of March 25th: "A concentration of enemy troops has been located just west of Bapaume. Every available machine will leave the ground so as to attack this concentration at dawn with bombs and small-arms ammunition and break it up before any attack develops."

The night was wild with hail and snow, yet the R.F.C. did as they were bid. But this was only the start of the battle. Between March 25th and 27th nine new divisions arrived to reinforce the German Second Army. The wedge between the two halves of the British Fifth Army widened and another appeared between the British and French troops—a wedge which could have cut in two the lateral railway which served the whole front. In other words, the whole Allied front could have been separated if the two wedges had not been checked. The war could have been lost at that point. The German advance had to be halted but the Allied armies were unable to achieve this. The task fell to the R.F.C.

G.O.C. of the Royal Flying Corps in France at that time was Major-General Salmond who was not a man given to over-dramatizing a situation. There was, therefore, no doubt about his seriousness when he issued the following order on March 26th:

Bomb and shoot up everything you can see . . . Very low flying essential. All risks to be taken. Urgent.

Every available aircraft took off at dawn. Flying at 500 feet, they roared and bounced their way eastwards. Those pilots who dared to glance down at the ground racing by below saw a clammy, sodden, grey-yellow landscape. But the sky was so thick with aircraft that the threat of mid-air collision gave few opportunities for examining the dismal countryside. Soon, little puffs of smoke ahead indicated the nearing front line. Occasionally, a bigger explosion would send out tails of black smoke and red flame and the debris seemed to settle with impossible slowness.

Then the aircraft were passing over the remains of trenches. Dark shapes lay like huge bubbles in muddy puddles. Some of them moved. Orders had called for "very low flying" and the British pilots ignored the red tracers which were soon streaking towards them and the anti-aircraft shells which went whistling past. The leading pilots pulled their aircraft even nearer the ground and the others followed. A new noise reached the following pilots—the rending sound of crashing British aircraft. But still the swarm of biplanes bore down towards the Germans.

Small-arms fire and bombs thudded down into the masses of grey uniforms at point-blank range, but perhaps the greatest morale breakers were the aircraft themselves. "Several British Tommies flew so low that the wheels of their aeroplanes touched the ground," wrote a bugler of the 8th German Grenadier Regiment. "My company commander, Leutnant Nedee, had to fling himself flat on the ground, but for all that he was struck on the back by the wheels of one of the machines, thus being literally run over."

When the first attack ended, the British survivors battled against the prevailing winds back to their bases, refuelled, re-armed and once more set off eastwards on the nightmare journey—and, this time, there were the twisted and sometimes charred remains of British aircraft to sign-post the way. The weather remained bitterly cold but the continual effort of struggling with stick and rudder bar, necessary to avoid crashing at such low altitudes, made the pilots sweat in their fur flying clothes. Time and again, the R.F.C. treatment was repeated.

That night the Flying Corps messes were filled with tired and excited men. The question on everyone's lips was "have the attacks succeeded?" Confirmation came soon. General Gough telephoned Haig and told him that the enemy attacks were weakening and that the Germans were nearing exhaustion. The Royal Flying Corps had turned the tide. There was no doubt in any mind of the debt owed to the airmen and the message which King George V sent to Haig that night must have had the whole-hearted endorsement of every Allied soldier on the Western Front.

I wish to express to General Salmond and to all ranks of the air services of the British Empire in France today my gratification at their splendid achievements in this great battle. I am proud to be their Colonel-in-Chief.

Such was the achievement of the men of the Royal Flying Corps at a time when there was so much bitter and stupid controversy in London over their future. For those on the Western Front the day of the "Great Battle"—March 26th—marked the birth of Britain's new air force. On that day, although they had not yet won the war, they had certainly prevented it from being lost. Whatever was going on across the Channel meant nothing to them, morale was high and the *esprit de corps* had never been stronger.

April 1st dawned a fair day, with good visibility, and the airmen could not have cared less what fancy name was given them. It was no time for resting on laurels or pondering on the passing of the Royal Flying Corps. Instead, the flying and fighting continued at a fair pace. Bombing attacks had been carried out on Douai station and the nearby German barracks from the early hours. After sun-up there came reports of German air activity south of the Somme. German two-seater aircraft were flying low and strafing British troops while, above enemy scouts were circling protectively. It was a situation which promised some stirring aerial combats—the type of fighting which the British pilots enjoyed.

Among the aircraft which made for the spot was an S.E.5 flown by Captain G. E. H. McElroy, a young pilot who was to notch up an unofficial score of 52 enemy aircraft destroyed before he was killed at the end of July. McElroy arrived in the area at a considerable height and saw three German scouts below him. Confident of his superior position, he dived down to a successful surprise attack.

He picked out one aircraft and succeeded in getting to within 100 yards without being seen. Carefully lining up his sight, McElroy fired. It was too late then for the German to escape. Twist as he might, the German pilot felt the majority of the one hundred rounds McElroy fired hit his machine or his body. One wing of the German scout then dipped, almost gracefully, earthwards and the aircraft remained in a jerky spin until it crashed into a field just north of Ignaucourt.

Not far away, at Bearcourt, Lieutenant Viscount Glentworth of No. 32 Squadron discovered four German scouts attacking two S.E.5s. Singling out one of the enemy, he dived but, unlike McElroy, did not surprise his victim who immediately set off in a crazy race for safety only fifty feet above the muddy, potted ground. Glentworth stuck to his tail, trying to ignore the naked, splintered trees which flashed past his aircraft as he tried to steady his sights on the German. At last, for a few seconds only, the cross-wires appeared glued on the grey shape ahead and Glentworth fired. The German flew straight into a clump of trees where his aircraft disintegrated.

Another ground chase, this time with different results, came the way of Lieutenant W. J. A. Duncan flying an S.E.5 of No. 60 Squadron. He dived at an enemy aircraft which had been firing at British troops. Unexpectedly, the German set off at high speed and low level towards the *British* territory. Just as suddenly, the German landed in a field and Duncan, anxious not to let his prey escape, landed nearby and ran towards the German, brandishing his service revolver, but the enemy pilot had been wounded in the shoulder and was in no mood for further resistance.

Even the slow reconnaissance aircraft had their triumphs that day. Captain F. McD. Turner and Second Lieutenant A. Leach were busy taking photographs of enemy positions when they were attacked by five Fokker Triplanes. Leach turned, grabbed his gun and fired thirty rounds into one of the enemy machines, which immediately caught fire and crashed. Another enemy aircraft then joined in the fight and Turner was forced to turn back. Leach had finished his first drum of ammunition and fired the whole of his second drum at another Triplane which, as the last few bullets were whistling towards it, turned on its back and dramatically fell to pieces in mid-air.

By sunset on April 1st, 1918, the newly formed Royal Air Force had shot down seventeen enemy aircraft. By the end of that week the total had grown to fifty-seven, with a further thirty-seven driven down out of control. Over the same period the R.A.F. had lost forty-seven aircraft.

Towards the end of March morale among the Germans had been high because they had realized that the end of the war was in sight, with Germany the victor, but, by the end of that first week in April, their feelings had swung to the opposite extreme. But this was too early for the British to take life easily or for the Germans to admit defeat. The fighting had to continue.

Back in Whitehall the personal feuding continued while whole gaggles of committees were trying to finalize such details as uniforms, the names of ranks and the names of units for the R.A.F. Over in France life continued much as before. True, the words "Royal Air Force" appeared on official documents but, to the men servicing the machines on the ground and to those flying them, it was the Royal Flying Corps which was carrying on the war.

New and better aircraft were arriving from England. Some brought new problems but most helped improve the fighting ability of the pilots and gunners. There were aircraft like the Bristol Fighter, or the "Brisfit" as it was christened. The first prototype of the Brisfit flew during September, 1916, and by March, 1917, several bugs had been scotched—the engine radiators, for instance, were found to obscure the pilot's vision.

No. 48 Squadron, which had as a flight commander the legendary Captain W. Leefe-Robinson, V.C., took delivery of the new aircraft in France. Great things were expected of this aeroplane. Its armament comprised one fixed Vickers machine gun, mounted centrally under the engine cowling, and a single or twin Lewis on a Scarff ring in the rear cockpit. The aircraft carried, in addition, bomb racks under the wings. For its day, the Brisfit was a veritable flying fortress.

The first operational sorties of the Bristol F.2A, to give the aircraft its correct designation, were mounted on April 15th, 1917, when

Leefe-Robinson led a patrol of six aircraft over the lines. Over Douai they were spotted by five Albatros D.III Scouts led by the German ace Manfred von Richthofen. Only two of the new British fighters returned to their base at Bellevue. Two of them fell to von Richthofen and another two, including Leefe-Robinson, to other German pilots. Over the next ten days eight more Brisfits were lost, although five of these failed to return because they had run out of fuel. The aircraft had, indeed, made a spectacular debut, but not in the way which the R.F.C. had hoped.

Naturally the blame was put on the aircraft. Pilots had had sufficient experience with two-seater aircraft to know that the correct procedure when meeting an enemy was to place the aircraft in such a position that the observer could bring his guns to bear, and this they had been doing. It was left to a young man who was convinced that he should have been made a single-seat pilot to discover the correct way to use the Brisfit and, at the same time, to bring about a dramatic change in its fortunes.

Second Lieutenant Andrew McKeever was a young pilot newly sent out to No. 11 Squadron after training in England on the Bristol. His ambition had been to fly as a single-seat scout pilot and his dissatisfaction led him to muse on the possibilities of the Brisfit's forward-firing Vickers gun which, up to that time, had been overlooked.

It was on June 20th, 1917, that McKeever first had the chance to put his theories into practice. He had just completed an uneventful reconnaissance patrol and was droning back steadily towards the British lines, when he spotted an Albatros ahead. The German saw the Bristol at the same time and both pilots were elated at their immediate prospects. The German was excited because, by this time, the Brisfit was regarded as "easy meat" in the German Air Force. He knew exactly how he should tackle this aeroplane. McKeever, on the other hand, was confident that the German was in for an unpleasant surprise.

The Albatros bore down on the British machine, certain that, as soon as he was seen, the British pilot would swing his aircraft round so that the rear gunner could bring his guns to bear. This was the moment the German would open fire, just as the British aircraft presented a difficult-to-miss broadside aspect.

But, as the gap between the two aircraft rapidly diminished, the

German began to have qualms, for the British machine showed no signs of turning. Could it be that the British pilot had not yet seen him? The answer came suddenly when, a few seconds later, McKeever eased back a little on his control stick, the Bristol's nose inched up and a stream of red tracer leaped out towards the Albatros. Thrown completely off guard, the German pushed his aircraft into an almost vertical dive. The Brisfit was a manoeuvrable machine, despite its weight, and McKeever immediately followed on the German's tail. One more burst from the forward-firing Vickers was enough to ensure that the German would never pull out.

This was McKeever's first victory—the first of thirty aircraft confirmed shot down by this remarkable Canadian while flying Bristol Fighters. More important was the fact that this victory confirmed the suspicions which several pilots had been nursing—that the Brisfit should be flown as a single-seater. The front gun was the main attacking weapon. The task of the observer in the rear cockpit was to keep a look-out behind. Once these truths were realized, the Bristol Fighter, which had started its career by being one of the most unpopular aircraft in France, became an invaluable addition to the R.F.C.'s armoury.

The R.F.C. was also receiving improved single-seat aircraft. The first S.E.5s arrived at the front in April, 1917. This aircraft, designed and built by the Royal Aircraft Factory, can lay safe claim to being one of the most successful aircraft of the war. It was the mount of many aces who, as the R.F.C. and, later, the R.A.F. began to achieve air superiority, were amassing most impressive scores and, somewhat to the annoyance of the War Office and Air Ministry, were receiving tremendous publicity at home. Mannock, McCudden, Bishop and Beauchamp-Procter all used the S.E.5 or its development, the S.E.5a.

The S.E.5a's challenger was the Sopwith Camel, probably one of the greatest fighter aircraft of all time. In the hands of a novice it could be a death trap but, with an expert at the controls, it was second to none. The Camel first arrived in France on July, 1917, and from that time until the signing of the Armistice it accounted for no fewer than 1,294 enemy machines. But it also killed many British pilots. The trouble lay with the Clerget rotary engine. If a pilot forgot to weaken the petrol mixture immediately after take-off, the engine choked, stalled, and the almost inevitable result was a spin towards the ground with too little height for any hope of recovery.

Trouble also came from the torque effect of the rotary engine, in which the cylinders revolved around a stationary crankshaft. The weight of the revolving engine was such that there was a tendency for the whole aircraft to turn in the opposite direction to the engine. Because of this, the nose of the aircraft tended to drop during a right-hand turn and to rise when turning left. In the hands of an expert these vices could be used to improve still further the Camel's tremendous manoeuvrability. For the novice, however, the result of a clumsy turn was a spin.

The Bristol Fighter, S.E.5 and Camel were, despite some vices, winners. They played a vital part in gaining for Britain the air superiority which was to win the war, but it must not be thought that the lot of the British pilots was easy merely because they had better aircraft. Far from it. Cockpits were still wide open to any punishment a wayward climate could provide, parachutes were still forbidden and a large number of aircraft were still fitted with rotary engines with their accompanying stench of castor oil. In a rotary engine the fuel was led to the cylinders through a hollow crankshaft. Normal lubricants would have dissolved in the petrol: only castor oil was proof against the fuel.

The smell became part of every pilot's life, for almost every man had learned to fly on a rotary engine, even if he were one of the lucky ones later chosen to fly aircraft with in-line or radial engines. But it was not just the smell which caused discomfort. The invisible, but very obvious, fumes would blast back from the engine and condense around parts of the aircraft fuselage in an oily smear. The fumes also condensed around the pilot. Some swore that you could always tell how long a pilot had been flying by the size of the condensed castor oil globules swinging on the fringe of his furry flying helmet. The joke that the boys of the R.F.C. never suffered from constipation wore a little thin by the end of the war.

Aero-engines of all types underwent steady improvement over the war years and, as well as increasing speed, they enabled pilots to fly higher, so confronting them with the little-understood problems of oxygen starvation. Not one pilot had ever been medically tested for his ability to withstand reduced atmospheric pressure. Ear ache—

the needle sharp pain of a tortured ear drum which no amount of massage or head-shaking would assuage—and bleeding noses were common. Even those pilots who, at a later date, would have been found fit for high altitude flight found conditions at 20,000 feet most unpleasant. McCudden, in his books, has recorded how he used to cruise over the lines at 20,000 feet so that he would have a few thousand feet in hand when he spotted an enemy below. He invariably felt sick and dizzy after these fiights but never allowed this to deter him from repeating the performance whenever it was possible.

The last eighteen months of the war was the era of the great aces. It is not, as I have said, the purpose of this book to relate their stories. They have been told many times before and will continue to be told in the future. But a history of the Royal Flying Corps cannot be left without mention of the part played by the "aces" in the conflict and a word about the attitude of the R.F.C. HQ and, later, the Air Ministry, towards these men.

No war was ever won just by the actions of a few gifted and aggressive pilots. If you subtract the efforts made by the aces between 1914 and 1918, it is probably true to say that Britain would still have won the war in the air—if every other pilot had still managed to achieve as much as he did. The crucial question is: would the other pilots have achieved as much if they had not been inspired by the spectacular success of the great flyers? The answer is, almost certainly, 'No.'

The 'aces' inspired other pilots, they inspired ground crews, soldiers and even the public back at home. They raised morale everywhere and, equally important, accounts of their deeds led hero-worshipping young men to join the R.F.C. and R.A.F. There are few, if any, of the Second World War aces who will not admit to being inspired to join the Service by tales of the exploits in the air over the Western Front.

Yet, despite the valuable part played by aces, the War Office and Air Ministry have always appeared embarrassed by the presence of these men. From the time of Albert Ball there has been a tendency to cover up the part played by outstanding individuals. No doubt, it is an attitude which stems right from the earliest days of the R.F.C. when, as we have seen, the exploits of this collection of brilliant individualists threatened to bring personal publicity. It was felt that undue publicity for one man might engender discontent among the others and destroy the sense of unity which the new Corps wished to breed. It is an attitude which is mistaken, because publicity for those who merit it has always served far more to inspire than to breed discontent.

Contrasted with this official attitude was the tendency to award Victoria Crosses for "political" reasons—in other words, the award, although it may well have been made in recognition of some heroic deed, was made primarily because it was felt propitious to boost morale at a certain moment. This does not mean that some V.C.s were undeserved, but it does mean that deeds of valour were frequently performed and were not recognized by the ultimate in awards because it was felt that little would be achieved by the award. This system certainly caused far more discontent than any undue publicity accorded to aces.

These are lessons which still have not been learned in their entirety. A student trying to collate the scores of aces from both World Wars will find many differing sets of figures from which to choose. If he applies to the Air Ministry—the one organization which could be expected to provide a firm answer—he will be given a "recommended" list but will be told that this is not official because the Air Ministry do not recognize aces as such.

Despite the efforts of officialdom, the fighter pilots received—and always will receive—the major attention. A more positive approach to newspaper publicity during the First World War could have avoided the impression that the aerial effort was confined to daring young men in single-seat aircraft. We have already seen the vital rôle played by the reconnaissance pilots, but there remains one other type who did not have the opportunity to play a significant part in the war effort until later, and that is the bomber.

Bombing sorties were carried out against specific targets from 1915 onwards. But these raids were always performed by aircraft designed for other uses and were against tactical targets. When World War Two began, long-range strategic bombing was an accepted art which owed its existence largely to the newly-formed, still bickering Air Ministry.

For most of the 1914–18 War, British opinion held that it was morally wrong to bomb cities where women and children might be killed, mainly because Germany had the ability to carry out raids of this type while Britain did not. When it became obvious that Britain would also be in a position to carry out raids of this kind, there was a move in some quarters for discussions, through the medium of neutral Spain, with the object of an agreement with Germany to stop such attacks. The move failed, largely through the correct assumption on the part of those busy bringing the R.A.F. into being, that a valuable function could be performed by aircraft used solely for carrying the war into German cities. This line of thinking did not stem from the "reprisals" call so beloved by Members of Parliament, but from the realization that many valuable war commodities were produced in towns hundreds of miles from the front line, and that continuous attacks on these targets would not only sap the German war effort but might cause fighters to be withdrawn from the front in order to play a defensive role over the Fatherland.

But these proposals for a strategic bombing force were resisted, though not on moral grounds, from yet another source. Up to this time, all aerial operations had been directly linked with one part of the Front and with one formation of the Army. There had been no call for a unified air command. When the line of British thinking on this subject became apparent, the French raised strenuous objections as they believed that the armies would be deprived of air power. They argued strongly that any such force should be under some joint Allied command and, moreover, that it should only be used for strategic bombing if and when the army command could not use it some other way.

Attempts to overcome this stalemate took much time and almost threatened to delay the formation of a genuine strategic bombing force until too late to have any effect on the course of the war. England felt so strongly in favour of this force that, at one time, it was proposed to base the aircraft entirely in England, despite the operational difficulties which would have been caused. But the discussions eventually resulted in agreement and the Inter-Allied Independent Air Force was born on October 17, 1918. Trenchard was appointed Commander-in-Chief but his post came under the supreme command of the Generalissimo, Marshal Foch.

Fortunately, however, Britain had not awaited the results of the protracted wrangling before starting some form of strategic bombing. The R.N.A.S. had paved the way, as early as the summer of

1916, when its aircraft carried out attacks in the Saar industrial area, hoping to delay the manufacture of steel for U-boats. Then, German attacks on Britain in the following summer provided the incentive to create a special bombing force of R.F.C. aircraft. A batch of fifty D.H.4 aircraft, originally destined for Russia, provided the core of the force and, with some F.E.2b "pusher"-type biplanes and the Handley Page bombers of No. 16 Squadron, R.N.A.S., formed the 41st Wing, R.F.C., under the command of Lieutenant-Colonel C. L. N. Newall, who was later to be Chief of Air Staff during the Battle of Britain in World War Two. The Wing came under the ultimate command of Trenchard who was still commanding the R.F.C. in France at that time.

Operations started on October 17th, 1917, when eight D.H.4s of No. 55 Squadron bombed a factory at Saarbrucken. The damage achieved was not significant but this attack did mark the start of a new career for R.F.C. pilots and, from the first results, it seemed to be a career which would not be over-costly in men and aircraft. Germany's ground defences were far better prepared than England's had been the previous year, but the opposition did not worry the attacking aircraft unduly. Unfortunately for the R.F.C., this state of affairs did not last for long. German defences, both on the ground and in the air, increased both in strength and efficiency and soon the raids were being carried out against well-drilled and pugnacious opposition.

On July 31st, 1918, for instance, twelve D.H.9s—a bigger and better version of the "4", set out to bomb Mainz at first light. Three pilots turned back with engine trouble. Of the remaining nine, only two were destined to cross the lines again after the attack.

The first indication of heavy resistance came soon after crossing the lines when some forty German fighters set about the bombers, which battled gamely on. The British leader, however, decided that it would be impossible to reach Mainz in the face of such opposition and turned his formation towards Saarbrucken. Four of the bombers had fallen to the fighters before this target was reached, and the remaining five dropped their bombs on the railway.

The German fighters maintained their attacks throughout the raid, and afterwards, and three more British aircraft were shot down before the pitiful remnant of the attacking force recrossed the lines.

But the German defences were not always as efficient as this and, on one occasion at least, came to the help of the attacking force. Two Handley Page aircraft of No. 216 Squadron approached Mannheim during the evening of August 25th, 1918. The aircraft were flown by Captain W. B. Lawson and Lieutenant M. C. Purvis, and they had been briefed to attack a factory belonging to the Badische company. The two pilots had reasoned that success would most surely be gained by making a very low-level attack, and Lawson, who was in the lead, began his run-in from north-west of the target at 5,000 feet and, ignoring the searchlights and machine gun fire from the ground, glided rapidly down to only 200 feet. A fact which disturbed him more than the anti-aircraft fire was the effectiveness of the factory's blackout. It was almost indistinguishable from its surroundings. But then, as the searchlights swept low, trying to keep the bomber in their beams, they threw the whole area into sharp relief. Lawson's bombardier saw his target clearly and dropped his bombs. Purvis had been following close behind at 500 feet and the searchlights tracing his course did not illumine the scene, but those trained on his leader remained alight long enough for him to carry out a successful attack as well.

The inevitable balloon barrage was also employed by the Germans but this did not cause undue hardship to the R.F.C. Normally, the balloons could be seen well ahead and overflown. Occasionally, however, a crippled aircraft could not rise above the barrage and its pilot then had the unpleasant choice of a long detour in an ailing aircraft—or trying to fly through the barrage. The latter course was taken by Second Lieutenant L. G. Taylor, who was flying an F.E.2b, one night during January, 1918.

With his observer, Second Lieutenant F. E. Le Fevre, he had taken part in a raid on Treves and his aircraft had been damaged. Unable to gain height, and with his engine labouring painfully, he was making his way back across Luxembourg when Le Fevre suddenly pointed ahead. Stretching across the approaches to the town of Esch, was a balloon barrage reaching a height of some 4,000 feet. There was no chance of flying above the barrage and the sound of the engine did not make a wide detour an attractive proposition. Taylor did not know how far apart the cables were but decided to take a chance and fly through them. Le Fevre did his best to better their chances by opening fire on a balloon straight ahead, in the hope of causing a gap in the barrage.

As they approached the barrage, Taylor craned back more and more as he searched for a gap in the cables. He could not see them at all. Then, as he was looking vertically upwards at the balloons above him, he was certain that his luck had held and he was through. As he relaxed, there came an unpleasant sensation of flying backwards. He pushed forward on the control stick to try and gain flying speed and avoid a stall, but without any effect. It now seemed that the aircraft was stationary in mid-air and he could not understand why it did not stall.

Neither of the men realized that they had flown into the cables, one of which had cut into both the upper and lower wings and rapidly sawn its way inwards until stopped, just short of the central nacelle, by the heavy steel of a flare rack carried under the lower wing. It seemed to the two men that they were sinking slowly downwards without stalling—an impossible feat. As they neared the ground, however, the speed of the descent apparently increased alarmingly. No sooner had they made out the vague shape of trees below them, than they were smashing through the upper branches with a loud rending noise. The nacelle drove its nose into the ground and the two men immediately scrambled from the wreck.

They were amazed to see the wings sawn neatly almost in half. The lower wing had crumpled up under the nacelle during the fall. Perhaps the only satisfaction from the incident was the sight above them. The orderly line of the balloon barrage had received a severe shaking and several balloons had been brought down with the aircraft. The two men were eventually taken prisoner.

Regardless of losses, the bombing aircraft continued their raids by night and day. The Handley Page Company had designed a newer, even bigger bombing aircraft, the 0/400, which had the range and load-carrying ability to attack Berlin from England. Pilots were trained and a squadron began forming. On the Western Front the British fighters held almost undisputed sway which meant not only that individual pilot's scores of aircraft destroyed were mounting rapidly but, even more importantly, that the vital reconnaissance work could go on with little fear of interruption. British morale was high.

Even so, the last few weeks of the Great War were by no means easy for the Royal Air Force. Strategic bombing continued and, nearer the front line, the fighters were always busy carrying out ground attack sorties against German troops and retreating convoys. Higher in the air, the many dog-fights were complex and still costly to both sides. On October 30th, 1918, for instance, British Scouts destroyed no fewer than sixty-seven German aircraft—but forty-one R.A.F. machines were struck off the register as a result of enemy action. Twenty-nine airmen were killed or missing and eight were wounded.

Then Germany accepted the terms of the Armistice. On November 11th the British pilots in France suddenly found themselves with nothing to do, while those training to raid Berlin in the new Handley Pages never had a chance to put their theories into practice. For the final seven months of the war the air and ground crews had been in the Royal Air Force, but this had meant nothing to them. They still thought of themselves as the R.F.C. and retained their R.F.C. ranks. It was the R.F.C. which, inexperienced, ill-equipped, yet willing and inventive, had taken the field in France. Many mistakes had been made and many costly lessons learned. Yet, however dire the situation might have been, the spirit of the Corps had never faltered. They had been given a weak, vacillating lead from the politicians at home, but the majority of their own leaders in the field had been brilliant and far-sighted men. It was too much to expect the character and outlook of the Corps to change for the last fraction of the War.

The debt which the nation owed to the R.F.C. was immediately apparent when the 1914–18 War drew to a close but, as the years passed, it became obvious that these men had done far more than just win a war. With demobilization many pilots returned to civilian life. Many had experienced enough of flying under such crude conditions but others found flying in their blood. Some toured the country, barnstorming and giving joy rides to anyone willing to pay. These men helped show the British public the potentialities of aviation. Others continued in flying in more serious vein and blazoned the great air routes across the world to make possible the intricate network of airlines which we take for granted today.

But perhaps the important minority were those who remained in the R.A.F. The Service suffered a few lean years immediately after the war and there was little aircraft construction. Then Trenchard made a triumphant come-back as Chief of Air Staff. Under his firm guidance, the many lessons learned during the war were consolidated. He laid down a strong basis for the R.A.F. and most of the traditions existing today owe as much to Trenchard as they do to the handful of volunteers which arrived in France during the summer of 1914.

And, when the world toppled into another conflict in 1939, it was the costly lessons learned by the R.F.C. and the same unconquerable spirit which they had shown which, once more, ensured that Britain would eventually be the victor.

It is a debt which can never be exaggerated.

Bibliography

The following does not comprise a full list of books dealing with flying in the First World War but merely indicates publications which have provided much useful background information for this volume.

A Short History of the R.A.F.: Air Ministry.
The Romance of Air Fighting by R. W. Anderson.
Grey Steel by H. C. Armstrong.
Testing Time by C. Babington-Smith.
Trenchard, Man of Vision by Andrew Boyle.
A Pioneer in Flight by M. Busk.
The Birth of the Royal Air Force by J. A. Chamier.
Leader of the Few by B. Collier.
Heavenly Adventurer by B. Collier.
The Air Weapon by C. F. S. Gamble.
The Aeroplane by C. Gibbs-Smith.
War Flying in Macedonia by Heydemarck.
To Know the Sky by Prudence Hill.
A History of No. 24 Squadron by A. E. Illingworth.
Over the Balkans and South Russia by H. A. Jones.
The War in the Air by H. A. Jones & W. Raleigh.
The Fated Sky by Sir Philip Joubert.
Captain Albert Ball by R. H. Kiernan.
Empire at War by Sir Charles Lucas (Ed.).
First Through the Clouds by F. W. Merriam.
Air Dates by L. G. S. Payne.
Squadrons of the Royal Air Force by Major F. A. Robertson.
An Outline of de Havilland History by Martin C. Sharp.

The Central Blue by Sir John Slessor.
Recollections of an Airman by L. A. Strange.
From Many Angles by Sir F. H. Sykes.
C.F.S.—the Birthplace of Air Power by J. W. R. Taylor.
In the Clouds Above Baghdad by J. E. Tennant.
Flying and Sport in East Africa by Leo Walmsley.

The following magazines and newspapers have also provided valuable information: *Blackwood's Magazine, Royal Air Force Flying Review, Flight, Aeroplane, The Times.*

Index